Franco-German
Relations

Political Dynamics of the EU series

Series Editors:
Professor Kenneth Dyson and
Professor Kevin Featherstone

LEGITIMACY AND THE EU
David Beetham and Christopher Lord

THE COMMON FOREIGN SECURITY POLICY OF THE EU
David Allen

FRANCO-GERMAN RELATIONS
Alistair Cole

TECHNOCRACY IN THE EUROPEAN UNION
Claudio M. Radaelli

Franco-German Relations

Alistair Cole

An imprint of **Pearson Education**

Harlow, England · London · New York · Reading, Massachusetts · San Francisco
Toronto · Don Mills, Ontario · Sydney · Tokyo · Singapore · Hong Kong · Seoul
Taipei · Cape Town · Madrid · Mexico City · Amsterdam · Munich · Paris · Milan

Pearson Education Limited

Edinburgh Gate
Harlow
Essex CM20 2JE
England

and Associated Companies throughout the world

Visit us on the World Wide Web at:
http://www.pearsoneduc.com

First published 2001

ISBN 0 582 31997 8

British Library Cataloguing-in-Publication Data
A catalogue record for this book is available from the British Library

Library of Congress Cataloging-in-Publication Data
A catalog record for this book is available from the Library of Congress

10 9 8 7 6 5 4 3 2 1
04   03   02   01

Typeset by 35
Produced by Pearson Education Asia Pte Ltd.
Printed in Malaysia,LSP

Contents

Series Editors' Preface

At the start of the new century, Europe remains in a process of profound transition. The ramifications of the end of the Communist regimes in Eastern Europe, the collapse of the Soviet Union, and German unification are still being unravelled. At the same time, the process of European integration has intensified, with the onset of the single European market and the launch of Economic and Monetary Union. The linkage between both sets of developments is provided, of course, by the prospect of the European Union (EU) being enlarged to include many of the eastern states. The EU now looms large over the full continental landscape. The connecting theme of these changes is of the 'Europeanisation' of domestic politics and society.

With this in mind, the emphasis of this new series is very much on the dynamics of the European Union. Together, each of the volumes will analyse and reflect on the implications of such changes for the European integration process in the next decade.

The series also seeks to encourage undergraduate students to reflect theoretically on the implications of these changes. Just how adequate are different analytic frameworks for understanding what is happening in a given area of integration? The series will usefully complement more descriptive and institutionally-based accounts of European integration. At the same time the editors avoid imposing a single theoretical approach on what they recognise to be a wide range of varying experiences across different areas.

In addition to encouraging theoretical reflection, the series seeks to give a strong empirically-grounded content to each volume in the form of brief case studies, which are designed to illustrate important aspects of the phenomenon under investigation. These case studies focus in particular on the theme of power: of where power lies and of how it is exercised.

Finally, the series encourages authors to reflect on scenarios for development in the policy field or issue-area with which they are concerned. In this way, the theoretical and empirical foci of the volumes are brought together.

This third volume in the series extends the coverage to a new dimension of EU politics: that of the relations between national governments. No relationship has been more important to the development of the integration process than that between France and Germany. From Robert Schuman's declaration on 9 May 1950 presaging the European Coal and Steel Community to the present day, the progress of integration has crucially depended on the understanding established between these two states. The personal relationships of Adenauer and De Gaulle, Brandt and Pompidou, Schmidt and Giscard, Kohl and Mitterrand have underscored the scope for further integration, brokering compromises and overcoming domestic opposition. The bargaining coalitions of EU states have been defined by reference to the Franco-German relationship. Others, like Britain and Italy, have found it difficult to break into this bilateral relationship for very long or with great effect, even when they had the will to do so.

Despite the political significance of the Franco-German relationship for the course taken by the EU, it has received only limited academic study. No doubt the task is a daunting one, requiring expertise on both national systems, foreign relations, and the EU framework. Cole has met the challenge here, by synthesising knowledge gained across these different sub-fields and advancing our analysis of the various contours of Franco-German relations. Students and researchers will find in this volume a lucid exploration and an insightful analysis of the bilateral relationship that is the defining core of the history of European integration. This is a key building-block to a wider understanding of the past, present and future of the EU.

Professor Kenneth Dyson
Professor Kevin Featherstone
University of Bradford

Preface

My research interest in the Franco-German relationship can be dated quite precisely. In November 1991, I was asked by the then recently arrived Professor of German Politics – Eva Kolinsky – to present a paper to the research seminar of the Keele Centre for Modern German Studies on French reactions to German unification. With a great degree of apprehension I agreed. The result was a first insight into the fascinating bilateral relationship apparently occupying the centre of European gravity. Writing the paper coincided with the end-game of the negotiations leading up to the Maastricht summit, and my intellectual interest was naturally fuelled by the unfolding of events during the critical 1991–93 period. The Keele paper eventually became an article in *German Politics* (December 1993). By the time I decided to write a book on the Franco-German relationship another five years had passed. In a very real sense, this book owes its existence to the support of former colleagues at Keele (Eva Kolinsky) and Bradford (Kenneth Dyson and Kevin Featherstone) who encouraged the endeavour and were tolerant with postponed deadlines. I thank them.

The Franco-German relationship is commonly presented as the driving force underpinning European integration. The book tests this central proposition by seeking answers to three principal research questions. To what extent does the Franco-German relationship exercise leadership, joint or otherwise, within and beyond the European Union? Has there been a policy convergence between France and Germany during the past decade? Is there a changing balance within the Franco-German relationship? Through investigating responses to these three interlocking research questions, the book addresses issues involving the dynamics of the Franco-German relationship, the governance of the EU (mainly from a state-centric focus), the properties of the EU policy process, and the direction of change in post-cold war Europe.

The focus of the book is by turns historical, institutional, comparative, policy-oriented and EU-specific. The book starts by setting out the historical evolution of the Franco-German relationship. It then proposes a framework for analysis, which situates the Franco-German relationship within the main paradigms of European integration and comparative politics (neo-realism, historical institutionalism, domestic politics, and the policy process). After observing the operation of the bilateral relationship between France and Germany, the book considers in some detail whether the Franco-German relationship leads the EU, the underlying assumption of much of the literature. Two policy-specific chapters then elucidate the role of the Franco-German relationship with respect to economic and monetary policy and defence and security policy. The penultimate chapter appraises the evolution of the Franco-German relationship in the new social democratic era, concluding that the dynamics of existing relationships and the importance of distinctive national traditions far outweigh in significance cross-national partisan attachments. Addressing the theoretical paradigms and research questions evoked earlier on, the book concludes that the direction of change is towards a rather weaker steering role for the Franco-German relationship across the whole dimension of EU policy. The EU policy process has a dynamic quality, which is beyond the control of individual member states, or even of the powerful Franco-German relationship. Although France and Germany are much closer on most substantive policy issues in the year 2000 than they were at the end of the 1960s, France is increasingly called upon to conform to the German policy standard.

Many people have assisted in bringing this project to fruition. The debt I owe to Professors Kolinsky, Dyson and Featherstone was alluded to above. I should also like to thank various colleagues for reading part or all of the book: Helen Drake, John Gaffney, Hans Mackenstein and Charlie Lees in particular. I am grateful to Douglas Webber for letting me have access to his book *The Franco-German Relationship in the European Union* (London: Routledge, 2000) before the official publication date. I would like to dedicate the book to my very good friend Peter Truscott, contemporary from student days, and MEP for Hertfordshire for most of the research period. Peter and Svetlana made research trips to Brussels and Strasbourg fun and opened many doors. Thanks. Last, but not least, the book is also dedicated to Caroline, who thought she would never see the end of it. Merci.

CHAPTER 1

The Franco-German relationship in historical perspective

Although other bilateral relationships have assumed great importance, and while other nations have endured lasting conflicts, Franco-German relations underpin the history of modern Western Europe more than any other. The contemporary states of France and Germany share many common historical roots. The precursors of the French – the Franks – were a Germanic tribe. The Carolingian empire of Charlemagne covered much of contemporary France and Germany (Leenhardt and Picht, 1997). Despite sharing certain generic roots, the chronology of state formation contrasted strongly in the two countries. Contemporary France can trace its lineage back to the Capetian monarchy of the tenth century. The French nation slowly expanded from its heartland in the Ile-de-France by a process of gradual territorial accumulation and military conquest. By the seventeenth century, an identifiable central authority had emerged in the form of the absolute monarchy. In spite of the ebb and flow of wars, territorial disputes and military occupations, the contours of contemporary France were largely intact by the late seventeenth century. As late as the early nineteenth century, 'Germany' was a disparate collection of enlightened despots (Prussia), imperial dependencies (in the Austro-Hungarian empire) and free states (Leblond, 1997). Although German national consciousness developed strongly during the nineteenth century, Germany was eventually unified in 1871 by force and military subordination. Unification involved the imposition of a Prussian order on the separatist southern states. The German nation state has experienced an uneven existence. It was partially dismembered in 1919 (with the loss of Alsace-Lorraine) and divided in 1949 (the division into west and east German states). When Germany was reunified in 1989, it agreed explicitly to respect the Oder–Neisse border, acknowledging the loss of many former eastern provinces to Poland.

Ever since the Thirty Years War (1618–48), which reduced Europe to ruins, hegemony within Europe has involved a contest between these two continental European states, and their precursors. From the seventeenth century onwards, France and Germany accumulated divisive memories of historical affronts. For Germans, the sacking of the Rhineland-Palatinate by Louis XIV at the end of the seventeenth century left a bitter anti-French legacy. For the French, anti-German sentiment was inherent in the creation of the unified Germany from the ashes of French defeat at the hands of the Prussians in 1870. Germanophobia was reinforced by the injury of the lost provinces of Alsace-Lorraine, by the patriotic war of 1914–19, by Nazism and by occupation. In the power politics of continental Europe, nation state interest was perceived as a zero-sum game, a conquest for European supremacy.

Two rival state traditions were anchored in the legacy of the French revolution and its Napoleonic aftermath, and the character of German unification. There were also many similarities between the two nations. The French revolution and German unification each contained within them the aspiration of national unification. Both processes involved an aggressive central authority imposing its will upon recalcitrant or rebellious provinces. Both produced states with continent-wide hegemonic ambitions. Moreover, there was a close linkage between developments in both countries. While German liberals were seduced by the national idea in the French revolution, nationalist reaction to French revolutionary excesses led to the development of the German national idea, notably in Prussia. Prussian troops were vital in the final anti-Napoleonic battles. The exchange of ideas and models continued beyond conflicts: in 1830 and in 1848, German liberals once again looked to France as the country of the Rights of Man and of enlightenment.

Contemporary post-war Franco-German relations have been shaped in reaction to the terrible legacy of three wars within three-quarters of a century. The Franco-Prussian war of 1870 completed the process of the unification of modern Germany. Germany's victory in the open military conflict with France was celebrated by the annexation of Alsace-Lorraine to the second Reich. From 1871 to 1914, Germany emerged as the pre-eminent industrial, economic and military power in continental Europe. German industrial takeoff contrasted with French demographic stagnation. While France was still a predominantly rural country in 1914, Germany had become an industrial locomotive.

The causes of the First World War of 1914–19 are open to contrasting interpretations: explanations include the outcome of great power politics, the legacy of imperialism, the logic of industrialisation and the arms race. The terrible human suffering was not open to doubt. The allied victory was consecrated in the punitive settlement of Versailles (1919), which declared German war guilt, restored Alsace-Lorraine to France and imposed heavy reparations on the losers. The polarisation and fragmentation of the German polity during the Weimar Republic (1919–33) reflected deep divisions within

German society. The social and economic circumstances of Weimar were not propitious to the establishment of a stable liberal democracy. The political institutions of the Weimar Republic never had time to take root. Hyperinflation and unemployment induced a sense of political crisis based on social and economic dislocation, military defeat and failed revolution (in the form of the 1919 Spartacus uprising). The radicalisation of German society occurred to the detriment of liberal democracy. Economic and social crisis gave birth to the rise of political extremism from the mid-1920s onwards, notably during the early 1930s. The emergence of the German Communists (KPD) in the late 1920s was overshadowed by the rise of the NSDAP and Hitler's accession to power in 1933. Analysis of the Nazi experiment lies outside the scope of this book; there is a strong argument that the economic autarky of the Nazi regime was destined to result in war (Milward, 1979), as was its ideological mission and world vision.

The consolidation of liberal democracy in France followed a somewhat less tortuous path than in Germany. Defeat in the Franco-Prussian war discredited the monarchist idea and its adjacent institutions (such as the military). After three decades of divisions between Catholic monarchists and anti-clerical Republicans, of political crises and of civilian/military conflicts, the Republic established itself as the natural form of government for a majority of the French (Cole, 1998a). The Third Republic survived intact throughout the turbulence of the Weimar and Nazi years; it eventually succumbed to foreign invasion in 1940.

After Germany's defeat in World War One, the temptation to humiliate the defeated aggressor was strong. The hard-line stance adopted by French premier Poincaré in the Versailles negotiations of 1919 was aimed at dismembering the defeated German Reich and punishing the historic enemy. France recovered control of Alsace-Lorraine and forced heavy war reparations on Germany. Official inter-war French responses to Germany oscillated between hard-line enmity (the Poincaré approach to the Versailles settlement) and attempts to build bridges and to evolve new interdependent relationships (the Briand approach). These alternatives would resurface after the defeat of Nazism in 1945. The Poincaré approach became synonymous with punishing Germany. The Briand approach, on the other hand, signified developing a working partnership between the former enemies and promoting European union. Some German politicians, such as Chancellor Stresemann, also attempted to overcome mutual enmities and to build a new understanding with France. There were areas of common interest. Both Briand and Streseman sought to protect Europe from the rising US threat. The arguments in favour of closer collaboration bore a striking resemblance to those of the 1950s. Streseman believed that a multilateral structure, in the form of a European union, would allow a defeated Germany more influence than any bilateral understanding (Pedersen, 1998). The French premier Briand sought a European union as a means of restraining Germany and embedding Franco-German collaboration (Morgan, 1993). These plans did not withstand the death of Chancellor Stresemann and the rise of German extremism. The idea of European union as a solution to Franco-German conflict proved to be a stubborn one, however. In 1940, former French premier Léon Blum proposed 'the incorporation of the German nation within an International Community sufficiently powerful to re-educate the German nation, to discipline it, if necessary to dominate it' (cited in Rideau, 1975: 82). Whether through coercion or cooperation, there was agreement on the need to control Germany in the interests of lasting peace.

Germany's invasion of France in March 1940 led to an 'armistice' being signed between the victorious German armies and Marshall Pétain. The authoritarian wartime Vichy regime in France maintained an illusion of independence, celebrated by cultivating the symbols of French counter-revolutionary patriotism. This was tolerated in return for collaboration with Nazi war and policy objectives (notably, as demonstrated by the *Rafle d'Hel'Viv* in 1942, the arresting of Jews later sent to concentration camps). Nazi control became more vigorous after November 1942, when the German army occupied the whole of the country (Paxton, 1972). The impact of wartime occupation and collaboration continues to ricochet through contemporary French politics; the importance of the trials of war criminals such as Barbie, Touvier and Papon demonstrates this, as does the wartime record of politicians such as former President Mitterrand (Péan, 1994).

France, Germany and the reconstruction of Western Europe, 1944–58

However many declarations of profound mutual friendship are made, postwar Franco-German relations cannot elude past historical conflicts. While national identities are rooted in distinct historical legacies, however, postwar Franco-German relations have built upon a measure of convergence of ideas and interests, a joint management of political projects and an institutionally embedded existence. The project of European integration has underpinned the bilateral Franco-German relationship. It has also provided a constraining multilateral framework for the conduct of Franco-German relations. It has enabled one state – the Federal Republic of Germany – to recreate a sense of positive identity from a dark collective memory. It has empowered another – France – by allowing it to pretend to the role of a great power. In both cases, the advantages have outweighed the constraints imposed by Community membership.

The triumph of what Morgan (1993: 120) terms the 'Briand' approach was not a foregone conclusion. During the early post-war years, Germany was divided into four occupation zones – the American, the British, the Soviet and the French. France was recognised as a victorious power by the USA, USSR and Britain in the 1946 Potsdam conference. The French government initially adopted a hard-line stance to its former occupier. It was resolutely hostile to the creation of a unified (west) German administration, in contrast to Britain or the USA. It only revised its unyielding position once the emergence of a west German state became inevitable. French strategy bore comparison with that adopted after the First World War. Humiliated by her experience of wartime occupation, the post-war provisional government – headed by resistance leader Charles de Gaulle – adopted a traditional Rhineland strategy designed to keep Germany weak and divided (Morgan, 1991). This involved a bid to split off the Sarre (a German coal-producing area administered by the League of Nations from 1919 to 1933, and by the French from 1945 to 1953) and other western areas from Germany and annex them to France. De Gaulle also proposed the creation of a separate political authority to administer the Ruhr, the heartland of German industrial power. The first French post-war plan, drafted by Jean Monnet, was similar in its desire to punish Germany, advocating the permanent dismemberment of the German state and the dismantling of the German steel industry. Monnet realised the critical importance of economics – France had to limit Germany's capacity to produce steel and coal, the raw materials of military conquest.

Such a hard-line stance was unrealistic and it was thwarted by the Anglo-American alliance. It ran against the logic of Marshall aid, and the imperatives of cold war reconstruction. France could not prevent the USA and UK supporting German economic recovery in their occupation zones, or assisting democratic rebirth. She could appear neither to oppose the return of democracy in Germany nor to forestall any prospect of Franco-German reconciliation. There were many common interests with the former enemy, especially in the areas of security and economic policy. French policy gradually shifted with the development of events in Eastern and Central Europe. American pressures for a united European response to Soviet aggression proved overwhelming. However, it should be stressed that the crystallisation of a west German state and the revival of the German economy occurred in spite of initial French opposition. Even after the creation of the Federal Republic of Germany (1949), France and Germany continued to harbour territorial disputes with each other, notably in relation to the Sarre. Only in 1956 did French premier Mendès-France agree to hold a referendum in the disputed Sarre territory. This took place in 1957 under the government of Auguste Pinay; a large majority voted in favour of being restored to Germany.

The 1950s were a period of a joint Franco-German drive towards closer European integration, accepted by both countries as a precondition of restoring European peace. Having failed to dismember western Germany, French governments resorted to the Briand approach: reaching agreements with Germany in order to bind her to France. This stance was above all associated with Robert Schuman, who took over as foreign affairs minister in 1948. Schuman was convinced that Franco-German reconciliation would serve French interests in post-war Europe (Bonnefous, 1995). The best way of tying down Germany was to bind it to the goal of European integration. Any revival in German power would benefit Europe as a whole and France in particular. Regional integration also fulfilled basic German security needs. European integration would remove borders and create opportunities for the revival of German industry. Moreover it would signal Germany's return to the community of European nations. The first West German Chancellor, Konrad Adenauer, envisaged a privileged Franco-German partnership, not least to avoid any possibility of a Franco-Russian alliance aimed against Germany. Adenauer considered it to be in Germany's interest to demonstrate its acceptance of a framework of collective security and a process of regional integration. The ultimate objective of German unity could only be achieved with the consent of the main international players.

As demonstrated in the following examples, Franco-German agreement was a necessary but not a sufficient condition for moves to closer European integration in the 1950s.

Europeanising coal and steel

The European Coal and Steel Community (ECSC) initiative of 1950–51 was a landmark in shifting attitudes towards Franco-German relations. Whereas the first Monnet plan (1946) had sought to dismember Germany in order to guarantee France access to German coal and steel, the Schuman plan (also inspired by Monnet) advocated a European solution (Milward, 1984). Schuman proposed the creation of a single market in coal and steel, which would guarantee France and other countries access to German natural resources, while allowing the Germans to increase energy production. Each signatory country would have access to the others' markets. Internal tariff barriers would be phased out; a common external tariff would be levied. The plan would be implemented and policed by a High Authority with supranational powers, composed of commissioners nominated by each country. The regulation of coal and steel would escape the direct control of national governments. The symbolism was potent – coal and steel provided the raw materials of military conflict, so Europeanising coal and steel would make war impossible.

However this innovative solution also responded to the vital national interests of France and Germany. Dedman (1996: 61) considers the Schuman plan of 1950 to be a 'second French attempt (after the Monnet plan of 1946) to reshape Europe's economic and political environment to suit the needs of the domestic French economy'. Access to German coal and steel would accelerate France's post-war industrial takeoff. The ECSC would rescue Monnet's modernisation plan by guaranteeing access for French industry to German raw materials. Moreover, the plan created a protected market for French steel in southern Germany for a three-year period.

German motivations were rather more complex and political considerations were uppermost. The 1949 Basic Law created a semi-sovereign West German state. The occupation statute prevented the Federal Republic from engaging in an autonomous foreign or defence policy and placed limitations on its foreign trade. To lift these constraints, the German Chancellor Konrad Adenauer engaged a strategy of close collaboration with the UK, USA and France. The ECSC provided a good example of Germany gaining influence by strengthening supranational institutions: it allowed Germany to recover full control of its steel industry by removing the obstacles imposed after Potsdam in 1945. Moreover, Adenauer achieved a symbolically important political act by insisting on equal terms for the Federal Republic in the ECSC negotiations. This was a step in the direction of autonomous statehood.

The problem of German rearmament

The question of German security and rearmament caused heightened friction between as well as within both countries. The legacy of German occupation was particularly potent, but so were the threats to Western security by the Soviet colonisation of Central Europe from 1945 to 1948. The onset of the cold war changed the nature of the security problem. Stalin's *de facto* incorporation of the eastern German zone into the USSR's sphere of influence (1948) entrenched the division of Germany into eastern and western German states. The Federal Republic was born in 1949 as the West German state, and as the bulwark against encroaching Stalinism. The Soviet threat increased French dependence on the USA as well, locking governments of the French Fourth Republic into the Western security alliance.

While the case for German rearmament became urgent and pressing after the outbreak of the Korean war in 1950, there was some dispute over the appropriate institutional structures to control the process. The creation of the North Atlantic Treaty Organisation (NATO) in 1949 represented a firm American commitment to the defence of the European continent against Soviet communism. British and American preferences were for German rearmament to be controlled by NATO, the solution eventually adopted.

The process was urgent; the American Secretary of State made clear his wish to see 'German soldiers in uniform by the Autumn of 1951' (Kergoat, 1991: 9). The Atlanticist option was not the only one, however. There were also powerful advocates of a Europeanised solution (Williams, 1964). In principle, France was opposed to rearming Germany. But a rearmed German army in NATO appeared much less palatable than a French-directed force. A European solution would tame Germany, while reducing US influence over the west European continent. The French feared that the NATO option would remove Germany from French control altogether. Initially sceptical, the USA also came around to a European solution as a long-term political response to the German problem.

The French solution to the problem of German rearmament was to create a European Army within the Atlantic Alliance (Dedman, 1996; Williams, 1964). The Pleven plan of 1950 proposed the creation of a European Defence Community (EDC), the core of which would be provided by a European Army. German troops would be rearmed only as units of the European Army, which would sign a cooperation agreement with NATO. French military planners expected German rearmament to be indirectly controlled by France. In the original plan, states would provide troops to the European Army, but would retain national control over units not pledged to the EDC. With 50 000 of 100 000 proposed troops, France would dominate the European Army. From the French perspective, there were close links between the Coal and Steel Community (ECSC) and the European Army (EDC). While ECSC had been intended to regulate Germany's re-emergence as an industrial power, the EDC proposals were a means of using supranational mechanisms to control German rearmament.

German Chancellor Adenauer had his own agenda. The EDC provided a second example of a supranational solution that would enhance German sovereignty. Initially hostile to full German rearmament, Adenauer seized an opportunity to consolidate the Federal Republic's role as a normal nation and to enhance its political independence. The German chancellor insisted on West German equality with other countries within collective security structures (within NATO or the EDC) and made German rearmament conditional upon a recovery of full sovereignty and a renegotiation of the status of the three Western occupying powers. Adenauer agreed to the EDC, but demanded French concessions. Under German pressure, the French had to accept *fusion complète*; all national forces were to be fused into a single army from the start. In the 1952 Treaty of Paris, the European Defence Community thus contained provision for a completely supranational European Army.

The Treaty of Paris (1952) went much further than the initial Pleven plan in the direction of a supranational army. There was powerful political opposition within France to the proposed dissolution of the French army into a pan-European force. Although France had launched the proposed EDC, the French National Assembly failed to ratify the Paris Treaty in 1954, the proposal defeated by an alliance of Gaullists, left-wing socialists and Communists (Wall, 1991). The failure of the EDC created considerable unease and anger in the Federal Republic, which entered NATO shortly afterwards, proposed and supported by Britain. By 1955, West Germany was a fully sovereign state with the last vestiges of the occupation statute removed. The failure of the EDC proved to be a lasting setback for grandiose political schemes of European integration that went to the heart of national sovereignty. Indeed, the EDC was far more ambitious in its objectives than any European Act since.

The Common Market

After the failure of the European Army, economic integration again became the spur for closer relations. Although France and Germany were the major players, Italy and the smaller European countries could also influence the process of integration at critical junctures. Thus the Benelux countries took the initiative on the Common Market, fearful of the consequences of Franco-German dissension. Even so, the Treaty of Rome signed in 1957, which created the European Economic Community (EEC), was 'essentially a compromise between German interest in market liberalisation, and French interest in support for agriculture' (Pedersen, 1998: 80). The Treaty (reprinted in de Guistino, 1996) built on the model of economic-based integration experimented in the ECSC. The Treaty envisaged the creation of a common market between the six signatory countries (France, Germany, Italy, Belgium, Netherlands and Luxembourg) with a phased removal of all internal tariff barriers and a common external tariff. It promised the creation of common policies in agriculture and transport and pledged mechanisms for closer economic and social coordination. It established a new set of political institutions, loosely based on the architecture of the ECSC: 'The tasks entrusted to the Community shall be carried out by the following institutions: an Assembly, a Council, a Commission, a Court of Justice' (cited in de Guistino, 1996: 95). These pillars of the EC's organisational and political existence will be referred to at regular intervals throughout this book. The Treaty went beyond economic cooperation; it envisaged a federalist finality, in the form of an 'ever closer' political and economic union between the six signatory states. Germany and France both believed they would gain in the long run from more integrated European structures. In the shorter term, the treaty guaranteed support for French agriculture in crisis (Noël, 1995).

De Gaulle, Adenauer and the directorate.
Franco-German relations in the 1960s

The return to power of General de Gaulle in France in June 1958 challenged the integrationist agenda established by the Treaty of Rome. The general was careful not to reject the Common Market; coming shortly after the defeat of the EDC Treaty (coordinated by de Gaulle himself) this would have sent entirely the wrong signals to Germany (Grosser, 1988). But de Gaulle's preferences were far removed from the avowed federalism of Europe's founders. To an ever closer union, the Gaullist paradigm was that of a Europe of nation states. This might be summarised as a strong Europe with weak institutions under French leadership, a conception considered in some detail in Chapter 4. A strong Europe was essential, in order to counter American cultural and economic hegemony, and to defend Western security interests against an aggressive USSR. French leadership was a *sine qua non* for such a Europe; Germany remained a semi-sovereign state; Britain was too close to the Americans. French pretensions to a leadership role were strengthened by France's procurement of an independent nuclear deterrent by 1960. The nation state – with its contradictions, symbols and identities – would remain the focus of political organisation. Nation states provided a stable bearing in the rough sea of international anarchy. It was through the nation state that order and prosperity could be organised.

To achieve the central objective of restoring France to its rightful place as a leading world power, de Gaulle adopted what Pedersen (1998) has labelled the *Directoire* approach. France would lead Europe in privileged alliance with Germany on the basis of close intergovernmental cooperation. De Gaulle's Franco-German orientation contained a mixture of political expediency and conviction. Wounded *amour propre* was a driving motivation. One of de Gaulle's first acts as President of the Fifth Republic was to propose a Franco-British–American 'directorate' over the affairs of the West (Soutou, 1996). In a 1959 memorandum, de Gaulle called for a tripartite leadership of NATO (by France, the UK and the USA). This memorandum – published two days after the first visit of Konrad Adenauer to Colombey-les-Eglises – was rejected by the USA (McCarthy, 1993a). Such an affront to the rank of France by the Anglo-Saxon democracies encouraged de Gaulle to turn towards Germany.

A strong Europe with weak political institutions also signified intergovernmental collaboration at the summit of the Community. De Gaulle's Europe was explicitly predicated upon a dominant Franco-German axis. This bilateral relationship was conceived in a directory sense as an alternative to an ever closer union under the political leadership of a federally minded European Commission. De Gaulle did not question the economic advantages of the Common Market, but the Common Market did not provide a structure for determined political leadership. This could only be provided by nation states acting in partnership with each other. In the Fouchet Plan of 1961–62, de Gaulle proposed an intergovernmental reform of the EEC, based on shifting the focus of decision-making away from supranational institutions (the Commission) to regular meetings of national governments (Soutou, 1997; O'Neill, 1996). The federal direction of an ever closer union was anathema to General de Gaulle. The Fouchet plan offered the Germans a *de facto* joint management of the EEC. This inter-governmental form of European cooperation was rejected by Belgium and the Netherlands, for whom supranational institutions such as the Commission guaranteed the rights of small countries. The Germans were initially less hostile. Adenauer accepted the need for a close alliance with France, notwithstanding the counsels of powerful Atlanticist forces ranged against this option within his own party. But the Germans also eventually rejected the Fouchet plan, since de Gaulle had publicly linked accepting the plan and repudiating British membership of the EC.

De Gaulle's priorities were not identical to those of Konrad Adenauer, the Federal Republic's first chancellor, although there were many points of convergence between the two leaders. Adenauer was principally preoccupied with tying Germany into the Western alliance, via the European Community and NATO. German normalcy would be achieved by immersing Germany in multilateral structures, as well as by developing new bilateral relationships and restoring trust. Multilateral structures would bind Germany to the West. Adenauer's strong support for international cooperation was a rational strategy: the powers that West Germany gave up to the ECSC or to NATO were not really sacrificed at all, because they had been exercised by the occupying authorities. Alongside support for new international organisations, Germany would also gain from building bilateral relationships; with the USA and France in particular (Paterson, 1998). Adenauer strongly believed that the stability of the German state required an entwining relationship with France. Franco-German reconciliation was a precondition for a lasting European peace and for rebuilding German prosperity. Although initially distrustful of de Gaulle, in time the French and German leaders developed an effective, highly personal relationship. Adenauer was a dedicated Francophile, but alliance with the USA was even more important, not least for security reasons, with the onset of the cold war in 1948 (Garton-Ash, 1994).

Adenauer's vision was both more integrationist and more Atlanticist than that of de Gaulle, but there was a convergence in positing Franco-German reconciliation at the centre of European cooperation. Security considerations were important. For the first time in its history as a nation, Germany had a friendly country to its west. Drawing France into a binding bilateral alliance would preclude any possibility of de Gaulle forming a Franco-Soviet partnership aimed at Germany, and the Franco-German alliance would strengthen the Western alliance against the Soviet bloc. Germany also valued a close relationship with France as a symbol of Germany's return to the European community of nations.

De Gaulle and Adenauer held their first meeting in September 1958 (Grosser, 1988). From 1959 to 1963, de Gaulle played the card of the Germans as privileged allies. The seduction strategy involved high-level summits and a state visit to West Germany in September 1962 (McCarthy, 1993a). This state visit was followed shortly after by the signing of the Elysée Treaty in January 1963. This assertion of Franco-German friendship was politically contentious, coming as it did only weeks after de Gaulle had vetoed British entry to the EEC. It accurately reflected the Gaullist vision of European priorities. The original document implied that Germany would be forced to choose between France and the USA in international forums such as NATO. This was too provocative for the West German lower chamber, the *Bundestag*, which insisted on adding a preamble reaffirming Germany's participation in GATT and NATO in strongly pro-Atlanticist terms (Soutou, 1996). The defence clauses of the Elysée Treaty were largely stillborn as a result. The Elysée Treaty was still an important symbolic assertion of Franco-German reconciliation and alliance; that the two countries signed a treaty, rather than a simple convention or memorandum, demonstrated the importance both placed on close cooperation. The Elysée Treaty also had a more practical application. It created a complex set of institutions designed to ensure the durability of Franco-German contact. These are considered in Chapter 3.

Did the Elysée Treaty promote European integration? One plausible interpretation of the 1963 treaty is that it created an alliance within the alliance. The strategy of the *directoire* was a direct challenge to multilateral supranationalism and in particular to the Monnet method of staged progress towards supranational leadership of the EU. During the long Gaullist interlude, the two countries in many respects held conflicting political visions. These divergences became clearer once Adenauer had left office in 1963. They centred on the role of supranational institutions, the importance of the Atlantic Alliance and the role of the USA in Europe. In the absence of fundamental agreement between France and Germany to pursue integration, European cooperation languished from the mid-1960s to the mid-1980s.

Franco-German cooperation within Europe was not always consistent with the centrality of the German–American security relationship. German chancellors after Adenauer were embarrassed by defence and security developments in the latter part of de Gaulle's presidency, notably France's withdrawal from NATO in 1966, her courting of the Soviet Union and the Eastern European people's democracies, as well as by the confrontational stance adopted within the EEC. On the other hand, the French, together with the other occupying powers, recognised the right to a united Germany in the 1971 Berlin agreement (Morgan, 1991).

From the German perspective, France was often an awkward partner after de Gaulle's return to power in 1958. De Gaulle placed the Germans in a difficult position; his demand that Germany choose between France and the USA was unrealistic. When forced to choose, Germany preferred the security offered by the US nuclear umbrella over the dubious French alternative, especially because de Gaulle refused to extend nuclear protection to the Germans (Deporte, 1991). De Gaulle's dual veto of British entry into the EC, in 1963 and 1967, embarrassed the Federal Republic. His empty chair policy of 1965, leading to the Luxembourg compromise of 1966, directly challenged the community mode of governance favoured by the Germans (Henig, 1997).

Adenauer's departure in 1963 began a new phase in Franco-German relations. The next two German chancellors, Erhard (1963–66) and Kiesinger (1966–69), were much less sympathetic to French foreign policy aims. Neither Erhard nor Kiesinger were of comparable stature to Adenauer; neither enjoyed warm personal relations with de Gaulle. The French president's assertive stance hardened attitudes, as did his polycentric view of the Atlantic Alliance and European security arrangements. De Gaulle refused to recognise the shifting balance of power within the Franco-German alliance, notably resisting German demands for a devaluation of the franc in August 1968 (Dyson and Featherstone, 1999). After de Gaulle, no French president could pretend to maintain the Germans in such an unequal relationship, not least because by the early 1970s the German economic miracle had shifted the balance of power within the bilateral relationship. One of the first acts of de Gaulle's successor Pompidou was to accept the inevitable devaluation of the franc and implicitly to recognise the changing equilibrium of the Franco-German relationship (Simonian, 1985).

From directorate to hegemony?
Franco-German relations in the 1970s and 1980s

The equilibrium of the Franco-German relationship from the early 1960s through to the late 1980s rested upon a fine balance between political prestige and economic power. France enjoyed the political and diplomatic prestige of being a World War Two victor, with occupation rights in Berlin and a permanent seat on the UN security council. Moreover, since 1960, France had been a member of the highly selective club of nuclear powers

(Gordon, 1995). In the 1963 Elysée Treaty, there was no question of according the Germans any oversight over the French *force de frappe*. In practice, the exhortations for closer defence collaboration ran against French unilateralism, and the canons of Gaullist nuclear doctrine (the Weak's defence against the Strong), which blatantly contradicted those of NATO (Cole, 1997).

As a loser in the Second World War, West Germany had none of the trappings of great power status, with which Gaullist France had cloaked itself. West Germany's strengthening on the economic and diplomatic front during the 1970s, however, enhanced her standing and introduced new strains within the relationship. Germany's economic prowess gradually increased her self-confidence and esteem (Markovits and Reich, 1997). By 1970, Germany had become the undisputed economic locomotive of the European economy. Economic interdependence turned to Germany's advantage, notably in its bilateral relations with other EC states. The German economic miracle outpaced the French economic miracle; the balance of economic exchanges was strongly in (West) Germany's favour. Its status as the leading European economy, combined with its geo-strategic location on the Western European frontline, ensured that Germany remained at the forefront of American security concerns. Germany was strengthened by its role as the principal continental American ally (Szabo, 1990). France's self-exclusion from the inner circles of NATO allowed the Federal Republic to occupy a security role that might otherwise have been contested by its French ally. The pivotal role performed by the Federal Republic in NATO demonstrated that interdependence with the West was a means of exercising foreign policy influence. Furthermore, the Bonn Republic had specific security concerns in relation to the countries of Central and Eastern Europe that could lead it to adopt stances in opposition to those of France.

Franco-German rivalries were manifest in relation to Eastern and Central Europe (Simonian, 1985). Disguised beneath an idealistic rhetoric, the Bonn Republic adopted a hard-nosed foreign policy (Garton-Ash, 1994). The German chancellor Willie Brandt's *Östpolitik* of the early 1970s demonstrated a new self-confidence in Germany. *Östpolitik* responded to a real security concern for the Federal Republic: how could it build stable relations with the neighbouring Communist states of Central and Eastern Europe, while promoting a climate propitious to eventual German unification? German planners hoped (and French planners feared) that *Östpolitik* would attract Eastern European countries into the German sphere of influence. From the French perspective, *Östpolitik* demonstrated not only that West Germany was becoming less easy to control, but also that it constituted a serious rival to French influence in relation to Eastern Europe and the USSR. It appeared to be in direct competition with de Gaulle's attempts to build alliances with Eastern European popular democracies from 1963 to 1968. On the other hand, the Federal Republic's recognition of East Germany in 1971 was welcomed by France, because it appeared to consolidate the existence of two German nations.

The relationship between Chancellor Brandt (1969–72) and President Pompidou (1969–74) provided a case study of the tensions that could undermine the Franco-German relationship (Simonian, 1985). Domestic political settings, personal political styles and rival party affiliations could produce routine misunderstandings. Chancellor Brandt's European initiatives were based on social democratic principles in the sphere of social policy and upon integrationist overtones in European policy, notably the German chancellor's proposal for direct elections to the European parliament. They did not appeal to de Gaulle's successor as president, the conservative Gaullist Georges Pompidou (1969–74). Pompidou attempted to counter-balance growing German influence by accepting British entry into the Community, and engaging a close dialogue with British premier Heath. In line with traditional balance of power politics, British entry was perceived in part as a means of securing French influence vis-à-vis the Federal Republic. Far from promoting economic convergence with Germany, President Pompidou made a determined push for domestic growth financed by high inflation. This was particularly significant as there were acute pressures for greater Franco-German convergence in monetary policy (see Chapter 5). Even when the personal equation faltered, however, France and Germany lay behind the most important European policy initiatives. The Hague summit of 1969, which formally adopted resolutions on monetary union and foreign policy coordination, testified to this (Garton-Ash, 1994).

Brandt's replacement by Helmut Schmidt inaugurated rather less tense relations between France and Germany. Schmidt's long tenure of the office of German chancellor (1974–82) roughly coincided with the presidency of Valéry Giscard d'Estaing, the non-Gaullist conservative president who replaced Pompidou (1974–81). The Giscard–Schmidt partnership had more of the trappings of a 'special relationship' than its predecessor (Simonian, 1985). Giscard d'Estaing did not fundamentally challenge the canons of the Gaullist heritage (a strong Europe with weak institutions). Indeed, the creation of the European Council in 1974 strengthened intergovernmental bargaining as the key dynamic of European Community decision-making. Giscard d'Estaing firmly believed that the functions of political leadership should be exercised by heads of government, rather than the president of a supranational Commission. On the other hand, President Giscard d'Estaing went further than any of his predecessors in accepting moves to closer European political and monetary union; the creation of the European monetary system in 1978–79 bore testimony to this (Chang, 1999).

On the German side, Chancellor Schmidt was certainly not a Francophile, nor was he primarily interested in European integration. Nonetheless, Schmidt's rigorous style of domestic economic management had an impact upon EC institutions, and upon the Franco-German relationship in particular. The bilateral Franco-German relationship was strengthened by close cooperation between Schmidt and Giscard d'Estaing. Important Franco-German initiatives occurred in the spheres of monetary policy (the creation of the European monetary system in 1978–79) and political integration. A trade-off occurred between Giscard d'Estaing's lobbying for the creation of the European Council, as a biennial summit meeting of heads of government, and the French president's acceptance of German chancellor Schmidt's demands for direct elections to the European parliament. To some extent, this trade-off was revealing of competing preferences for intergovernmental (France) versus supranational (Germany) visions of political union.

The election of Mitterrand as Socialist president in France caused an abrupt cooling of Franco-German relations. President Mitterrand argued vaguely for a rebalancing of European alliances, away from an exclusive dialogue with Germany, and held summits with Spain, Italy and the UK. The personal antipathy between Mitterrand and Schmidt was longstanding. Throughout the 1970s, Mitterrand's Socialists had dismissed the German social democratic model as one to be avoided. Mitterrand specifically rejected the implicit linkage of the Barre plan between convergence with German economic performance and internal economic modernisation. With Mitterrand's Socialist–Communist government adopting Keynesian reflationary policies from 1981–82, aimed primarily at reducing unemployment and stimulating growth, relations reached a new low between the new French president and Chancellor Schmidt. French proposals for a European-wide economic relaunch – in the form of the Chandernagor memorandum – were blocked in October 1981 by an alliance of Schmidt and Thatcher (Drake, 1994).

As McCarthy (1993b: 1) observes, however, France and Germany were 'condemned to partnership'. France was moving closer to German positions even before Mitterrand's economic U-turn of March 1983. In a landmark speech to the German *Bundestag* in January 1983, Mitterrand urged the new German chancellor Kohl to deploy US cruise and pershing missiles in response to the Soviet SS20s and to resist the sirens of pacifism from within German public opinion (Szabo, 1990). In March 1983, President Mitterrand chose the 'European' option of maintaining the franc within the European monetary system, rather than continuing with the Keynesian economic policies pursued since 1981 (Cameron, 1996).

Close cooperation between Kohl and Mitterrand underpinned moves to closer European political and economic integration in the 1980s and 1990s.

With the resolution of Britain's budgetary contribution achieved at the Fontainebleu summit in June 1984, the French and German leaders cooperated closely on the principal moves towards closer European integration; the Single European Act and the Maastricht Treaty being the two obvious examples. Under Mitterrand and Kohl, important steps were also taken to reinvigorate and institutionalise the Franco-German relationship and to extend the scope of its intervention (see Chapter 3).

Helmut Kohl's European vision emerged as a constant feature of his long career. Kohl shared a generational belief with other leaders such as Mitterrand that theirs was the last political generation that could be relied upon to move decisively to European union. European unity was a question of war and peace. As representatives of the wartime generation, political responsibility lay upon this generation of political leaders to move decisively to European union. Such beliefs grew in intensity after German unification.

Kohl and Mitterrand shared a European vision, but it was not an identical one. Kohl's European vision was 'pure Adenauer'; he advocated a close political relationship with France, consistent with a close security partnership with the US and NATO (Paterson, 1998). Mitterrand's Europe was more interventionist in a technological sense; far less Atlanticist, with certain Gaullist overtones (Cole, 1997). Different appreciations of economic and monetary union were also apparent (Chapter 5). However, both leaders had a sense of mission, and of the responsibility conferred on a particular generation to complete the process of European unification. Their fruitful collaboration withstood the pressures placed upon it by the unforeseen process of German unification.

The Franco-German relationship and German unification

Preceding German unification, post-war Franco-German collaboration had been based upon a delicate and shifting equilibrium between the two countries, according to which German economic supremacy was counterbalanced by French political influence within Europe. To the extent that it kept Germany divided, and deprived it of great power status, the 40 years of cold war and the post-war division of Europe had generally benefited French interests. Germany was sometimes unfairly portrayed as an economic giant, but a political pygmy. French claims to exercise a leadership role were demonstrated in its pursuit of a Gaullist foreign policy, which Germany could not imitate. France's status as a permanent member of the UN security council, its neo-colonial relationship with francophone African states and its nuclear deterrent all conferred vestiges of great power status, assiduously cultivated by French policy-makers (Moreau-Defarges, 1994).

Germany was constitutionally barred from deploying troops outside of the NATO area, but developed an unswerving Atlanticism as a gauge of its commitment to the Western alliance.

The events leading to German unification and their aftermath sorely tested the cohesion of the Franco-German relationship. Although French foreign policy had officially supported the goal of German unification since the presidency of General de Gaulle, its politicians and officials were unprepared for the rapid unfolding of events from 1989 to 1991 (Cole, 1993, 1997). The principle of German unification was explicitly recognised in the Berlin agreement, signed in 1971 by the four occupying powers. But it had never previously been a pressing current issue because of the post-war division of Europe. The revolutionary events of 1989 abruptly called this bipolar division into question.

The speed of events partly explained the sense of unreality surrounding the momentum that culminated in German unification in October 1990. From the moment the Berlin wall fell on 9 November 1989, Kohl immediately appeared to grasp the opportunity of a possible unification of Germany. The German chancellor presented an audacious programme for unification – known as the Ten Point Plan – only days before the Bush–Gorbachev Malta summit in November 1989 (Tréan, 1991). Kohl's plan irritated many of Germany's traditional allies, especially the French. The Ten Point Plan for unification was a personal initiative; it had not been discussed with British, French or Russian leaders. Even foreign minister Genscher expressed surprise at the move (Pruys, 1996). The determination illustrated by Helmut Kohl himself to exploit the issue of unification for its maximum political benefit transformed his leadership reputation. Kohl's main contribution to history was his courageous and decisive pursuit of the goal of unification – from an early date and whatever the costs. In fact, German unification did not take the course outlined in the Ten Point Plan, but this act as political voluntarism was undoubtedly important in associating Kohl's name with the historical process of unification.

Nobody associated with French foreign policy believed in the possibility of German unification in the autumn of 1989. The various options formulated by foreign policy advisers did not include unification (Morgan, 1991). As late as autumn 1989 the GDR continued to be envisaged as an Eastern European 'popular democracy' comparable with the others: reform pressures, it was imagined, would express themselves within the parameters of the East German state. The most daring case scenario was that East Germany would eventually be accorded an 'Austrian statute'. Initial French reservations over the perspective of German unification were largely shared throughout Europe: in the USSR, foreign minister Gérassimov dismissed unification as an intellectual exercise (Tréan, 1991). In the USA, President

Bush welcomed the principle of unification, but carefully avoided being more specific. In London, Mrs Thatcher dismissed any German unification in the immediate or longer term future; she never really accepted the idea of unified Germany. Opposition to Kohl's plan from close allies such as Mitterrand was due in part to a lack of consultation, but also the plan did not mention the four wartime victors, who had continuing legal responsibilities in relation to Germany, notably their troops stationed in Berlin. Helmut Kohl's plan was deliberately ambiguous over borders; it appeared to call into question the existing Oder–Neisse border with Poland, an ambiguity that was only clarified after the East German election of March 1990. Kohl's refusal to specify that the Oder–Neisse border represented the final border between Germany and Poland implied that a new unified German state might have demands on parts of current Polish territory.

The Franco-German special relationship had little impact on the process of German unification (Cole, 1993). Far more important was Gorbachev's agreement of July 1990 that a unified Germany would remain within NATO, and that Soviet troops would withdraw from East Germany in return for massive financial assistance. Far more important also was the role played by the Americans. The US demand that German unification could only take place within NATO removed it from the realm of fictional politics; the Americans thereby signified their willingness to cooperate with an enlarged Germany as an alliance partner. The role of the USA in constructing the 'two plus four' negotiating formula provided an important diplomatic breakthrough (Costigliola, 1994). In contrast, attempts by Mitterrand and other European statesmen to influence events were largely without consequence. In response to Kohl's Ten Point Plan, Mitterrand appeared to attempt to resurrect a Franco-Russian axis to frustrate aspirations for German unity. On 6 December 1989, Mitterrand and Gorbachev made public a joint declaration which stipulated that any realtering of European borders was premature and would have a destabilising effect. Mitterrand also made highly symbolic visits to Poland and to East Germany, where he praised the 'East German identity' in a television broadcast. Mitterrand vigorously contested media interpretations of his actions (Mitterrand, 1996).

Chancellor Kohl personally involved himself in the details of German unification. He actively intervened to prevent the propping up of the East German regime before the GDR elections of March 1990, in the expectation of hastening the process of unification. Kohl's decision on the currency union between the two Germanies, operative in July 1990, was imposed upon a hostile *Bundesbank*, causing the resignation of its president, Karl Pöhl, shortly afterwards. Moreover, after initially alienating Germany's European allies, Kohl personally involved himself in smoothing out bilateral relations, most especially with France and President Mitterrand. In order to demonstrate

Germany's good intentions, Kohl reiterated that Germany would remain irrevocably tied to the EU. In the all-German election of December 1990, Kohl was elected as first chancellor of the unified German state.

There was a direct link between German unification and the new drive towards greater European political and economic integration (see Chapters 4 and 5). At crucial moments before, during and after unification, Kohl came down on the side of European integration, as against a more exclusive concentration with German affairs. The membership of a unified Germany in NATO, and a commitment to increased European integration, were the corollaries of German unification. The engagement in favour of a single European currency at the Maastricht summit – interpreted by some as running counter to Germany's economic interests – confirmed the linkage in Kohl's mind of the processes of German and European unification. A parallel linkage was operated by French politicians, who attempted to ensure that the unified state would be tied as closely as possible to the EC, and that the Franco-German axis would continue to provide an effective co-direction of the Community.

Conclusion

The main French fears fostered by unification were those of a nation discovering itself to be a junior partner in a relationship within which it had long pretended to seniority. They concerned, most obviously, the potential economic and political power of the new Germany, making it a more formidable rival in all spheres of national competition. As we argue in Chapter 5, binding in the economic Leviathan became a recurrent French justification of monetary union. The Franco-German relationship became even more valued after unification, however, for its capacity to contain Germany and safeguard French influence. Any threats to the Franco-German relationship – for example, from a resurgent Britain – were fought with determination.

French fears were also rooted in what was perceived to be a new strategic reality. French policy-makers suspected Germany might be tempted to look towards the East at the expense of the European Community. The Franco-German alliance, they reasoned, was not Germany's only option. She could also rely on closer relations with the USA, or expansion to the East. To some extent she could look to alternative configurations within the European Union, especially as the EU enlarged to take in the new democracies of Northern, Central and Eastern Europe. Germany no longer needed France in the same manner to demonstrate its commitment to Europe and liberal democracy. France had only its European policy, and needed Germany more than ever. A unified and confident Germany would face few constraints.

French fears of a united Germany thus oscillated between those of dealing with a hegemonic rival within the EU and that of a loose cannon outside of it in Central and Eastern Europe.

Germany often reacted with bemusement to such fears, convinced she had demonstrated her indelibly Europeanised and democratic character. In 1994, Klaus Kinkel, Germany's foreign affairs minister, confronted the fears of her partners head on. Germany remained committed to NATO; Germany retained close ties with the USA (with President Clinton looking to Germany as the USA's principal European partner), and Germany remained committed to a strong European Union (*The Economist*, 1994). Although the balance has shifted in its favour, the evidence presented in the ensuing chapters suggests that the new Germany continues to place great importance on the Franco-German relationship. Since German unification, there has been less place for sentimental symbolism, but France has remained Germany's principal political and economic partner. A new balance of power weighted in favour of Germany has not prevented close Franco-German cooperation on many policy issues. Before considering these cases in more detail, we will propose a theoretical framework of analysis for studying the Franco-German relationship.

CHAPTER 2

A framework for analysis

The Franco-German relationship does not easily fit into pre-existing theoretical frameworks. Our starting point is that it is impossible to dissociate studying the Franco-German relationship from the broader field of European integration. And yet European integration studies provide only partial insights; paradigms drawn from international relations and political science are necessary complements.

Any framework for analysing the Franco-German relationship must pose several complex research questions and address distinctive literatures. The research questions underpinning this study might be classified according to three broad dimensions. These concern the strategic, institutional and policy dimensions of the Franco-German relationship. Each research question can give rise to competing conceptual interpretations. Through elucidating these research questions and their related interpretations, we aim to achieve a syncretic synthesis that is operational for analysing the Franco-German relationship.

The leadership of the European integration project

The first series of questions relate to the role of France and Germany in the leadership of the European Union. Theories of European integration have had little explicitly to say about bilateral relationships. Supranational integration theories of neo-functionalism or neo-federalism posit outcomes that look beyond the nation state as the focal point of analysis. Indeed, their underlying presuppositions downplay the nation state as an object worthy of analysis. They focus attention on supranational actors (the Commission, the Parliament, the Court), on transnational forces (such as international business) which englobe and surpass national realities, or on cross-national political movements. Bilateral relationships are invisible when the phenomena observed are of such a level of generality. On the other hand, much analysis of the Franco-German relationship confines its focus to the 'couple' and assumes rather than demonstrates its influence and internal cohesion.

These observations give rise to several research questions. What evidence exists that France and Germany exercise joint leadership (or 'hegemony' in the realist lexicon) within the European Union? Has the changing equilibrium within the Franco-German alliance since German unification altered its leadership role? Has German leadership supplanted a joint directory of the EU? These initial research questions are primordial. They explicitly address the core themes of leadership posed throughout the book and implicitly contribute to theorising the nature of the European integration project principally from a state-centric conceptual focus.

The most appropriate conceptual tools to understand these research questions are those of neo-realism (from the discipline of international relations) and (liberal) intergovernmentalism (from political science). A fundamental postulate of both neo-realism and intergovernmentalism is that states matter – and that some states matter more than others. Neo-realism is rooted in expectations of rational state behaviour; nation states all act in rational ways to maximise their interest. Relations between states are determined by their position within the international hierarchy. Economically and militarily stronger states are expected to seek advantage by developing a hegemonic relationship with weaker neighbours. Only a balance of power between states of approximately equal standing can control the inherent anarchy of the international system (Milner, 1991). From neo-realism, we deduce inter-state rivalry to be the fundamental reality of international politics. Given its underlying assumptions, realism 'does not expect states to form cohesive and highly institutionalised structures' such as the EU (Pedersen, 1998: 5), although power alliances and inter-state coalitions (such as the Franco-German relationship) would seem compatible with realism.

Franco-German leadership?

There exists a powerful neo-realist interpretation of the Franco-German relationship within the European Union (Baun, 1996; Chang, 1999). From the perspective of neo-realism, the Franco-German relationship is predicated upon the mutually reinforcing strategic calculations of France and Germany. The post-war Franco-German relationship survived and prospered because it fulfilled specific functions. It allowed France to exercise a preponderant weight within the European communities while facilitating Germany's readmission into the international concert of nations. There was a fundamental complementarity in strategic and economic terms. France and Germany were forced together in the defence of Western Europe against the threat of Soviet aggression. Ultimately protected by US strategic leadership, France and Germany were able to channel their energies into the development of the European communities. The constitutive bargain of the Treaty of Rome set the EEC on a path that manifestly favoured the interests of its two leading members. The EEC not only symbolised historic reconciliation between France and Germany, but also allowed each country to pursue its enlightened economic self-interest: a common market underpinned the revival of German industry; a common agricultural policy protected French farmers and promoted French farm produce. The European communities allowed Germany to become a world player far more rapidly than had it continued to be isolated. One version of the realist paradigm interprets the Franco-German relationship as a directorate designed to serve the interests of France and Germany (Pedersen, 1998; Chang, 1999). The European Union was created on the basis of a series of inter-state bargains, in which France and Germany divided the key roles. The nature of the initial bargains biased the Community in favour of France and Germany, which were able subsequently to exercise a joint leadership over European affairs. The real political leadership was the international 'regime' formed by France and Germany within the European Union.

The internal equilibrium of the Franco-German relationship was relatively harmonious during the long period from 1949 to 1989: the relationship enabled one power to control itself (Germany) and to accept that a traditional enemy (France) had a right to exercise a partial control over its destiny (McCarthy, 1993a). One of our principal research questions relates to the evolution of the Franco-German relationship since 1989: has German unification fundamentally altered the internal equilibrium of the Franco-German relationship, and, if so, what are the consequences of asymmetry?

Neo-realist and liberal intergovernmental accounts presuppose a leading role for nation states – and for France and Germany in particular – in the process of European integration. This is implicit in the writings of scholars such as Hoffmann (1995), Milward (1984), Taylor (1983) and Moravscik (1991, 1993, 1998). In his study of post-war European reconstruction (1984), Milward concluded that European integration is consistent with the survival of the nation state. Supranational organisations such as the ECSC and the EEC were set up for the specific purposes of nation states. Indeed, European integration strengthened nation states. European integration allowed common tariff barriers to be introduced to protect Western European markets. Integration also allowed Germany to be tied into Europe – and German economic reconstruction was vital for the recovery of other Western European states. Above all, European integration facilitated the re-emergence of the Federal Republic as a nation state. The most eloquent contemporary exponent of intergovernmentalism is Andrew Moravscik (1991, 1993, 1998). The essence of the Moravscik argument is that 'the EC can be analysed as a successful intergovernmental regime designed to manage economic interdependence through negotiated policy coordination'

(Moravscik, 1993: 473). Since their origins, the European communities have been based on inter-state bargains between the leading states (especially France and Germany), whose cooperation is predicated upon the need to minimise transaction costs and costly competition. In *The Choice for Europe*, Moravscik (1998) claims to have demonstrated inter-state bargaining to be a far more potent dynamic in the EU than the input of supranational leadership, European institutions, or transnational business groups.

Moravscik's central thesis is that European integration strengthens the authority of national leaders through concentrating national negotiating power in their hands during treaty negotiations, the defining moments of EU institution-building. Not only are national governments the most important actors, but there is a hierarchy of power between them. Only the big states really count, and France and Germany count more than most. Small states are either bought off with side payments, or coerced into acceptance of package deals. There is no integrative effort to 'elevate the common interest', but rather a lowest common denominator bargaining style. This liberal intergovernmental approach points to the weakness of the Commission and other community actors in treaty negotiations between member states. The role of France, Germany and Britain as harbingers of change is examined in more detail in our study of the Single European Act in Chapter 4.

German hegemony?

At the core of realist theory lies the hegemon: a dominant power able to impose its will on weaker members of a regional community. Keohane (1984) defines hegemony according to three principal characteristics: a hegemon enjoys a material preponderance of capabilities, a military primacy and sufficient political influence to organise relations with other regional players. 'Hegemonic stability theory' assumes the existence of a regional hegemon able and apt to impose its domination upon weaker members of a region and to limit the inherent political anarchy and economic instability of the international system. The USA is the obvious paradigm. Several attempts have been made to apply hegemonic stability theory to the case of Germany (Marsh, 1992; Lankowski, 1993; Hueglin, 1995), but this is problematical. Although Germany is the most significant European economic power, its lead over its main competitors and neighbours is not that great; indeed, if measured on a per capita basis, there was a tendency for Germany's relative lead to stagnate during the 1990s (Chang, 1999). Military hegemony does not accurately describe the situation of post-war Germany; in most respects the 'economic giant' remains a military pygmy. Germany has substantial political leverage, but its influence within the EU depends upon building coalitions with like-minded countries. On the other hand, Germany has demonstrated its capacity to exercise regional leadership in those areas that matter most, notably in monetary policy and economic standard setting (Kaelberer, 1997). On account of its economic influence, Germany performs the most important rule setting and agenda defining roles in the EU. By promoting the use of qualified majority voting (QMV) across all areas of decision-making, some have argued that Germany has sought a pan-European institutional basis for its primacy (Pedersen, 1998). There is a far closer structural fit between the German polity and the political system of the European Union than that of any other country; this gives Germany an informational and resource advantage by comparison with other states. Widening the EU to the East will create an old-fashioned sphere of interest.

On balance, however, scholars have had great difficulty in applying the realist paradigm to Germany, a state whose domestic ideology of consensus, interdependence and smallness appears to most observers to be more important than the structural qualities of German power (Le Gloannec, 1993a; Markovits and Reich, 1997).

The supranational challenge

Intergovernmental paradigms have been vigorously contested by 'Institutionalists' who have adopted the modern mantle of neo-functionalism (Puchala, 1999). The emerging 'new orthodoxy' (Webber, 1999a: 579) in EU theoretical studies is that the EU is a multi-tiered, quasi-federal polity, with a gradual shift of competencies to supranational actors, namely the European Court of Justice, the Commission and, most recently, the Parliament (Stone Sweet and Sandholtz, 1997; Armstrong and Bulmer, 1998). Although concerned with the overall leadership of the European integration project (hence their inclusion in this section), supranational paradigms pose a rather different series of research questions, namely: how has the Franco-German alliance managed the transition to an increasingly supranational polity? How do France and Germany cope with the effects of policy change which challenge their respective national traditions?

The most appropriate theoretical paradigms for comprehending this series of research questions are those of neo-functionalism and historical institutionalism. Neo-functionalism has vied with liberal intergovernmentalism in providing a general framework for European integration. Three basic ideas underpinned the neo-functionalist paradigm developed by Ernst Haas and others from the late 1950s (O'Neill, 1996). First, that Western nations were economically interdependent, and they shared overwhelming common interests. Second, the regulation of economic management was best assured at a supranational level, where economies of scale could be maximised. Third, the complexity of socio-economic processes would encourage governments to transfer competencies in specific sectors to the supranational level. Early functionalist accounts of European integration used the example of the European Coal and Steel Community to illustrate, as they saw it, the primacy of economics, the importance of technical integration and the dynamic of functional spillover. Because of the technical linkage between policy sectors, neo-functionalists predicted a permanent pressure for the transfer of new competencies to the supranational centre. The Common Market created by the Treaty of Rome in 1957 ideally required a single regulatory authority to ensure fair trade, which, in turn, could only be controlled by a supranational authority with adequate political legitimacy. Technical pressures would spill over into the political domain. Gradually, a supranational authority would take over the responsibilities and competencies of the nation states. Both citizens and political actors would eventually shift their loyalties towards a new centre.

The originality of the neo-functionalist approach was that of spillover. There are different uses of the concept of spillover. In its original sense, functional spillover predicted a process of technically driven integration as a result of the linkage between policy sectors. This was the spirit present in Monnet's advocacy of sectoral integration, of the ECSC variety, as a stepping stone to a more integrated European polity. Neo-functionalist writers also referred to political spillover. For Ernst Haas (1958), European integration would occur naturally as a by-product of the interaction between national political actors anxious to benefit from technological advances. Political actors would come to look naturally to the supranational level as the benchmark of efficacy and the focus of their loyalty. Political actors might also use spillover as a cultivated strategy; taking a long-term view, state actors can decide that it is in their interest to strengthen supranational institutions, because they gain from the 'constitutive bargain'.

Traditional political actors were marginalised in the neo-functionalist scheme, which predicted the increasing importance of powerful supranational organs and a waning of influence of national governments. Indeed, insofar as political actors were important at all, integration would favour supranational over national actors. From a neo-functionalist perspective, the Commission – rather than nation states such as France and Germany – would lead the integration process.

Neo-functionalism suffered from its inability to explain the Gaullist brake on integration in the 1960s. As integration has deepened since the mid-1980s, and the linkages across policy sectors have become more powerful, there have been various attempts to rehabilitate neo-functionalism (Tranholm-Mikkelsen, 1991; Mazzucelli, 1997). For the new generation of neo-functionalists, the Single European Act created a momentum for a single currency, as an effective minimiser of transaction costs. In turn, EMU will lead to pressures for tax and fiscal harmonisation, to ensure that currency exchanges occur on a level playing field. The economic and monetary policies of member states are not only benchmarked; they become collectively owned. Mazzucelli (1997) points to the linkage between completing the internal market and capital liberalisation as proof of an adept political usage of neo-functionalism.

The most elaborate formulation of the modern variety of neo-functionalism is that of historical institutionalism. Pierson (1996) can be taken as a sophisticated exponent of this perspective. He argues that political development must be understood as a historical process; institutions develop a life of their own and are difficult to rein in at will. The historical institutionalist argument emphasises the temporal dimension of politics; there is a lag between decisions and their long-term consequences. Once decisions are made, they are difficult to undo and they shape the direction of future decisions. Member states such as France and Germany (and even more so all the others) gradually lose control of the process of European integration. There are various forces undermining member-state control. These include the unintended consequences of past decisions, the autonomous actions of European institutional actors, the restricted time horizons of national decision-makers, changing member-state preferences over time and the importance of path-dependent policy processes.

While nation states might have retained the initiative until the mid-1980s, the 'institutionalist' critique identifies the Single European Act as representing a paradigm shift. The Single European Act changed the rules of the European game and created a dynamic and unpredictable process that has empowered a range of new transnational and supranational actors. The research questions that follow logically from this supranational perspective – which we formulated above – concern national state resistance to Europeanised and globalised political and economic processes. Our next series of research questions are concerned with the operation of the Franco-German relationship as a bilateral relationship.

Institutions and actors of the Franco-German relationship

In the above section we considered the impact of the Franco-German relationship on the leadership of the European Union; we now address more squarely the institutions and actors of the Franco-German relationship itself. Several pertinent research questions must logically be posed concerning France and Germany's bilateral relationship. How important is Franco-German bilateral institution-building? Does the Franco-German relationship operate as a bilateral 'regime'? Which actors drive the Franco-German relationship? In order to elucidate further these empirical questions, we intend, where appropriate, to refer to contrasting analytical explanations.

Institutions and regimes

Institutions have been defined as 'the rules of the game in a society, or, more formally . . . the humanly devised constraints that shape human interaction' (Pierson, 1996: 126). Far from being merely rules of the game, however, new institutionalist thinkers argue that institutions come to embody essential values and procedures that shape the policy process and structure human agency (March and Olsen, 1989). Briefly summarised, new institutionalism stresses the importance of formal institutions and rules, informal conventions, policy norms and symbols and policy instruments and procedures.

How important are the formal institutions of the Franco-German relationship? We argue in Chapter 3 that it is important not to over-emphasise the importance of the institutional forms of the Franco-German relationship. There is little evidence that Franco-German 'institutions' have developed a life of their own beyond the will of the principal agents, notably political leaders. Indeed, evidence is presented at various stages throughout the book to suggest the contrary. In the case of the Franco-German relationship, institutions stop far short of a binding rule-making capacity. Moreover, Franco-German institutions do not distribute resources – as do national or EU level institutions. Formal Franco-German institutions have had a mainly symbolic existence.

There are many ambiguities in the new institutional project. In relation to the Franco-German relationship, we can identify at least two understandings of institutionalism with contradictory implications. At the level of the nation state, institutionalism can be equated with the persistence of national traditions and contexts; the weight of national path dependencies is generally evoked to explain the resistance of national institutional and administrative actors to exogenous policy change. This is the sense of March and Olsen's original model. As applied to the development of the EU as a polity, on the other hand, historical institutionalism implies that the EU has developed its own institutions capable of inspiring loyalty and acting autonomously (Pierson, 1996; Armstrong and Bulmer, 1998). EU institutions are 'sticky', in the sense that they influence outcomes beyond member-state preferences. These two interpretations are obviously incompatible. The Franco-German relationship appears as an institutional hybrid; it is neither a genuine international organisation, nor a nation state. Consequently, institutional metaphors do not appear to be the most convincing for capturing the essence of the Franco-German relationship.

A more appropriate conceptual tool might be provided by regime theory. Developed in the realist tradition of international relations, regime theory sets out to explain why, and under what circumstances, states cooperate. International regimes are a specific form of realist compact. They are defined by Krasner (1983: 2) as 'sets of implicit and explicit principles, norms, rules, and decision-making procedures around which actors' expectations converge in a given area of international relations'. In a more precise definition, Young (1991: 13) describes regimes as structures bringing together a limited number of actors to manage well-defined activities, or resources in specific geographical areas. Regimes are loose, intergovernmental agreements to manage specific common interests. Regimes take states as the baseline, but recognise that some forms of mutually beneficial interstate collaboration are necessary (Pierson, 1996). Regimes do not challenge state sovereignty, and do not normally imply a high degree of institutionalisation. The regime label has been applied by realists such as Keohane (1984) and intergovernmentalists such as Moravscik (1993) to describe the European Union as a loose intergovernmental organisation. International regimes such as the European Union help states perform their domestic regulation tasks, and hence strengthen their decisional capacity. This has been much criticised (Wallace and Wallace, 1996; Featherstone and Ginsberg, 1996). Regime theory does not easily explain the very high level of institutionalisation of the EU. Regime functions do not require a supranational or a semi-federal union. We accept this criticism as a valid one. Inappropriate as a tool to render account of the complexity of the European Union, the regime concept might be more fruitfully applied to the Franco-German relationship as an institutional hybrid. The Franco-German relationship displays certain (bilateral) regime-like features. At its most effective, the Franco-German relationship appears as a bilateral quasi-regime. Rather than being a complex institutional entity, the Franco-German relationship is best understood as an informal, often invisible compact operating on a flexible basis to secure outcomes desired by both countries. The regime analogy points to the intergovernmental basis of international action, which appears specifically relevant when considering the Franco-German relationship. The efficacy of the Franco-German 'quasi-regime' depends on strategically astute political leadership, far more than upon embedded institutional structures.

Political actors

How important is political leadership for the effective functioning of the Franco-German relationship? Both realism and neo-functionalism underplay the role of national political leaderships. This is to misinterpret the importance of political factors and the role of human agency in the dynamics of integration. French and German leaders figure prominently in subsequent chapters both as the driving force and as a weather-vane of the Franco-German relationship. De Gaulle and Adenauer, and later Mitterrand and Kohl, all exercised a measure of strategic direction over the process of European integration at critical junctures in history. Not all of their contemporary leaders possessed a comparable quota of strategic vision. The role of the French president and German chancellor will be demonstrated in our analysis of the EMU negotiations (Chapter 5). Although an 'epistemic community' of central bankers and professional economists might have formulated the technical details of monetary union, and though the German *Bundesbank* and finance ministry were determined to control the process of implementation, Mitterrand (and Kohl) were the driving force behind placing EMU on the political agenda.

The study of political leadership requires cognisance of the complex interplay between structure, strategy and agency (Cole, 1997, 1998b). By structure, we refer to the combination of exogenous and endogenous constraints and opportunities within which political leaders operate. These are as likely to include exogenous variables, such as the nature of the international political economy, as they are to encompass domestic variables such as relations within the core executive, party political and coalitional factors, or the variables of public opinion or political culture. Political leaders attempt to navigate their way through this morass of constraints. By strategy, we refer to long-term leadership goals, and vision. By agency, we refer to the personal imprint left by leaders on policy outcomes, to their political skill and to their personal political styles. Appraisal of a particular political leadership requires an appropriate mix of structure, strategy and agency. As our analysis extends to bilateral relations (between French and German leaders) within multilateral settings (the EU and other international forums) we must also consider the external influences weighing upon a country, and the relationships between leaders, as well as their domestic leadership settings. The importance of the country or entity involved will obviously have a major bearing upon the resources at the disposal of the leader; the leaders of more powerful countries will be in a stronger bargaining position than the leaders of less influential nations. This explains the influence of Helmut Kohl, in spite of the existence of powerful domestic obstacles to his effective political leadership.

The model of two-level bargaining developed by Putnam (1988) provides a specific take on the role of political leadership. Putnam points to the importance of leaders building domestic coalitions that are consistent with foreign policy choices. In his innovative formulation of two-level bargaining, Putnam concludes that, 'It is reasonable to presume, at least in the international case of two-level bargaining, that the chief negotiator will normally give primacy to his domestic calculus' (Putnam, 1988: 457). If domestic variables outweigh international ones in determining state preferences, however, the interplay between domestic and international politics operates in both senses. Narrow domestic 'win-sets' are emphasised by political leaders in order to increase their bargaining power in international negotiations; the threat of an inability to deliver on a promise can be an important bargaining chip. But external 'constraints' can also be used at home to justify implementing unpopular domestic reforms. Externally-imposed reforms can serve a useful domestic policy function.

In Putnam's model, political leaders have a key linkage role. Not only are they directly exposed to domestic political pressures, but they are the agents of international negotiations. Core executive decision-makers – such as the French president and German chancellor – lie at the crossroads of domestic and international forces. Only leaders can use international pressures to resolve domestic policy dilemmas and plead domestic weakness to enhance a diplomatic bargaining position. There are 'transaction benefits' to be had from international summitry; political leaders like to be seen on the world stage, and their foreign policy role enhances their domestic prestige. There is particular solidarity between post-war French and German leaders, vested with a historic responsibility to promote European reconciliation. The most impersonal processes are negotiated by human agents, and French and German leaders have a long habit of working together.

The European Union has often been described an as elite-driven project. There was a strong bureaucratic politics content both in the Monnet method and in the underlying suppositions of neo-functionalism. In spite of its cultural manifestations at the level of the citizenry (the web of linguistic, cultural and educational exchanges) the Franco-German relationship is essentially also an elite-driven project. As we demonstrate in Chapter 3, French and German officials have performed an important part in sustaining sectoral and cross-sectoral bilateral contacts. In contrast, the Franco-German reflex is less automatic at the level of policy networks/interest groups, political parties and economic exchanges. These linkages will be developed in subsequent chapters.

National paths and policy convergence

The third series of research questions relate to the policy paradigms and processes underpinning the Franco-German relationship. Has there been a convergence of French and German policy interests, or, on the contrary, a further differentiation since German unification? Do common external pressures (such as Europeanisation and globalisation) strengthen the cohesion of the Franco-German relationship or, on the contrary, undermine them. What is the scope for policy learning between France and Germany?

Many new institutionalist and most cultural approaches are predicated upon varying forms of national distinctiveness. These portrayals stress the distinctive nature of national experiences and the primacy of path-dependent policy processes. States have different ideological cleavages that shape national interests and policy content (Bulmer, 1983). Each state has a different relationship to the outside world and states occupy different positions in the world economy. States will interact with each other on the basis of their political traditions and policy styles; interaction can produce learning, but it is unlikely to provoke convergence. A similar argument is used by Markovits and Reich (1997) in their study of post-unification Germany. National paths are shaped by domestic political traditions. National elites share causal beliefs about a nation's history. Cultural determinants are important in constraining foreign policy choices. Decisions take place within the parameters of acceptable choices, defined in accordance with ingrained national ideological traditions. Different countries have distinct traditions, and process change through particular conceptual lenses. Thus, in the case of contemporary Germany, Markovits and Reich introduce 'collective memory' as a powerful independent variable. Although elusive and ambiguous, collective memory and an enduring sense of war guilt impose limits on German national ambitions. Choices are non-rational, and ideology signifies patterns of behaviour that are inconsistent with rational explanations. Contemporary Germany remains characterised by an ideology of smallness which prevents it acting as a hegemon.

A contrasting variant of the domestic politics argument is that of domestic convergence (Bennett, 1991; Bennett and Howell, 1992). In an integrated regional organisation such as the European Union, a process of policy convergence gradually dissipates the distinctiveness of national context (specifically in relation to economic policy paradigms and social models) and facilitates the exchange of ideas, policies and goods. Adapted to Franco-German relations, a policy convergence thesis would emphasise not only the importance of endogenous political and economic factors in France and Germany but also that the state of the Franco-German relationship depends upon the converging internal pressures within France and Germany. The Franco-German relationship is grounded in reality because there is an essential consensus on outcomes and processes, and a narrowing of nationally distinctive positions over time (Trouille, 1994; Wood, 1995).

As we observed in our historical overview in Chapter 1, the national distinctiveness argument is clearly important. National context remains a primordial filter, and policy positions are viewed through nationally tinted conceptual lenses. It is not certain, however, that the reaffirmation of nationally distinctive positions can best explain the evolution of the Franco-German relationship. It is too static a portrayal. In the course of the subsequent chapters, we investigate the dynamics (and limits) of domestic convergence. There is evidence to suggest that the Franco-German relationship persists and flourishs because French and German policy positions have narrowed over time. A narrowing of distinctive national positions over time is – arguably – a prerequisite for engaging in long-term relationships and nested bargaining games.

Our central cognitive research question relates to the extent of, and the scope for, policy learning and policy transfer between France and Germany. State interests are not merely a reflection of structural power. States want to reduce uncertainty, as well as to pursue wealth and power. They need to find solutions to intractable policy problems. They can engage in positive sum relationships in international regimes, and they can also pool resources of expertise to attempt to resolve transnational policy dilemmas. The role of policy experts should be highlighted in this context. Causal beliefs and the search for technically feasible solutions can create 'a dynamic for persistent cooperation independent of the distribution of international power' (Haas, 1992: 4). Sharing policy expertise provides a means of building bilateral bridges; herein lies the importance of the web of informal contacts between French and German officials and experts. In the case of economic and monetary union and foreign and security policy, pooled Franco-German policy expertise affected strategic perceptions of how to advance shared national goals.

Throughout this book we present evidence to support an increased exchange of policy paradigms and ideas between France and Germany; this is part and parcel of the process of the narrowing of nationally distinctive positions. The process whereby member states are influenced by strong national models within their midst is demonstrated clearly in the monetary sphere, with the German model of monetary policy management acting as a benchmark for others. Best practice and a desire to imitate the most successful can produce a type of institutional isomorphism (Radaelli, 1999). The exchange between France and Germany in monetary policy is considered in Chapter 5. In a more indirect sense, the European perspective has affected cognitive assumptions about national and European models. French public policy in particular has become less self-sufficient, far more embedded in interdependent structures, and French elites have been more willing to engage in policy learning and to experiment with new discursive forms (Cole and Drake, 2000). Although in many respects there is a close structural fit between the German polity and the European pattern of multi-level governance, 'Europeanisation' has also challenged important features of the traditional German policy model.

Policy transfer requires human agency; ideas do not spread naturally, but require agents to assist in their dissemination. Political leaders are one obvious agent of policy change; policy entrepreneurs are another. Reference will also be made at various stages throughout the book to the role of 'epistemic communities' and 'advocacy coalitions' as agents of policy change. An epistemic community is defined by Peter Haas (1992: 3) as 'a network of professionals with recognised expertise and competence in a particular domain and an authoritative claim to policy-relevant knowledge within that domain or issue-area'. 'Advocacy coalitions' are well-established coherent coalitions (generally of technical experts) in particular policy fields. Unlike epistemic communities, however, where the emphasis is on elite consensus, the advocacy coalition approach emphasises the confrontation of alternative agendas in particular policy fields. These concepts can be usefully applied to the study of the Franco-German relationship. Thus, in their seminal study of economic and monetary union, Dyson and Featherstone (1999) stress the importance of an epistemic-like community of central bankers and professional economists in placing EMU on the policy agenda as a technically feasible and desirable policy project from the 1970s onwards. Dyson and Featherstone also identify the competition between rival advocacy coalitions (European and German within Germany; 'monetarist' and 'economist' within Europe) as representing an insuperable obstacle to the adoption of EMU prior to the earthquake of German unification.

Conclusion

This chapter has conceptualised various ways of understanding the Franco-German relationship. The paradigms presented are not necessarily mutually exclusive, though their principal advocates would probably consider them to be. For the purposes of analysing a bilateral relationship within a broader multilateral setting, intergovernmental theories offer a distinctive starting point. Without settling the argument between institutionalists and intergovernmentalists, the latter body of theories allows us to pose the appropriate research questions for the study of a bilateral relationship, notably those concerning the leadership of the European Union and the role of the Franco-German alliance therein. This conceptual choice need not commit us to any particular interpretation of the EU as a quasi-polity. Intergovernmental frames are appropriate for posing certain types of questions, but do not render full account of the EU in all its complexity.

The debate between intergovernmentalists and supranationalists has less relevance for the operation of the Franco-German relationship itself. We argued above that the Franco-German relationship displays certain bilateral regime-like features, especially within the specific multilateral setting of the

EU. The Franco-German relationship is undoubtedly the most important and most mature political relationship within the European Union. The Franco-German relationship appears as an institutional hybrid that falls somewhere between a formal institution and an informal bilateral regime. Although it is embedded in recognisable institutional structures, it is most effective as a set of relatively informal understandings and exchanges. The Franco-German relationship is brought alive, moreover, by human agents, of whom political leaders, national officials and policy experts are the most obvious exemplars. Our second series of research questions thus relate to the internal operation and the changing equilibrium within the Franco-German relationship during the period since German unification. The third series of research questions we pose concern issues of policy learning and policy convergence between France and Germany. We will return to these different research questions at various stages throughout the book and offer our preferred explanations in Chapter 8.

CHAPTER 3

Germany, France and the Franco-German relationship

Colourful metaphors abound when writers describe the nature of the post-war relationship between France and Germany. The three most popular are those of the Franco-German axis, the Franco-German motor and the Franco-German couple (Picht, Uterwedde and Wessels, 1990; Wallace, 1990; Bocquet, 1996). The metaphor of the Franco-German axis evokes the centrality of the Franco-German relationship to the European Union and its pivotal location. It highlights the dynamic qualities of the relationship and suggests that it is functionally necessary for the process of European integration. The Franco-German motor assumes literally that the two countries drive European integration. It is often used by politicians to justify maintaining an official bilateral alliance within the European Union as a form of enlightened leadership of the European integration project. The Franco-German couple is a rather more static appreciation, which invites unhelpful comparisons with domestic household disputes and is essentially insular. These metaphors all illuminate perceptions of the centrality of the Franco-German relationship. They also all assume its internal cohesion.

What exactly are these metaphors saying? If the argument is that the Franco-German relationship is united on the main issues facing the European Union, the evidence presented throughout this and other studies casts doubts upon the thesis of innate Franco-German cohesion. If the hypothesis is that the Franco-German relationship leads the EU, this necessitates closer observation of the genealogy of particular decisions and raises various methodological problems, notably to do with the secrecy of elite-level decision-making and the validity of memoirs and biographies. Actors close to French and German governments have certainly believed bilateral Franco-German cooperation to be a driving force of closer European integration. This was especially the case when Mitterrand and Kohl guided the destinies of the couple (Teltschik, 1990; Attali, 1993; Védrine, 1996; Mitterrand, 1996; interviews). It is difficult to establish with any measure of certainty whether anybody leads the European Union, but it would appear premature to exclude supranational actors from all influence. If the hypothesis is the weaker one, that the EU cannot 'progress' without Franco-German cooperation, this is also a matter of empirical observation rather than rhetorical acclamation. It invites a comparison of different levels and types of European Union decision-making. This task will be undertaken in Chapter 4. The main body of this chapter will investigate the internal operation of the Franco-German relationship. Before considering the various forms that this relationship can assume, and in recognition of the importance of domestic variables as potentially dynamic forces within the Franco-German relationship, this chapter sets out the national contexts that shape the negotiating positions and outlooks adopted by French and German governments. It then focuses on the purely bilateral aspects of the Franco-German relationship, and makes some initial judgements on the nature of the bilateral relationship between the two countries.

Germany in its domestic political setting

In the opinion of one high German civil servant, France and Germany are 'incompatible democracies' shaped by differing and conflictual historical experiences (Reeh, 1994: 237). Others disagree. On many issues, France and Germany instinctively agree and there is evidence of increased convergence during the past decade.

The Federal Republic of Germany in its initial version (from 1949 to 1989) was interpreted by Paterson (1998) as a 'semi-sovereign state'. Its institutions were invented by the occupying powers (the USA, the UK and France) in an attempt to create permanent checks and balances against the abuse of executive power. Its territorial boundaries (the division into West and East Germany) were a reminder of the division of post-war Europe into two mutually antagonistic blocs. Given that German leaders since Adenauer had steadfastly refused to 'trade' unification for neutrality – as Stalin had offered – recovering full sovereignty appeared a forlorn perspective, dependent on the improbable collapse of Communism. No one predicted the course of events of 1989. The Federal Republic was predicated upon the *de facto* division of Germany into two mutually antagonistic states. Its status as a frontline state reinforced its dependency upon US leadership in the global order (Szabo, 1990; Papcke, 1997). The foreign policy influence it could exercise was closely linked to its role in the American-led NATO alliance. The Federal Republic also developed a close alliance with France within Europe to ensure its rehabilitation as one of the European family of nations, and to support its own policy initiatives in Eastern Europe. Eternally torn between France and the USA, in the words of Garton-Ash (1994: 392), 'France was the most important power, but so was America'.

Germany's troubled history has contributed to defining the parameters of its contemporary polity (Markovits and Reich, 1997). Institutional checks and balances are predicated upon a mistrust of notions of undivided sovereignty, which directly related to Germany's Nazi past. Germany's post-war status as a conquered power has proved valuable in several respects. It helped to instil democratic values in a people abused by more authoritarian forms of government. It focused attention on the imperative of post-war reconstruction and provided the societal impetus for the Federal Republic to become the major European trading state. It facilitated the development of a social and economic model – the German social market economy – predicated upon economic growth, industrial harmony and cooperation. This soon became the envy of rivals. The consensual mode of German society favoured the development of professional training and the rise of a skilled workforce (Maurice, 1993). The political architecture encouraged power sharing, both vertically and horizontally, and lessened the fears of Germany's neighbours that an aggressive hegemon might rise from the ashes.

Germany's federal system of government proved itself well-adapted for the governance of the German polity. Although imposed by the occupying powers, the German model of 'cooperative federalism' allowed power to be dispersed by an elaborate system of political checks and balances and provisions for territorial integration. A form of institutionalised pluralism rested upon the dispersal of power across interlocking institutions; within the federal government itself (where the federal chancellor cohabits with strong ministers), between the federal government and the two chambers of parliament (the *Bundestag* and the *Bundesrat*), between the federal centre and the 11 (later 16) *Länder* governments (Padgett, 1994; Jeffery, 1995). Territorial integration strengthened political checks and balances; the *Länder* are directly represented in the upper chamber (*Bundesrat*) with a veto power over all issue areas affecting the *Land* governments (such as education and culture). The existence of a powerful second chamber (*Bundesrat*), controlled for much of the Kohl chancellorship by the opposition SPD, imposes a *de facto* grand coalition in important areas of policy. Moreover, the *Bundesrat* enjoys a large measure of scrutiny over European affairs. Not only does it dispose of the most efficient policy instrument for scrutinising EU law, but it has been strengthened by the constitutionally recognised right of the *Länder* to be consulted on European legislation that falls within their policy domain (Bulmer and Paterson, 1996). The Federal Constitutional Court is an effective constitutional arbiter, as demonstrated in landmark decisions on German troop deployment abroad and the Maastricht Treaty.

In very real terms, divided and coalition governments were the norm in the Federal Republic, notwithstanding the emergence of two disciplined *Volksparteien* after 1949. Only on rare occasions has the same party commanded a majority in both chambers. Even in these circumstances (as from September 1998 to March 1999) the interests of the Federal and *Land* governments do not automatically coincide. It is difficult to identify a single unitary 'German' political actor (Lees, 1999). Coalition building is more than ever the dominant mode of German politics. German chancellors exercise only a limited control over appointments and dismissals of government ministers; party, coalition, territorial and interest group balance all have to be respected when forming a government. Coalitions need to be constructed on specific issues – rather as in the governance of the European Union. The long-term effect of coalition government has been to strengthen policy sectoralisation, as coalition parties have colonised particular ministries; the best example is that of the FDP and the Foreign Affairs Ministry (Smith, 1994). Party logics coincide with ministerial disputes: rivalries between the Foreign Affairs Ministry and the Chancellor's Office over foreign policy have often been reinforced by political competition between the FDP and CDU, and, latterly, by the SPD and the Greens.

The domestic political setting within which a German chancellor functions is far more restricted than that of his French or British counterparts (Cole, 1998b). The forces militating against strong leadership include the compromises inherent in coalition management, the impact of factional politics within the governing coalition, the federal system, which vests a virtual veto power in the hands of state governments and the second chamber, the prevalence of sectoral corporatism as a model of state–group relations, and the impact of a particular institutional framework designed to dissipate decision-making authority across separate, but interdependent, institutions (Clemens and Paterson, 1998). The process of European political and economic integration has arguably reinforced the German chancellor's location within the core executive (Paterson, 1994). Direct contact with foreign heads of government allowed Kohl to develop close relations with French President Mitterrand, with Spanish Prime Minister Gonzalez, and with Commission President Delors. These relationships between key executive leaders were unavailable to foreign ministers, or even to finance ministers – each with their own less important networks. In addition, the Chancellor's Office has its own foreign policy experts, who maintain close contacts with their French interlocutors (in the Elysée office, in Matignon, in the Foreign Affairs Ministry).

Since 1990, new actors and interests (notably new parties and eastern *Land* governments) have added to the polycentric character of the German polity, making tasks of coordination and direction even more difficult. New types of political issue – notably the allocation of scarce resources, and the respect of cultural and territorial identities – have complicated the policy agenda (Welfens, 1993; Le Gloannec, 1993a; Jeffery, 1995).

Essential political decisions – such as over taxation increases and welfare cuts to accompany the introduction of the single currency – have been delayed, or buried by the *Bundesrat*. After a short respite, this institutional gridlock has carried over into the Schröder administration, where a CDU-dominated *Bundesrat* has decreed there is no political majority for welfare cuts.

At the heart of post-war German consensus lay *Modell Deutschland*, a social and economic model that became the envy of neighbours (Pulzer, 1995). German post-war economic performance could be measured across the range of economic criteria: growth, commercial balance, price stability and employment. During the 1960s, levels of economic growth averaged 8.2% in the 1950s and 1960s, and 4.4% between 1960 and 1973 (Dyson, 1996). Manufacturing exports were the driving force of German economic growth. A permanent economic surplus underpinned the economic consensus on the social-market economy. Ideas of social partnership, stakeholder capitalism and plant-level corporatism underpinned this socio-economic consensus. Social partnership implied partnership in industrial relations, collective wage bargaining, detailed regulation and a redistributive taxation and social security system (Dyson, 1996). During the 1990s, however, the German economy registered a sluggish economic performance, beset by the difficulties of digesting German unification and adapting to a changing international political economy. With the downturn and challenges to the German economy in the 1990s, the German social compromise became subject to increasing internal and external pressures. These themes are developed in Chapter 5.

France in its domestic political setting

The domestic political setting of post-war French politics contrasts in important respects with that of Germany. There was no real equivalent in the French case of the national division imposed on Germany from 1949 to 1989. On the other hand, France did lose an empire from 1948 to 1962, and, as in Germany, there was a close linkage between the process of national readjustment to a loss of prestige and moves to closer European integration. Restoring the rank of France as a great power was the leitmotif of post-war public policy. As a victor in the Second World War, France remained attached to symbols of national sovereignty and international prestige, symbolised by its permanent seat on the UN security council. Although an initiator of moves to closer European integration in the Fourth Republic (including the abortive European Army), during the early Fifth Republic Gaullist France appeared to favour maximum national independence in the sphere of defence, foreign and security policy. The withdrawal from NATO in 1966, and the building of France's independent nuclear deterrent were symbols of this obsession with rank (Fontaine, 1991).

Differences between post-war French and German polities are most obvious at the level of political institutions and ideological heritages. To the German model of institutionalised pluralism, the French post-war polity responded first with a form of unstable hyper-parliamentarism in the Fourth Republic (1946–58); later with a form of strong personal leadership developed under General de Gaulle. While the Federal Republic was the paradigm of decentralised federalism, the French Fifth Republic (1958–) was generally considered an example of strong personal leadership in the form of the elected president. Throughout the forty years of the Fifth Republic, the French polity gradually evolved from a presidential-centred polity to an executive-centred parliamentary democracy fundamentally comparable with similar parliamentary democracies elsewhere in Europe (Cole, 1998a). Whether under presidential, semi-presidential or governmental inspiration, core executive relations within the Fifth Republic have generally been more disciplined than in the Federal Republic, but this might only be by a matter of degree. There is no institutional embedding of coalition partners comparable with the German case, but coalition management has posed a greater or a lesser challenge to executive cohesion depending on political circumstances. The 'plural left' government led by Jospin (1997–) contains distinctive (and contradictory) positions towards the Franco-German relationship and European project within its ranks.

Although the model of the strong presidency is in convalescence, there remains a legacy of personalised decision-making in the sphere of European policy, and especially in Franco-German relations. In domestic politics, presidential pre-eminence in European affairs was for long so pronounced that Europe was considered to form part of a 'reserved sector'. During the Fifth Republic, the main European decisions certainly have been taken by French presidents (Cole and Drake, 2000). Presidential pre-eminence, however, did not imply that French presidents determined French policy towards Europe in isolation from other French political actors and institutions. Always overstated, the hyper-presidentialist thesis has become less tenable with the changing political environment since the 1980s (the push to more supranational forms of decision-making and closer integration), the inherent fragmentation of the EU policy process, and repeated instances of 'cohabitation'.

The political cultures of France and Germany have rested upon distinctive national ideological paths and institutional traditions (Gaffney and Kolinsky, 1991; Le Gloannec and Hassner, 1996). While Germany's model of cooperative federalism and institutionalised pluralism set out to disperse and share power, the French republican model has traditionally stressed the general will and the undivided nature of political legitimacy. The ideology of the One and Indivisible state was in some sense a defining feature of the Republic. We can identify several principal features of the traditional republican model of French politics and policies (Cole, 1998a). The existence of a powerful central state was a legacy of the process of nation-building, whereby centralisation and uniformity were imposed from above on rebellious provinces and local identities. This produced a model of Parisian centralisation, and – in comparative terms – a homogeneous political and administrative elite rigorously selected through a system of elite schools and competitive examinations. A natural corollary was the tradition of state interventionism in the economic and industrial sphere (*dirigisme*); the role of the state was to lead and to compensate for the lack of dynamism of domestic capitalism (Cohen, 1996).

At the level of political representation, the republican model vowed a distrust of intermediary institutions, such as parties, groups and regions, as threatening the general will. Although powerful provincial counterweights survived, these operated within the confines of Jacobin legality. There was a rather weak bargaining culture and divided, unrepresentative interest groups; the state determined which groups were representative. Contemporary French politics repeatedly highlights the paradox of a weak bargaining culture, producing strong social counterweights imbued with an ethic of direct action. The farming lobby acts as a powerful domestic constraint in the French case that has no real equivalent in Germany.

By comparison with the Federal Republic, the Fifth Republic has generally had executive-dominated governments, relatively weak political and judicial counterweights to a powerful executive authority and a high territorial concentration of power. French political leaders are able to negotiate with German and other partners without worrying excessively about sub-national interests. Even after the far-reaching decentralisation laws of 1982–83, which created directly elected regions, there is no equivalent of *Länder* governments and metaphors of multi-level governance have more resonance in the German case than the French. Parliamentary counterweights to executive authority have generally been much weaker in the French case. The lower chamber, the National Assembly, enjoys limited constitutional sovereignty and exercises weak parliamentary scrutiny, though the institution has acquired more powers and prestige in recent years. The Second Chamber – the Senate – is an archaic and ineffective institution, over-representing rural and small-town France at the expense of the urban areas of population. It lacks the legitimacy and expertise of the *Bundesrat*. Parliamentary control over EU affairs is less effective than in Germany. The constitutional amendment of 1992 ratifying the Maastricht Treaty allowed the National Assembly and the Senate to vote 'resolutions' on European laws, rather than merely expressing 'opinions', but the French Constitutional Council subsequently adjudged that parliament could not undermine the government's prerogatives in negotiating European laws (Ladrech, 1994). By contrast, the rise of judicial and regulatory counterweights to executive authority was a prominent feature of French politics in the 1990s. French public opinion has had a more direct impact on relations between governmental elites and the electorate than in Germany. Adapting the formula of Roberto Michels, there has been an 'iron law of anti-incumbency', whereby the outgoing French government has lost every decisive election since 1981. Assuaging domestic constituencies, and calculating finely tuned two-level bargains is a major preoccupation of French leaders.

The traditional model of French politics and policies has been subjected to intense pressure for change since the late 1970s. In the late 1990s, there were comparable forces provoking change across European countries. These include global economic change, the impact of European integration, pressures for economic convergence, a calling into question of certain types of political institution and the changing role of the state. As a leading European nation with a particular state tradition and historical legacy, these pressures have led to more visible changes in France than elsewhere. There has been a redefinition of the scope and activity of the state, a weakening of traditional bases of partisan identification and a rise of political movements contesting the underlying consensus of the Fifth Republican polity (Allison and Heathcote, 1999). On the other hand, there has also been an unprecedented measure of policy convergence amongst French elites (in favour of European integration, economic convergence and the single currency), and 'Europeanisation' has weighed increasingly heavily upon domestic French politics. I have developed these themes in some detail elsewhere (Cole, 1998a; Cole and Drake, 2000).

In summary, France and Germany each faced specific sets of domestic constraints and incentives. Both countries purveyed distinctive national models, in many ways the antithesis of their Rhineland neighbours. One of our central research questions – to which we return in the conclusion – is the extent to which the Franco-German relationship itself produced a convergence between these national models. Understanding the extent and limitations of convergence is facilitated by a fuller comprehension of how France and Germany view each other.

France and Germany in the looking glass

The Franco-German relationship is based not only on a network of bilateral structures, but also on deeply embedded representations of the adversary/partner and tacit motivations for cooperation. Before considering in more detail the bilateral relationship, it is appropriate to explore these paradoxical representations on both sides of the Rhine.

How does Germany view France? As surveyed in Chapter 1, friendship with France was the critical feature of the Adenauer period (1949–63). Early moves to closer European integration (especially the ECSC and the EEC) were legitimised in the name of Franco-German reconciliation. Indeed, Adenauer was even prepared to follow Gaullist France along the path to a bilateral relationship that was strongly contested domestically, and that many portrayed as going against the spirit of European integration and Atlanticism. Maintaining friendly relations with France fulfilled a major psychological need. For the first time since German unification in 1871, the Federal Republic had a friendly neighbour to its west. A close bilateral relationship with France has been highly valued by all German leaders, but misunderstanding and misrepresentation have often lain beneath the surface.

Official French pronouncements on the rationale of the Franco-German relationship could provoke German exasperation. During the unification period, Kohl found it hard to conceal his irritation with Mitterrand, for whom European integration was essential to 'tie in' the Germans and to prevent the temptation of neutrality. From a German perspective, this misrepresented the profoundly democratic character of post-war Germany. French politicians were prone to underplay the democratic safeguards existing within the German system (Sur, 1993).

If the Franco-German bilateral relationship has prospered, it is because it has fulfilled tacit German policy objectives. The Franco-German relationship has allowed German initiatives to be embedded in a broader bilateral framework. The Franco-German relationship performs the valuable function of reassuring other EC states over Germany's intentions and of framing German interests under a discourse of historical reconciliation. Germany has traditionally preferred joint Franco-German initiatives, rather than unilateral German ones that might raise suspicions of hegemony amongst Germany's European neighbours.

Less constrained by diplomatic conventions than her politicians, Germany's press often interpreted French policy towards Europe as being exclusively aimed against Germany. Thus, the Maastricht Treaty was a timid ersatz of the Versailles Treaty; EMU was a French plot to destroy the *Bundesbank*, even the Franco-German defence corps was a means of ensuring French leadership and controlling German military appetites (Rosselin, 1993). The French were suspected of protectionism, of *dirigisme*, and of wanting to protect the EU from the Central and Eastern European democracies. The French expected Germany to be the main paymaster and fiercely resisted any moves that threatened French agriculture. German public opinion indirectly voiced these concerns, notably in its longstanding opposition to the abolition of the *Bundesbank* and the sacrifice of the Deutschmark (Papcke, 1996). However, throughout the 1990s, a majority of German public opinion also held steadfastly to the belief that France was Germany's principal political ally.

How does France view Germany? One of the essential objectives of French foreign policy in the post-war period was to tie the Germans into the Western alliance through the process of European integration (Morgan, 1991). The geo-strategic position occupied by the unified Germany in the centre of Europe raised French worries that Germany might drift towards neutralism, towards a preference for an independent central European strategy, or even for a German–Russian entente, at the expense of a commitment to the EU (Papcke, 1996). Territorial irredentism was not completely imaginary; Kohl had, after all, hesitated over the Oder–Neisse border in 1989–90. The belief that Germany needed to be constrained in order to respect democracy was widely shared by French elites (Sur, 1993). Controlling Germany became the leitmotif of French strategic calculations, from EMU to the common foreign and security policy (CFSP). There were several variations on this theme of binding Leviathan (Dyson, 1999a). The traditional French foreign office view was that European integration would 'control' Germany in the French national interest. European responses to the problem of German power found even more favour after German unification; the corseting of Germany in restrictive institutions was an appropriate response to the new European balance of power. Alongside the strategic calculations of politicians, there was a pervasive fear of the new Germany, which emerged during the French Maastricht referendum campaign (Sur, 1993). Both sides used the latent fears of German domination to support their cause. For the supporters of the No camp, the Maastricht Treaty gave Germany a means of dominating the continent through monetary union. For the Yes camp, Franco-German collaboration constrained Germany, and prevented domination. Both representations were insulting to Germany; neither was willing to accord a democratic seal of approval to the unified German state.

The evolution of French public opinion during 1989–90 provides an illuminating case study of popular French fears over German unification. In the immediate aftermath of the collapse of the Berlin wall, French public opinion was largely favourable to the unfolding of events in Eastern Europe. The favourable attitude reflected a belief that a historic victory had been achieved over communism: in November 1989, 74% considered that the events in Eastern Europe had weakened communism in general (Cornut-Gentille and Rozes, 1991). But once that attention turned away from expressions of general satisfaction that communism had been vanquished, to the relative standing of France within Europe, French public opinion became more circumspect. In one SOFRES poll conducted in April 1990,

37% (against 19%) declared that German unification would weaken French influence within Europe, whereas 43% (against 20%) considered that German unity would make European political union more difficult. By the actual date of unification in October 1990, those considering that German unification would be a 'good thing' had fallen from over 60% when the Wall collapsed, to just 37% one year later (Morgan, 1991: 109).

Opinion poll surveys in 1990 and 1991 also revealed that there remained important areas in which there was little reciprocal understanding between the citizens of the two countries. French public opinion had for long been distrustful of Germany's economic preponderance: by May 1989, according to SOFRES, French public opinion had come to regard the Federal Republic as a more formidable threat to the French economy than the USA, only narrowly trailing Japan. In polls taken in September 1990, a clear majority opposed the idea that community funds should be channelled to the former East German *Länder*. To the traditional French fear of German economic hegemony was added the deeply rooted belief that a unified Germany would dominate the EC politically: 62% of a SOFRES sample polled in September 1990 considered either very or fairly likely that Germany would dominate the EC, as against 27% who considered this outcome unlikely or impossible (Cornut-Gentille and Rozes, 1991). In spite of decades of close cooperation between the two countries, opinion surveys illustrated that many traditional stereotypes remained intact: for the Germans, the French were above all nationalistic (57%); for the French, the Germans were above all disciplined (71%) (Cornut-Gentille and Rozes, 1991).

These societal images complete the presentation of France and Germany in their domestic political settings. We shall now turn to analysing the political operation of the Franco-German bilateral relationship.

The Franco-German bilateral relationship

There is no single form of Franco-German bilateral relationship, rather a series of multilayered relationships. They occur most obviously between political leaders, at the level of formal institutions, through informal networks, via party structures and through policy networks. The quality of these relationships can vary according to the level of interaction and the type of issue-area involved. In the ensuing section, we map out the different forms of the bilateral Franco-German relationship and consider how its operation varies according to the actors and issue-areas involved.

Personal relations

Personal relations between French and German leaders have always been important. The effectiveness of the 'special relationship' depends in part upon

the warmth of relations maintained between leaders, although such relationships are always underpinned by other, ultimately more consequential
considerations. De Gaulle and Adenauer enjoyed excellent personal relations, whereas those between the general and Erhard or Kiesinger were
far more difficult. Pompidou and Brandt distrusted each other; Giscard
d'Estaing and Schmidt enjoyed a relationship based on mutual confidence
(Simonian, 1985). From the moment of Kohl's inception as German chancellor, Mitterrand and Kohl endeavoured to recreate a great personal relationship, in conscious imitation of the de Gaulle–Adenauer partnership. This
was characterised by the famous image of the two leaders holding hands in
the cemetery of Verdun in 1984, a deliberate imitation of an earlier gesture
when, in 1962, de Gaulle and Adenauer had ostentatiously knelt together
in prayer in the cathedral at Reims. In contrast, relations between Kohl and
Chirac were often difficult, as demonstrated over French nuclear testing
(August 1995) and the German-inspired Stability Pact (1996–97). In many
respects, Gerhard Schröder has displayed a closer relationship with British
premier Blair than with either President Chirac or premier Jospin.

From September 1982 to April 1990 Mitterrand and Kohl reputedly held
more than 80 bilateral meetings (Haski, 1990a). Foreign ministers Dumas
and Genscher and special advisers Attali and Teltschik maintained even
more regular contact. The symbolism of leadership summits was important
– commitments undertaken by political leaders are difficult to retract. The
personal relationship is highly routinised; certain conventions are upheld
irrespective of the personalities of the leaders. The joint letters signed by
French and German leaders are a case in point. The political symbolism
of such appeals for European integration is of great importance, especially
when disagreements are the most serious. These meetings allow French and
German leaders to map out their visions of the future of Europe in relative
bilateral privacy. The development of international summitry has added
further arenas for frequent – though not exclusive – contact between French
and German decision-makers, who meet in fora as diverse as G7 economic
summits, the IMF and NATO. There is some evidence, much of it anecdotal,
of coordinated Franco-German responses in these fora, consistent with the
conception of the Franco-German relationship as a bilateral 'quasi-regime'.

Within this network of political leaders, French and German leaders
entertain the most dense relationships. Bilateral meetings with French
President Mitterrand served German Chancellor Kohl particularly well at
the height of the controversy over German unification; they allowed him
to make engagements that were difficult subsequently to challenge by other
German actors. French and German political leaders share a community
of interests in reserving the making of history-making decisions for themselves. In Kohl's opinion, only the German chancellor and the French

president could lead, direct and coordinate the process of European unification, while for Mitterrand it was the role of political leaders to preside and decide (Morgan, 1993; Drake, 1994). While the tendency in the long Kohl period was to centralise decision-making around the chancellor, this has become less true since Schröder assumed office; the Kosovo conflict witnessed a more even partnership between Schröder and foreign minister Fischer. In the French case, we intimated above that the French president has gradually adopted a rather less domineering role in European policy formulation (Cole and Drake, 2000) and 'cohabitation' has imposed a form of shared political leadership in Franco-German affairs between Jospin and Chirac. These developments have to some extent blurred the visibility of bilateral relations between French and German leaders, but they remain of primordial importance. The quality of the Franco-German relationship continues to depend in part upon the personal relations between French and German leaders.

Bilateral institutions

In the history of the Franco-German relationship, institution-building has often appeared as an end in itself, as a sign of good faith. France and Germany have invested considerable time and effort in institutionalising their relationship, in the belief that the relationship itself will produce a mutual learning process, and a narrowing of philosophical differences between the countries. The Franco-German relationship is held together by a complex mix of networks and structures. These include regular meetings of heads of state and ministers (especially foreign ministers), both bilaterally, and within multilateral structures (the European Council, G8, the IMF); various informal networks of elite civil servants; and bilateral party-based contacts in multilateral organisations such as the Party of European Socialists (PES) and the European People's Party (EPP). The Franco-German relationship thus operates both bilaterally and as an influential alliance within broader multilateral groupings.

The 1963 Elysée Treaty established a series of bilateral institutions (Soutou, 1996). The Franco-German summits were the most visible aspect of this institutional machinery. Since the signing of the Franco-German Treaty between de Gaulle and Adenauer in 1963, biannual summit meetings have been held between the French president, the German chancellor, representatives of the French and German governments and their advisers. There is a ritual about the Franco-German summits that is not altered by the changing personalities involved. This is demonstrated by the 72nd Franco-German summit, held at Potsdam in December 1998 (Haski and Millot, 1998). The summit was preceded by a joint Schröder/Chirac letter.

There was thorough political and administrative preparation in the run-up to the summit. Foreign ministers Fischer and Védrine held extensive talks. There were bilateral preparatory meetings between presidential, prime ministerial and chancellery advisors. On the eve of the summit there was an informal dinner for Schröder and Chirac. The summit itself mobilised over forty officials on each side. This high degree of mobilisation demonstrated the desire to relaunch the Franco-German relationship after the end of the Kohl years.

There were public relations advantages in bilateral leadership summits, as there were in more impromptu gatherings (such as flying visits, 'private' visits and working breakfasts). But the benefits went beyond public relations symbolism. Summits occasionally prepared the way for the launch of new initiatives, but were more likely to smooth over areas of Franco-German disagreement. Disagreements at lower levels could be unblocked by leadership summits, which also offered 'breathing space' to allow more time to resolve intractable differences. Above all, Franco-German summits excluded the Commission, as, to a lesser extent, did Franco-German collaboration in international fora. France and Germany have traditionally resisted Commission interference in their bilateral relationship. The most important function of the Franco-German bilateral summits is to allow the two countries to broker nested bargains. This is not new. In the Franco-German bilateral summit of January 1971, Germany inclined to the minimalist French view on EMU, partly in response to the official French stance of neutrality over Brandt's Östpolitik proposals, outlined by the French President Pompidou at a Franco-German bilateral summit the previous year (Simonian, 1985).

Franco-German bilaterals have always been used as a means of solving problems. Even public disagreements form part of the Franco-German method; airing public disputes allowed the two positions to be narrowed down, and areas of compromise and consensus to emerge. Many important decisions are taken 'behind closed doors' in informal Franco-German bilaterals; this was the case in the negotiations preceding the Maastricht summit (Dyson and Featherstone, 1999), in the Uruguay GATT round (Webber, 1998) and over successive reforms of the CAP (Webber, 1999b).

Apart from introducing regular summit meetings, the 1963 Treaty also contained provisions for cooperation in the spheres of security policy and defence, education, cultural policy and youth exchanges (Leenhardt and Picht, 1997; Vaillant, 1998). Arguably, Franco-German institutions have been the least successful where they have claimed to be the most ambitious, namely in the case of security and defence policy. While the Elysée Treaty proclaimed the desire of the two governments to harmonise their defence doctrines, their collaboration on defence matters was hampered by the *Bundestag's* insistence upon inserting its own strongly pro-Atlanticist prelude to the 1963 Treaty (Soutou, 1996). Moreover, the nuclear issue was specifically excluded from bilateral negotiation. The subsequent evolution of Gaullist foreign policy (and France's withdrawal from NATO) made effective collaboration even more difficult. These themes are explored in more depth in Chapter 6. The Elysée Treaty was far more successful in the sphere of cultural policy, where the Franco-German Youth Office (OFAJ) implemented a highly successful programme of youth exchanges (Marzal, 1997).

The drive to relaunch the institutional basis of the Franco-German relationship was a by-product of the fruitful Kohl–Mitterrand partnership of the 1980s. For Mitterrand and other French politicians, institutions were a means of binding in the Germans in areas of particular sensitivity. The twenty-fifth anniversary of the 1963 Treaty was celebrated by the conception of a new layer of bilateral institutions. The Franco-German Defence and Security Council and the Franco-German Economic Council were both created in 1988. New institutional structures were formed for purposes of coordinating policies on cultural policy and the environment. Some horse-trading accompanied their creation. The Germans were reluctant to agree to the creation of a Franco-German Economic Council; the *Bundesbank* feared any challenge to its independence in the sphere of monetary management. The Franco-German Defence and Security Council was requested by the Germans in an attempt to give the Federal Republic influence over French foreign policy.

The relevance of these committees was debatable. The Franco-German Economic Council had little influence on EMU, though informal Franco-German 'bilaterals' were essential throughout the negotiations. The Franco-German Defence and Security Council had a largely symbolic existence. The committee was not consulted before President Chirac proceeded with nuclear testing in 1995, nor before Chirac announced the end of conscription in 1996, two decisions that intensely angered the Germans (Vernet, 1996c). The Germans complained of the committee being used at best as a sounding board for unilateral French initiatives. On the other hand, the 1996 Franco-German defence agreement was officially adopted by a meeting of the Defence and Security Council co-chaired by Chirac and Kohl. The agreement was only then communicated to NATO and WEU partners. Preserving the appearance of Franco-German harmony was an important by-product of the relationship, but the history of Franco-German bilateral cooperation is at best uneven in this sphere.

Institution-building was not by itself indicative of the solid grounding of the Franco-German relationship. Officials complained of over-institutionalisation, and of excessive cost in time and resources. The Schröder government elected in 1998 announced its intention to cut back on the official paraphernalia of cooperation.

Informal and policy networks

Informal Franco-German bilateral networks were probably more important than formal institutions themselves. French and German officials and leaders have become used to working together. When it worked best, the Franco-German relationship became akin to the gentleman's club, with its own informal rules. The major unwritten rule was the need to reach positive sum agreements and to engage in nested bargaining games. Informal networks are not reserved for politicians. National civil servants involved in European policy issues have gradually increased their bilateral contacts with their homologues in other EU states (Lequesne, 1996). Although not unique, Franco-German administrative collaboration is of especial importance. Thus, Webber (1999b) demonstrates the high degree of Franco-German contact in the sphere of agriculture, one of the oldest areas of EU policy intervention. In her study of treaty negotiations, Mazzucelli (1997) contends that French and German national officials developed networks and adopted positions that went beyond those of their national masters. The role of civil servants was especially important in their agenda-setting capacity. They adopted a joint problem-solving approach that went beyond that of politicians. Frequent contacts did not always produce negotiated outcomes. Although officials from the French and German Permanent Representations were in constant contact during the Agenda 2000 discussions in 1998–99, insiders complained bitterly of the intransigence of their counterparts (interviews). However the joint problem-solving ethic was generally characteristic of administrative contacts.

The Franco-German relationship described thus far is an elite-driven project; elite-level contacts are routine. A distinctive Franco-German relationship is much less in evidence at the level of societal policy networks. Patterns of interest articulation take distinctive national paths in both countries; there is no French equivalent of the German model of social consensus. In one important sense, the Franco-German relationship does not really exist as an institutionalised relationship; it is unable to distribute resources or define rules. In a multi-level system of governance, lobbying is directed at national, supranational and even sub-national institutions, but not at informal bilateral quasi-regimes. There is little evidence of concerted Franco-German trade union action, for instance, or even joint bilateral environmental activism. Relations between French and German business associations are coordinated through the pan-European employer's association, UNICE. The area of farming possibly provides an exception; French and German farmers have on occasion coordinated their actions in favour of resisting CAP reforms. But it is an exception that confirms the rule.

Party political linkages

Political parties have often been underestimated or ignored as policy actors within the European Union. Recent work has stressed the importance of party channels as a conduit for contacts established both at the bilateral and multilateral levels (Gaffney, 1996; Hix and Lord, 1997). In the case of France and Germany, cooperation has been most in evidence amongst centre-left parties; the euro-ambivalence of large sections of the French right (especially the neo-Gaullist RPR) has acted as a brake on close bilateral links between the CDU and the French Gaullists. In contrast, contacts between the French Socialist and German Social Democratic parties, especially after 1995, provided some evidence for the importance of party. For a long time, relations between these two parties were highly strained; the SPD never forgave Mitterrand his part in bringing Kohl to power in 1982 (Ehrhart, 1991). Relations between SPD and PS gradually improved after Mitterrand's departure, and Lafontaine's capture of the SPD leadership in December 1995. Upon Lafontaine's initiative, the two parties agreed upon the creation of several policy sub-committees in December 1995. The documents produced by these committees – and the contacts established therein – provided blueprints for later collaboration between the Jospin and Schröder administrations, especially the close partnership between Strauss-Kahn and Lafontaine. In May 1997 – days before the first round of the French parliamentary elections – the PS and SPD published their Joint Declaration, in which the SPD agreed to the PS call for an employment policy chapter to be added to the European treaties and for 'intensive coordination in terms of economic policy' (Giret and Moatti, 1998). This gave the PS a badge of European respectability, offsetting Chancellor Kohl's scarcely veiled campaign intervention in favour of Chirac.

On a more general level, the Party of European Socialists and the European People's Party each provided a network for cross-national, party-based contacts to be intensified, although such contacts were not specifically bilateral. As we observe in Chapter 4, however, there was no tight Franco-German relationship within either of the main European Parliament party groups. Relations between the CDU and the parties of the French right (the UDF and the RPR in particular) were often tense, as became apparent during the Haider affair in early 2000. While the German CDU and SPD have occupied dominant or powerful positions within the two largest groups – the PES and EPP – French parties of all complexions have been ineffective within Strasbourg on account of their weak numbers and the preference of top-ranking French politicians for other institutional venues.

Conclusion

As has emerged in this chapter, the Franco-German relationship appears to be an institutional hybrid. French and German elites have placed great importance on developing their bilateral relationship in an institutionalised form. There is a sophisticated machinery of cultural, artistic and educational collaborative ventures, and an imposing paraphernalia of joint committees. The mobilisation of resources in the interests of Franco-German bilateral exchange is impressive.

While symbolically important, and although the bilateral paraphernalia of Franco-German cooperation has an obvious spillover in other institutional arenas (most obviously the European Union), it is debatable whether the institutional metaphor captures the essence of the alliance. The Franco-German relationship is not, strictly speaking, an institution; it does not engage directly in the allocation of scarce resources or the distribution of authoritative values. Domestic interests target sub-national, national or supranational institutions – but not the Franco-German relationship as such.

The relationship is driven by fairly informal, elite-level interactions, the nature of which is often difficult to evaluate, but which surpass in importance the role of formal Franco-German institutions. This elite-level collusion is a precondition for the effective operation of the Franco-German alliance in a broader institutional arena, such as in the EU. Informal understandings between French and German politicians, officials and policy experts is often enhanced by their practice of routine contact and the legacy of decades of working together. French and German officials invest more time in their mutual relationship than with those of other EU states (although each also has a wide range of other, important, bilateral relationships). France and Germany are the only countries tied by a treaty-based alliance within the European Union. These countries have an essential common interest in developing the European communities and advancing the project of European integration, though, as we observe in the next chapter, in many issue-areas France and Germany start from opposing positions. Indeed, the quasi-regime like quality of the Franco-German relationship involves a permanent exchange in order to reach common understandings on issues where national interests are often highly divergent.

This relationship can best be conceptualised as a bilateral 'quasi-regime', as an informal, intergovernmental, and inter-elite compact operating on a flexible basis to secure outcomes desired by both countries. The effectiveness of the Franco-German relationship lies in its flexibility and its informality rather than in its degree of institutionalisation. The essential regime-like quality of the Franco-German relationship lies in the presupposition that French and German leaders will attempt to reach agreement where possible, even against their initial preferences. On the other hand, the Franco-German relationship is not unilinear and it operates (or not) differently across various different levels and dimensions; this will become clearer in subsequent chapters.

The politics of the Franco-German relationship are, in part, symbolic politics. The institutional machinery is as important as a symbol of Franco-German reconciliation as for anything else. Political leadership lies at the juncture of symbolic and interest-based politics. There is evidence that French and German leaders have traditionally looked to each other for succour and support. Here we can usefully resort to Putnam's metaphor of two-level games. One of Putnam's more incisive insights relates to how international relations can strengthen the domestic standing of political leaders (Putnam, 1988). In the two-level game of international negotiations, leaders are wont to shore up each other's positions in an attempt to build trust and facilitate the implementation of jointly agreed promises. Respect for diplomatic forms is important; however influential their country, political leaders insist on interacting with other political leaders, rather than with lesser ranked officials (or even the Commission president). Leaders prefer informal institutional arenas – such as the intergovernmental conferences and European summits – at which foreign and finance ministers and their officials can be kept at arm's length. In the two-level game of Franco-German relations, there is some evidence to support the contention that the quality of relations between French and German leaders is an important weather-vane of the state of the Franco-German relationship itself. In the absence of determined co-leadership (as for much of the 1990s) the inter-state relationship can function efficiently, but it requires joint political leadership skills to act as a motor of European integration – or of anything else.

The Franco-German relationship and the European Union

France and Germany have both adopted visionary approaches to Europe; this separates both nations from Britain, which has consistently attempted to dampen integrationist ardour. In terms of substance, both France and Germany have envisaged a political presence for the EU that goes beyond the Union as an extended free trade zone. In Chapter 4, we start by presenting German and French approaches to European integration. In the main body of the chapter, we consider the operation of the Franco-German relationship at the level of the European Union itself. Our investigations are guided by the central question of whether the Franco-German relationship exercises leadership within the EU.

Germany and Europe

The European finality is part and parcel of the definition of modern German identity. The 'old' FRG (1949–89) was intimately linked to the European Communities and to the Atlantic Alliance; its identity as a German state was bound up with these two international organisations. West Germany benefited more than anybody else from increased intra-EC trade, rising German exports and improved foreign investment (Hueglin, 1995). Germany has also consistently favoured moves to European political union, although many ambiguities lay under the surface. German and French views of political union were markedly different during the Maastricht negotiations and had converged only imperfectly by the turn of the century.

Neo-realists have identified a German strategy of cultivated spillover; from this perspective the German vision of European political union involves a series of incremental adjustments that will eventually result in an integrated regional system modelled along German lines (Pedersen, 1998). Germany has certainly been willing to make short-term concessions in the interests of longer-term integration. This was demonstrated at the Maastricht summit, when Kohl abandoned the Deutschmark and the *Bundesbank*, in the interests of reconciling France and other EC states after German unification.

Although Germany has great structural power, many accounts refute the neo-realist supposition that Germany aspires to exercise a hegemonic role. Germany does not easily fit any of the classic definitions of hegemony. Her economic influence within Europe, while strong, cannot be equated with that of the USA during the early post-war period. German economic performance is dependent upon complex intertwined relationships with her principal European partners, most especially France. Moreover, the absence of German military ambition and weakness of her military resources runs counter to normally accepted definitions of hegemonic behaviour (Kaelberer, 1997). On the other hand, as the principal economic player in Europe, Germany has had an important agenda and standard setting role, within and beyond the EU, as is demonstrated most obviously in the economic sphere, a theme developed further in Chapter 5. Her economic primacy underpins her political influence, which, though not disproportionate, weighs heavily upon the strategies that her neighbours can adopt.

Ideas of European integration found a natural breeding ground in post-war West Germany. The nation state had lost all legitimacy after the 1933–45 period. Germany had to demonstrate a willingness to share power and live in peace with her neighbours. Unlike other states, West Germany – a semi-sovereign state – would recover influence by strengthening multilateral structures. Germany looked to federal European solutions, both as a means of solving domestic problems and of exercising influence on a pan-European level. There is a very close fit between the institutional structures of the Federal Republic and those of the European Union; the European level can be conceived intellectually as another tier in a complex decision-making system. There is an argument that German policy initiatives find leverage at the European level because the structures of governance at the sub-national, national and EU levels are so analogous. On the other hand, as demonstrated by Petersen and Bomberg (1999), the problem of coordination is especially acute in the German case, as no single central gatekeeper can harmonise negotiating stances. Indeed, the consensus view is that German policies are poorly coordinated at an EU level, reflecting the existence of varying centres of power: the *Länder* governments, the rival ministries (especially the Foreign Affairs and Economics Ministries), the *Bundesbank* and the Federal Chancellor's office (Bulmer and Paterson, 1987; Wright, 1996; Petersen and Bomberg, 1999). Against this, there is the argument that the governance of the European Union favours in some respects the German chancellor, who alone can impose a sense of political direction on the myriad of conflicting bureaucratic and policy rivalries (in the Chancellery, the Foreign and Economic Ministries).

Along with other EU countries, France found herself under increasing pressure to adapt her economic and social model to the German standard throughout the 1990s (Cole, 1998b). Germany conceived of the European Union as a stable community. Monetary stability was important above everything else. While Kohl was willing to make major concessions to Mitterrand at Maastricht, all German actors (in the Chancellery, the Finance Ministry, the *Bundesbank*) were inflexible in insisting that the single currency was implemented according to German rules. This theme is developed in Chapter 5. Germany envisaged a multi-speed Europe (Janning, 1996). Being part of a dynamic community was a reward, not a right. States had to demonstrate their ability to join a European hard core by their rigorous economic management and political vision. Germany advocated a democratic Union. The European Parliament must be strengthened. A stronger, more democratic Union was a necessity in itself, and would help to integrate and stabilise a unified Germany.

Unification challenged Germany's traditional role in the EU in several respects. First, it posed an increasing financial burden on the German state. The East German *Länder* were propped up by massive financial transfers, financed directly by West German taxpayers (and indirectly, through higher interest rates, by other EU citizens). In the light of the financial burden of unification, German policy-makers were reluctant to finance new European initiatives. Second, the urgent needs of renovation led Germany to adopt more interventionist-style policies, at least with respect to eastern Germany, which brought the German government into conflict with the European Commission on several occasions, and which were more commonly associated with France or Italy (Welfens, 1993). The burden of unification and the extension of the German social model to the new *Länder* threatened the social market economy that had underpinned German growth in the post-war period. Third, Germany was less able (and willing) to finance expensive side-payments to poorer EU states, or to subsidise French agriculture through the CAP. As measured by per capita wealth, Germany had regressed from second to sixth position within the 15-member EU (Welfens, 1993). By the late 1990s, Germany was urgently demanding a more equitable budgetary contribution in the Agenda 2000 negotiations.

France and Europe

France also believed in a European finality, though there were many contradictions in the French vision of Europe. This vision also varied according to political identity, partisan belief and generational attachment. But the Gaullist paradigm that prevailed until the mid-1980s – and remains influential – might be summarised in terms of six principal features: a cultural attachment to European values and civilisation, notably as embodied by France; a Europe prepared to protect its industry and agriculture; the promotion of common European policies where these do not endanger French interests; a marked anti-Americanism and advocacy of a more independent security and defence identity; a tight Community based on a Franco-German directorate, rather than a looser, more nebulous, grouping of nations; and a preference for intergovernmental over supranational institutions. France wanted a strong Europe with weak institutions (Le Gloannec and Hassner, 1996); a strong Europe, with its own industrial, political and cultural identity, but a Europe within which nation states remained the critical actors. France wanted to retain its role as a great power and to harness the resources of the Community to this effect. There was a discourse stressing the primacy of politics – but a fear of a genuinely supranational entity. Underlying the supranational discourse of French leaders, the European Union has always been regarded as a means of enhancing French national prestige. Through its privileged alliance with Germany, France used the European arena as a means of exporting ideas, policies and administrative styles. This Gaullist paradigm of a strong Europe with weak institutions was progressively modified from the mid-1980s onwards (Cole and Drake, 2000).

Transcending the Gaullist legacy was a feature of the Mitterrand presidency (1981–95) (Cole, 1997). In symbolic and substantive terms, Mitterrand's Europe was far more integrationist than that espoused by de Gaulle or his two successors (Lemaire-Prosche, 1990). In the broader interests of European integration, Mitterrand proved more willing to sacrifice elements of national sovereignty than any of his precursors had been, though arguably incapable of making the discursive break that such a shift implied (Schmidt, 1997). In the Single European Act of 1986, the French president accepted that majority voting should become the norm for many EC decisions. In the Maastricht Treaty, further provisions for majority voting were enacted, together with some strengthening of the powers of the European Parliament and the European Commission, traditionally anathema to French presidents. Mitterrand's successor Chirac initially maintained an ambiguous attitude towards further European integration after fighting a euro-ambivalent election campaign in 1995. Any lingering doubts over France's commitment to the single European currency were dispelled in a press conference in October 1995. Chirac undertook bold initiatives in the sphere of European defence (Bosnia) and institutional reform (negotiating the Amsterdam Treaty) before his government slumped to defeat in the snap June 1997 National Assembly elections.

While politicians in the Federal Republic saw the EU as another layer in a multi-layered system of governance, there was also a degree of structural fit between French political and administrative traditions and those of the European Union. The European institutions were modelled along French lines; hence the role of *Cabinets*, and *Directions Générales* in the Commission.

The French model of the *concours* was that adopted for recruitment to European institutions; this might explain the reputation for effectiveness of French civil servants within the Commission and elsewhere. France was reputed for its efficacy in placing its nationals in key directorates in areas of overriding national interest (such as DGV1, Agriculture), while no such reputational mastery has been attributed to Germany. In contrast to Germany, France offered a model of strong, centralised EU coordination rivalled only by the British and the Danish (Wright, 1996).

France and Germany shared a common belief in the desirability of a more integrated Europe, but diverged in their understanding of what this entailed. Both countries had common interests in strengthening the EU – and accepting the sacrifices this supposed. The French vision of *grandeur* – Europe as an extension of France – would be meaningless without a stronger EU, if necessary one in which the French could occasionally be placed in a minority. France needed the EU to develop, or face the consequences of a loss of international influence. Germany needed the EU to be as effective as possible, including in the foreign policy sphere. Though their initial positions were often very different, both countries depended upon a more integrated EU. Franco-German divergences were narrowed throughout the 1990s, as inter-state exchanges intensified, notably through preparations for the launch of the single currency in 1999. We now turn to consider the operation of the Franco-German relationship in more detail at the level of the European Union itself.

The Franco-German relationship within the European Union

There are two principal dimensions of the Franco-German relationship within the European Union. First, EU affairs have been at the heart of the bilateral Franco-German relationship; the primary objective of Franco-German institution building has been to attempt to harmonise negotiating positions within the EU. Second, the Franco-German relationship has been an important force within the EU, bringing forth the metaphor of the Franco-German relationship as the motor of European integration. The two countries certainly lay behind many European initiatives. France and Germany usually seek each other's support when launching new initiatives. There are well documented occasions when compromise between the two has unblocked blocked situations; such was the case, for example, over the start date for Stage Two of Economic and Monetary Union on 1 January 1994 (Dyson and Featherstone, 1999). When France and Germany disagree, so the argument runs, new European initiatives are rarely forthcoming and stand little chance of being implemented. The supranational decision-making machinery (the European Commission) depends to some extent upon the cooperation of the member states – and of France and Germany more than any other – for its effective operation, notably for the implementation of directives.

The 1963 Treaty encapsulated the bilateral regime character of the Franco-German relationship. It sets out that the two countries should attempt – as far as possible – to reach common agreement on bilateral, multilateral and international affairs. In a Community where movement has been synonymous with progress, historical evidence has suggested that when Paris and Bonn were in disagreement, European movement was less likely to occur. Franco-German disagreement could frustrate movement; this was an outcome Germany in particular set as its mission to avoid. As demonstrated on repeated occasions in the 1990s, Germany would go out of its way to avoid French isolation within the EU and other international organisations. In the currency upheavals of 1992–93, the _Bundesbank_ intervened massively to safeguard the parity of the franc when it was under attack from international capital (Andrews, 1993; Reland, 1998). During the GATT negotiations of 1992–93, German Chancellor Kohl brokered a compromise with the Americans in order to prevent French isolation on this issue (Webber, 1998). Germany took seriously the mutual assistance clauses of the 1963 Treaty. It was imperative not to isolate her principal European partner. To this end, Germany occasionally adopted policy stances against its instinctive preferences, as in the case of the GATT round, where Chancellor Kohl appeared to go against the free trade preferences of the German and American business communities in order to appease French interests.

Upon closer observation, however, the metaphor of the Franco-German motor as the engine of European integration needs to be examined more closely (Ziebura, 1996). We argue in the next section in favour of differentiating between various levels of European Union decision-making. The impact of the Franco-German relationship appears greater in constitutive 'grand bargains' than in spheres of more recent EU policy intervention or in details of policy implementation.

The Franco-German relationship and history-making decisions

The argument that France and Germany acting in tandem have exercised the most important influence in history-making decisions has been strongly put (Moravscik, 1991, 1993, 1998; Garrett, 1992; Gerbet; 1993; Bocquet, 1996; Petersen and Bomberg, 1999). The list of successful Franco-German initiatives might arguably include the early initiatives of the 1950s (such as the Schuman Plan), the European monetary system of 1978–79, the Single European Act of 1986 and the Maastricht Treaty of 1992. On the other hand, the claim for Franco-German domination has often been rather loosely made. The European Defence Community (EDC) was killed by Franco-German dissension in the 1950s. The foundation of the European Community itself involved the smaller European powers of the Netherlands and Belgium, who forced the pace on integration after the setback of the EDC. The 'Gaullist consensus' acted as a brake on integration from the mid-1960s to the mid-1980s. The European 'snake' dissolved in an atmosphere of mutual Franco-German recrimination in 1976. Metaphors of the Franco-German motor have a tendency to underplay the role of supranational and non-governmental actors, such as the European Commission and international business.

The case for Franco-German bilateralism can be judged by reference to the three principal history-making negotiations undertaken since the relaunch of the EU in the mid-1980s: the Single European Act, the Maastricht Treaty and the Amsterdam Treaty.

The Single European Act

The Single European Act has been open to various interpretations, the most rigorous being those of inter-state bargaining (predicated on domestic convergence) and the international political economy.

Inter-state bargaining accords a specific place for the Franco-German relationship. For Moravscik (1991) the trade-offs between the major EC states could explain the negotiation of the Single European Act. The leading roles were performed by Germany, France and Britain, with the latter being alternatively co-opted into the Franco-German directorate, or coerced with threats of expulsion. Moravscik contends that the Single European Act resulted from a policy-based convergence between Mitterrand, Kohl and Thatcher. Domestic political factors were essential in understanding this policy-based convergence. Given that Germany and Britain shared a common approach to more supply-side economic policies, policy convergence involved France falling into line. French President Mitterrand's economic U-turn of 1982–83, and the changing centre of gravity within the domestic French governing coalition (the decline of the Communist Party) were the critical variables at play. After his decision to abandon unilateral Keynesian reflationary policies in 1983, Mitterrand sought to transform proven internal constraints (France's economic interdependence) into European-level opportunities (defining a new European role for France). In this way, changing domestic circumstances, and the move to conservative economic policies, underpinned changing perceptions of national state interest. The moving closer of domestic and external win-sets allowed Mitterrand to engage upon his European mission.

The French convergence with German (and British) macroeconomic trends made inter-state bargaining possible. The three big states accepted the need for an opening of intra-EC trade and service liberalisation, in an effort to redress Europe's declining competitiveness against the USA and Japan. Internal market liberalisation was acceptable to all three states, while the other options – strengthened monetary coordination, a common defence policy or EC procedural reform – met with resistance from at least one of the big three. The heads of government of the largest member states performed the leading roles. Supranational actors (such as Commission President Delors) or transnational business interests were of marginal importance. Moravscik's account differs from classic realism by the emphasis placed on domestic policy pressures. Policy preferences were not static, but were rooted in changing domestic incentives.

Although the Franco-German tandem led the dance, the lowest common denominator style of decision-making ensured that substantive policy outcomes closely mirrored British preferences, so much so that Thatcher was able to recommend the Act in spite of the procedural reforms (more majority voting) contained therein.

This view has been strongly contested. For Helen Wallace (1990: 150), for example, the Single European Act owed its impetus 'to a shrewd alliance between the Commission and the business community'. The European round table of business organisations operated as an effective pressure group and the Commission espoused the business cause of free markets. Contemporary neo-functionalist theorists (Sandholtz and Zysman, 1989; Stone Sweet and Sandholtz, 1997) share the view that supranational actors and transnational business forces drove the moves to market deregulation inherent in the Single European Act. Policy-specific case studies in the spheres of telecommunications, energy and research and development lend powerful support to this view (Schmidt, 1999; Eberlain and Grande, 1999). The issues involved were so complex, both at the formulation and implementation stages, that coalitions were shifting and issue-based, and there was no overarching national view. Indeed, nation states themselves were divided in pursuit of their essential interests, a point accepted in Moravscik's account.

Even if the argument of nation-state control at the constitutive stage is accepted, the unintended consequences of the Single European Act soon made themselves felt (Pierson, 1996; Armstrong and Bulmer, 1998). The Act unleashed a dynamic process beyond the control of any nation state, or, indeed, of the Franco-German relationship. This is demonstrated in the policy case studies below, where France and Germany were each subjected to powerful supranational pressures. The Franco-German relationship was as likely to operate as a defensive rearguard action as to be the motor of further integration. Neither France nor Germany – together or separately –

was able to control the consequences of the Single European Act. French
and German traditions were equally challenged in the domain of regulatory
politics, where the supranational actors of the Commission and the Court
demonstrated a capacity for innovation (Majone, 1996). The liberal interpretation of competition policy by Commissioners Brittan and van Miert
posed almost as great a challenge to German ordo-liberalism as it did to
the traditional French model of economic management and monopoly public
service (Thatcher, 1997; Cole, 1998a, 1999b; Schmidt, 1999).

The Maastricht Treaty _ Kohl committed Germany to EMU.

There is an even stronger case for Franco-German bilateralism in the
Maastricht Treaty, although other national actors (Britain, Italy, Spain, the
Netherlands, Denmark) made an impact, as did the Commission and its
President Delors. Moreover, the problem of ratification introduced a hitherto
neglected actor – public opinion. France and Germany certainly adopted
an attitude of close cooperation throughout the Maastricht negotiations.
The decision to launch the intergovernmental conferences on political and
economic union came at the December 1989 Strasbourg summit. Mitterrand
adeptly exploited Kohl's desire for French (and European) support by
linking his backing for German unification with the German Chancellor's
agreement to the two intergovernmental conferences (on political and economic union). The Maastricht pre-negotiations were driven by the Franco-
German couple. French and German political leaders performed a vital role
in giving political direction to the Maastricht negotiations. Common initiatives came in the form of joint letters published by Mitterrand and Kohl in
April and November 1990, and in Franco-German bilateral initiatives in
new spheres such as foreign and security policy (Haski, 1990b; Johnson,
1990). The close collaboration between French and German negotiators
ensured that the official Franco-German stance prevailed in crucial areas
such as economic and monetary union, defence, foreign and security policy
and Article 100c (visa policy). The complex trade-offs over EMU and CFSP
are considered in later chapters.

Franco-German cooperation was much less convincing in the sphere of
political union than in the economic sphere. Political union was an ambiguous concept over which no one could agree. While the Germans looked to
strengthen supranational institutions (the Commission and the Parliament),
France and Britain refused to allow any right for Commission initiative in
the area of CFSP and were generally hostile to enhanced Commission influence. The European Parliament was a source of major disagreement. While
Germany looked to strengthen the Parliament in order to counter the EC's
perceived democratic deficit, the French retorted that democratic sovereignty

was vested in national governments and parliaments. Indeed, Mitterrand initially proposed to create a second European parliamentary chamber, composed of representatives of national parliaments, with a right to veto the decisions of the directly elected European Parliament (Duverger, 1991). The contradictions between the French republican tradition and Germany's cooperative federalism were laid bare in the Maastricht negotiations.

In their joint letter of 10 April 1990, preceding the Dublin summit, Mitterrand and Kohl advocated transforming the EC into a genuine 'political union'. The contents of this letter were reputedly drafted in the German Chancellery Office (Baun, 1996) and it became clear that Germany had far broader and wider reaching aims for political union than France. For France, political union signified building Europe as a super-state with an influence in world affairs; for Germany, political union involved notions of citizenship and democratic control. For France, closer European integration should be based on tighter intergovernmental cooperation (in the Council), rather than moves towards strengthening supragovernmental institutions. Hence the traditional opposition of French governments towards the European Parliament, the European Court of Justice, and the Commission. For Germany, building a democratic Europe signified strengthening democratic institutions, first and foremost the European Parliament. The French resisted the German proposal that the President of the Commission should be allowed to select his Commissioners, without reference to national balance; and that the President of the Council should be elected for two years, not replaced every six months. In spite of close Franco-German bilateral collaboration, German negotiators made little progress in the intergovernmental conference on political union (Baun, 1996). The co-decision procedure was eventually inserted into the treaty in order to ratify the minimal requirements of German domestic policy. Nonetheless, the final treaty locked the EC more firmly into economic integration (the single currency by 1999) than it made real concessions to the principle of political union. To this extent, it responded more accurately to French priorities than to German ones.

The Germans were not entirely consistent in their advocacy of closer political union. German negotiators fiercely resisted French proposals for 'economic government', but this could be interpreted as one model of political union. Failing to cede ground on economic government, they met with resistance, from France in particular, to their version of political union. The German preference for a 'communautarisation' of foreign and security, justice and interior policies was effectively abandoned in favour of an intergovernmental pillar structure advocated by the French. Although there were agreements for European policy in new areas such as foreign and security policy (second pillar) and justice and home affairs (third pillar), these were limited to intergovernmental cooperation and outside of the Community's normal decision-making procedures.

Did the Maastricht negotiations really confirm the centrality of the Franco-German relationship? In this specific instance, there is strong evidence of Franco-German bilateralism, due in part to the historic circumstances surrounding the summit. The Franco-German relationship provided the mechanism to enable Kohl to overcome domestic opposition (from the *Bundesbank* and the Finance Ministry) and to agree to French demands for monetary union, in order to tie in French support for unification. For there was a strong linkage between French and European support over German unification, and concessions made to Germany's European allies at the Maastricht summit. This explains why Germany appeared to compromise more of her initial objectives at the Maastricht summit than any other nation. Tsebelis's (1990) metaphor of nested games is appropriate in this context.

The Amsterdam Treaty

In the words of the *Financial Times* editorialist of 17 June 1997: 'take away the Franco-German anchor and the EU falls to the pettiest of squabbling'. The Amsterdam summit demonstrated that the Franco-German relationship could not blindly impose its will against the interests of other member states, and that the Franco-German relationship could be undermined by dissension between and within the French and German governments. On the other hand, France and Germany continued to perform the role of principal agenda-setters.

Franco-German cooperation in preparation for the intergovernmental conference launched at the Turin summit in March 1996 and completed in Amsterdam in June 1997 was very close. Somewhat like at Maastricht, France and Germany combined their efforts in an attempt to pre-structure the negotiations. This took the classic form of bilateral meetings of ministers and officials. There was also an innovation in the form of the Franco-German seminar, a body that organised a series of bilateral, inter-ministerial meetings devoted to the intergovernmental conference. In line with precedent, Chirac and Kohl published a joint letter on 7 December 1995, setting out their joint objectives for the summit (Quatremar, 1995).

There had been some movement in national state preferences since the Maastricht agreement. France had moved closer to traditional German positions on several institutional issues, notably on the extension of qualified majority voting. French proposals on institutional reform for the IGC included extending the use of qualified majority voting (QMV) within the Council; re-weighting votes within the Council in favour of the large countries; and strengthening the role of the Commission in specific instances (such as employment policy) (Martin, 1996). In areas of vital national interest (such as CFSP), however, France continued to argue for the right of national veto, hence resisting all abandoning of the Luxembourg compromise. Germany agreed cautiously with proposals to re-weight votes in the Council and to extend the use of QMV, but advocated finally laying the Luxembourg compromise to rest (Martin, 1996). France and Germany were joined by Britain and Italy on the issue of re-weighting of votes within the Council in favour of the largest countries. These proposals were fiercely opposed by the smaller EU nations. Franco-German collaboration also lay behind the limited proposals for 'strengthened cooperation', whereby any group of EU countries could use EU resources to deepen their collaboration in specific areas.

There remained areas where no common position could be achieved. Traditional divergences over enlargement became entangled with issues of institutional reform. From the French perspective, finally reconciled to Eastern enlargement, it was imperative to safeguard a capacity for resolute EU action, given the imminent enlargement of the Union. The French response to enlarging was a measured deepening, hence the proposals for 'strengthened cooperation' and more majority voting. On condition that it was not isolated in the minority, there was no reason to oppose an extension of QMV. Germany agreed in principle, but refused to make EU institutional reform a pre-condition of future enlargement negotiations; the political and economic imperative of enlargement to the countries of Eastern and Central Europe outweighed the inconvenience of institutional uncertainty.

Even where they were united, the Amsterdam summit demonstrated that France and Germany do not always win in EU constitutive politics (Lemaître, 1997b). The Franco-German proposals on CFSP were modified under pressure from Britain; the proposals for 'strengthened cooperation' in this sphere and for the fusion of the WEU and the EU were rejected. These issues are explored further in Chapter 6. The 'cohesion' countries (Spain, Portugal, Greece and Ireland) united effectively to fight off threats to the cohesion and structural funds. Most importantly, France and Germany were defeated on the two main chapters of institutional reform; the smaller nations combined to defeat Franco-German proposals to re-weigh voting within the Council of Ministers, and to limit the number of Commissioners. Although the scope of QMV was expanded quite extensively, Franco-German dissension prevented further moves in this direction.

The Franco-German relationship was unable to prevail in an IGC with fifteen members stubbornly defending national interests. The impact of the

Franco-German relationship was reduced by France and Germany adopting contradictory positions on important issues. The new French plural left government was isolated on the main issues at Amsterdam. The conservative German chancellor would not agree to the French Socialist-led government's central demands: that the EU should borrow to reflate the economy; that the Commission should be given new competencies in employment; and that the EU budget should finance a new employment policy. Kohl resisted all of these, and they were all rejected in the form proposed by the French. France appeared weak and isolated in the absence of an effective Franco-German relationship; it needed the special relationship far more than Germany, which demonstrated an uncharacteristic unwillingness to agree with France in the name of Franco-German solidarity.

The Amsterdam summit demonstrated above all that there were limits to the traditional belief that Germany would make more sacrifices than others in order to maintain the Community ship on course. At the Amsterdam summit, the Germans acted to defend their narrow national interest, as perceived by Christian Democratic Chancellor Kohl. Germany blocked moves to introduce QMV in social policy, in spite of an extension of QMV being a formal German negotiating position. Kohl also refused to allow the EU to define a sphere of competence in employment policy. The German chancellor's position demonstrated clearly the weight of domestic political priorities. Agreeing to increased EU responsibilities in the social and employment fields would, Kohl feared, play into the hands of his domestic political opponents. In the case of France also, the domestic political calculus was manifestly more important than Franco-German solidarity; the Jospin government had to be seen to be respecting its electoral promises. Faced with Franco-German dissension, the Amsterdam summit could not reach agreement on institutional reform, its ostensible function. The Amsterdam summit determined that changes to institutional rules could wait until the Community had grown to 21 members. The stalemate at Amsterdam increased pressure on France, Germany and the other states to reopen the dossier of institutional reform barely two years later.

A rather uneven pattern emerges from this overview of history-making decisions. The Franco-German relationship was only one influence on treaty outcomes. The evidence for bilateralism is stronger in relation to Maastricht than either the SEA or Amsterdam. In each case, Franco-German negotiating strategies were closely coordinated, a degree of contact that was necessary to attempt to bridge distinctive national positions. In each case, the details of policy implementation escaped from tight control of the Franco-German partnership. The SEA strengthened supranational actors, and in particular the European Commission. The Maastricht Treaty encouraged a close German supervision of the implementation of monetary union that was aimed against French policy positions. In the case of Amsterdam, Franco-German dissension at the summit produced a general lack of enthusiasm for monitoring implementation.

The Franco-German relationship and the EU policy process

As we observed in Chapter 3, there is no easy correlation between the intensity of a relationship and its impact. Webber (1999a) contends that the degree of coordination of the Franco-German relationship depends principally on the importance of the policy area for the two countries. Issue areas considered to be important by one or other partner will be the subject of intense coordinating activity in order to try and harmonise responses. Intense bilateral relations can be a smokescreen for major policy differences. Indeed, Franco-German contact is often the strongest in areas where the two states are in disagreement. This caveat aside, the intensity of the bilateral Franco-German cooperation appears to set it apart from other bilateral coalitions. The object of Franco-German bilateralism is invariably the elaboration of common positions in European negotiations or in fora such as the IMF. The interesting question is whether the Franco-German relationship can provide leadership (or 'joint hegemony' in the expression of Chang (1999)) in the EU policy process as a whole. Such a leadership role is inherent in the metaphors of the Franco-German relationship as the motor of European integration. Evidence of leadership was to some extent uncovered in the survey of treaty negotiations, but does this extend into management of the EU policy process?

Our responses to these questions have for long been hampered by a lack of empirical research. Fortunately, with Webber's (1999a) book on *The Franco-German Relationship in the European Union* we dispose of a set of detailed policy case studies (albeit of uneven quality) into the operation of the Franco-German relationship within the EU. Following on from the lead given by Webber, we propose to measure the influence of the Franco-German relationship by contrasting an established policy sector (agriculture), and an area of more recent EU importance (competition policy) before drawing some general conclusions on theses of Franco-German 'joint hegemony' within the European Union.

The centrality of the Franco-German relationship: the case of agriculture

Agricultural policy formed part of the initial constitutive bargain between France and Germany. France's insistence on a common agricultural policy was traded against Germany's pressure for an opening of industrial markets. The laborious introduction of the CAP from 1961 to 1964 has been well analysed by Webber (1998, 1999a). In its Article 3, the Treaty of Rome advocated 'the adoption of a common policy in the sphere of agriculture' (de Guistino, 1996: 95). After his return to power in 1958, de Gaulle linked support for the survival of the EEC with the creation of a common agricultural policy on terms favourable to French agriculture in crisis. Proposals for a common agricultural policy were tabled by the European Commission in December 1961. There were many differences between France and Germany in this sphere. With a large agricultural sector, France (supported for once by the Dutch) favoured a strong CAP that would safeguard essential national policy objectives – to retain a sizeable population on the land, to secure agricultural self-sufficiency, to protect French farmers and to favour exports. To pursue these objectives the French sought open access to other European and international markets, especially Germany. Hence the French insistence on the three core features of price and income support, import levies and subsidised exports (Baltas, 1999). With a less proficient farm sector, a tradition of agricultural protectionism and higher farm prices, Germany initially opposed this initiative. German farmers feared any lowering of farm prices and the competition of French agricultural produce in their home market. French and German domestic conditions were quite different. The farming lobby exercised a domestic political weight in France that had no real equivalent in Germany (the weight of the Bavarian farming lobby notwithstanding). Hard bargaining between the six member states took place in numerous council meetings between December 1961 and January 1962 when agreement over a common agricultural policy was finally achieved. The French and Dutch linked their acceptance of a common industrial market (1.1.62) to the CAP. De Gaulle's insistence on the CAP forced the Adenauer administration to side with France against the initial preferences of the German farming and business lobbies.

This inter-state bargain set the EC on a path from which it subsequently became difficult to diverge. It guaranteed a distribution of resources that manifestly favoured one member state (France) over others. By far the largest item in the EU budget, financing the CAP became the principal cause of the massive financial transfer from Germany to France and, later, the southern European countries. Thirty years later, the budgetary priority to agriculture remained intact, notwithstanding the growing importance of structural and cohesion funds and budgetary retrenchment. Even after successive reforms in the 1990s, and in spite of strong external pressure in the Uruguay GATT round, the core features of the CAP (price and income support, import levies and subsidised exports) had been modified only at the margins.

By any objective material measure, French and German interests often differed in this primordial sphere; the economic interests of French farmers

(Euro-centric and protectionist) and German industrialists (global and neo-liberal) often seemed at loggerheads. But Germany repeatedly used its good offices to prevent French isolation over the CAP (in the mid-1980s, and the early and late 1990s), irrespective of the political identity of the coalition in power. Agriculture enjoyed the prestige of being the longest established common policy and the pressure of an established policy community able and apt to resist any change. Because the CAP was part of the initial constitutive bargain, it was rather different from any other policy sector. From a German perspective, the political priority of the Franco-German relationship outweighed the material inconvenience of making side-payments to French farmers. German governments were also subject to strong domestic pressures from the German farm lobby – long converted to the merits of the CAP – especially effective when the CDU–CSU coalition was in power.

Inter-state bargains are possible because the agricultural sector remains essentially intergovernmental. Farm policies are deliberated by negotiations between agricultural ministers and their officials, either bilaterally, or in the Council of agricultural ministers. Supranational institutions are relatively weak in this sphere. The Commission does not have the ability to circumvent the Council – as it could, for example, in competition policy. Governments resist Commission interference in this quintessential sphere of distributive politics. The reactions of French and German governments to attempts by the Commission to impose CAP reform in 1992–93 and 1997–99 amply demonstrated this. During the Uruguay GATT round of 1992–93, French and German governments rejected the farm deal negotiated with the USA by Commissioner MacSharry without a mandate from the Council (the Blair House agreement of November 1992). French opposition to Commission proposals for 're-nationalisation' in 1997–99 scuppered the agricultural reforms proposed by the Commission in the Agenda 2000 negotiations (see Chapter 7). The Commission is in a relatively weak position because it depends on national governments to police and implement the CAP. The European Parliament is also marginalised in the sphere of agriculture, where only the consultation procedure applies.

The Franco-German relationship under stress: the case of GATT

The case study of the 1992–93 GATT Uruguay round is so important for several reasons – it elucidates diverging French and German attitudes towards the USA; it allows observation of the dialectical qualities of the Franco-German relationship in action, and it allows contrasts to be drawn between the impact of French and German domestic governing arrangements on international negotiations (McClean, 1994; Epstein, 1997; Webber, 1998).

The General Agreement on Trade and Tariffs (GATT) was a free trade agreement signed in 1947 with a mission to eradicate barriers to international free trade. Covering 70% of world trade in 1992, the GATT agreement had enabled tariffs to be reduced from 40% to 5% over the period since 1947 (Lemaître, 1992). There had been eight GATT trade rounds during this period. The 'Uruguay' round, opened in 1986, was heavily centred on agriculture. Pushed by powerful multinational firms, the USA was determined to cut EU subsidies for farm exports and to open up European markets to greater US penetration. The EU initially opposed any negotiation over agricultural trade liberalisation, with the French and German agriculture ministers in the forefront of opposition; the CAP was, after all, the only example of a fully integrated common European policy. The 1990 Brussels GATT summit collapsed as a result of the tough EU negotiating stance.

Pressurised by Germany (world export champion in 1988 and 1990), France eventually agreed to join in the GATT round in 1992, in return for German support on farm subsidies. The desire to avert a trade war with the USA – and to rein in burgeoning agricultural expenditure – explained why the EU undertook an important reform of the CAP in 1992, which agreed big cuts in guaranteed farm prices and contained provisions for the 'set-aside' of arable land. The close understanding between Mitterrand and Kohl facilitated this agreement.

French and German attitudes towards the importance of the GATT round differed in spite of the close cooperation of their leaders. France and Germany were perceived to represent distinctive positions on international trade, particularly in agriculture. The traditional French line was that CAP formed part of the *acquis communautaire* and could not be called into question. France argued in favour of regional protection, and advocated strengthening Community preference by maintaining a high common external tariff. Paris demanded that agriculture and culture be exempted from GATT rules, arguing in favour of European cultural exceptionalism. Germany feared that a 'fortress Europe' policy would harm its global interests. For most of the negotiations, Germany coordinated its strategy with Britain, Denmark and the Netherlands in the 'group of four' (Webber, 1998). Though in a minority, France was not completely isolated; it was supported on various occasions by Spain, Italy, Ireland and Belgium.

The GATT example demonstrated the importance of domestic constraints on international bargaining positions. To use Putnam's analogy, French negotiating positions were enhanced by a very narrow domestic win-set and a compliant German partner. Successive French governments (led by Bérégovoy and Balladur) pleaded with international partners that any unsatisfactory deal would spark civil unrest in France itself, and endanger future participation in the international GATT organisation. In November

1992, the French parliament passed a resolution saying it would veto any agreement 'contrary to France's fundamental interest'. There was a fundamental consensus across the French political spectrum to resist American pressure: the Balladur government, elected in March 1993, acted no differently from its predecessor. A French veto – openly evoked by Bérégovoy, Mitterrand and Balladur – would have damaged the Franco-German entente, but was seriously branded as a last resort.

The Franco-German relationship was critical in understanding the outcome of the Uruguay GATT round. France calculated that Germany would never come to an agreement against French interests. This calculation was not fundamentally misguided. Though hostile to the manner of negotiating the Blair House agreement, Germany initially opposed the French demand for counter-sanctions against the USA, leaving France isolated in the European Council. However, the German stance gradually shifted once the consequences of French isolation became clearer. At a critical meeting of the Council in August 1993, Kohl shifted towards the French position (Webber, 1998), a move opposed by the Economics and Foreign ministries, and representatives of German industry. Though formally resisting the French call for renegotiation of the Blair House agreement, Germany aligned itself with important French demands: namely the creation of a World Trade Organisation to apply the rules (resisted by the Americans) and important side-payments to appease French agricultural and film interests. These demands were contained in the GATT agreement signed in April 1994.

Several conclusions can be drawn from this important episode. First, only Germany was capable of playing the role of mediator between France and the USA. Second, German Chancellor Kohl placed a high priority on the Franco-German relationship, to the extent of advocating policy positions opposed by the Americans and German business. Third, the dialectical quality of the Franco-German relationship was more important in explaining the outcome of GATT than the role of the Commission, or the exogenous pressures placed on the Europeans by the Americans.

Challenging the Franco-German relationship. Implementing the single market

In history-making decisions, 'intergovernmental' EU sectors and international negotiations, where states are the primary actors, accounts stressing inter-state bargains are often convincing. The above examples all demonstrate the importance of the Franco-German relationship, whether in a leadership sense, or as a mechanism for mediating differences. But state-centric theories do not tell the whole story. Indeed, as what is now the European Union has developed since the mid-1980s, we find much evidence of the Franco-German relationship being challenged by powerful supranational forces. The Single European Act appears in many accounts as a watershed, not least for the ability of the Franco-German relationship to 'lead' the European communities.

The institutional changes wrought by the Single European Act should be briefly recalled. The Single European Act required almost 300 changes in Community legislation. In accordance with its treaty-defined role as a force of proposition, the Commission was responsible for drafting directives to implement single market measures, to be ratified by qualified majority votes in the Council. As the complexity of the process became apparent, the Commission evoked Article 90.3 of the Rome Treaty to issue certain directives by-passing the Council altogether, a practice upheld by the European Court of Justice in 1993 (Schmidt, 1999). Given the supremacy of EC law, governments subsequently were obliged to translate these requirements into national legislation.

While liberal intergovernmentalism focuses on inter-state bargains, contemporary supranational theorists argue that the Single European Act has decisively shifted power away from states – including the Franco-German relationship (Puchala, 1999). As the European Community/Union has developed since the passage of the SEA, it has challenged the national state traditions of all member states, including, in important respects, those of France and Germany. The EU has come into its own as a regulatory, quasi-federal polity (Majone, 1996). Unable to distribute resources except at the margins, the Commission can make a difference through its power to define the rules of market competition. As EU institutions seek to expand their power base at every opportunity, one might expect their orientations to conflict with the preferences of at least some member states some of the time.

Even when united, France and Germany were on occasions unable to prevent determined Commission action. This can be demonstrated in the field of competition policy and public services (Eberlein and Grande, 1999; Schmidt, 1999; Schneider and Vedel, 1999). Before the Single European Act, the European Community (EC) had largely ignored public services and state assistance to industry. Though the legal basis of the treaties is against state aids, public monopolies and assisted sectors, until the mid-1980s the Commission intervened only very rarely in national practices of industrial management. Pressures for radical policy change came from the entrepreneurial action of the EC after the passage of the Single European Act. It was centred in the Competition Directorate General (DG4, now DG1) and the activism of individual commissioners such as Peter Sutherland, Leon Brittan and Karel van Miert. The harmonisation of national legislation as a prelude to opening the single market gave the Commission a large legal base to issue directives in specific sectors. Strengthened by the tough competition regulations of the Treaty of Rome and the SEA, the Commission developed several mechanisms to break up state monopolies. Favoured measures included privatisation, the strict regulation of state subsidies, the opening up of specific industrial sectors to competition and the creation of independent regulatory agencies.

The Commission did not always need the approval of the Council or the Parliament for these single market measures, and there were instances – as in telecommunications – of the Commission imposing change on reluctant national governments (Thatcher, 1997). Even when France and Germany combined to resist Commission activism – as in postal service liberalisation – their efforts were only partially effective, succeeding in delaying inevitable change. On the other hand, where vital national interests were at stake – as in the case of French energy policy, where vast resources had been invested in monopoly public services – the Commission found it politically difficult to ignore the preferences of powerful member states. In the case of the French energy conglomerate EDF-GDF, determined national resistance prevailed in part over Commission activism. The French firm had to accept a staged opening of energy competition in its domestic market (from 1999 onwards), but was able to resist demands for its break-up, and retained its status as a public service organisation (Cole, 1999b).

As it emerged in the 1980s and 1990s, the EU regulatory framework was rather different from the traditional French (and to a lesser extent German) industrial models. This was most obvious in relation to state aids to industry, an area in which both France and Germany came into conflict with the Commission. There are many examples of disputes between France and the Commission, with the saga of the state-owned bank Crédit Lyonnais dwarfing all others. Equally portentous was the case of problems with the former East German *Länder*, which brought the German federal government into conflict with the EU Commission. The German government argued that genuine competition had swept aside East German industry, and that the German state had no option but to intervene to assist the transition in East Germany. The German EU Commissioner Bangemann took a less sanguine view, and refused certain state aids to industry in eastern *Länder*. Germany was also in the line of Commission fire for its failure to open up many public works contracts for competition.

The above analysis suggests that in areas of more recent EU competence such as post-SEA competition policy, telecommunications, research and technology, and the environment, Franco-German bilateralism is unlikely to prevail. Supranational actors (the Commission, the Parliament and the European Court of Justice) are more likely to be influential actors, as are transnational interests and networks. A *forteriori*, national state actors are less able to dominate proceedings than in traditional sectors such as agriculture.

The Franco-German relationship and the institutions of the European Union

It is difficult to uncover evidence of close and systematic Franco-German leadership within the official governing institutions of the European Union. The convention that member states should reach consensus – even in areas where qualified majority voting prevails – makes it impossible to measure Franco-German voting rolls within the Council, for instance. In specific issue-areas such as agriculture, it has been claimed that tight Franco-German coordination has ensured that decisions made by the Council are pre-shaped in negotiations involving a subset or subsets of member governments (Webber, 1999b). However, such claims are difficult to substantiate.

If evidence of systematic Franco-German cooperation is difficult to uncover within the Council, it is doubly so within the Commission. Commissioners are in theory completely independent of member-state control, hence of bilateral coalitions. Nationality is supposedly irrelevant and policy sector is undoubtedly a more pertinent variable. 'Going native' can be a useful strategy for Commissioners to demonstrate their European collegiality. In the crisis over the Santer Commission in 1999, it was noteworthy that only the French government seriously attempted to shield French Commissioner Cresson. Franco-German friendship did not extend to covering clientelism.

Neither is there any evidence of privileged Franco-German coalition building within the European Parliament, where French parties have been too divided to be effective, and are fragmented across and within the main European Parliament groups. It is undoubtedly at the level of the European Parliament that the Franco-German relationship matters least. Franco-German dissension often appears flagrant. Differential attitudes towards the democratic deficit and the role of the European Parliament spill over into a lack of a specifically Franco-German coordination in Strasbourg. In recent years, moreover, the French and German delegations in the European Parliament have been of unequal effectiveness, due to the chronic divisions of the French representation. While French MEPs have been notable absentees (often combining European and national or local office), German members have been more disciplined and assiduous. The strengthening of the parliament at Amsterdam – where the co-decision procedure has been extended to most spheres of EU policy – is likely to heighten the unpredictability of the parliament's actions and accentuate Franco-German divergence in this institution.

The big picture falls rather short of 'joint hegemony'. On the other hand, the bilateral Franco-German machinery exists to coordinate positions, and there is a long practice of Franco-German fine-tuning at the bilateral level. There is an argument that consensus-oriented policy norms of the EU institutions (the Commission and the Council) actually promote Franco-German agreement, usually as a means of avoiding French isolation (Webber, 1999a). As the example of the Agenda 2000 negotiations demonstrates, during the period observed Germany would often go out of its way to make sure that France was not isolated, even when this meant adopting policy positions at variance with its initial preferences.

Widening and deepening the European Union

Initially conceived as an ever closer union of six member states, the EU expanded to include 15 countries by 1995, with further enlargements likely to increase the number to 27 by 2005. More often than not, enlargement has comprised an area of Franco-German discord. Successive enlargements were initially opposed by French governments, for whom a broader Community threatened vital national interests. German governments supported enlargement in atonement for their role in provoking past European division, through a belief in European reconciliation, and because successive enlargements enhanced Germany's role at the centre of Europe.

The earliest Franco-German dispute over enlargement could be traced back to the arrival of de Gaulle in 1958. De Gaulle's double veto of British membership of the EU in 1963 and 1967 caused serious frictions between the two countries. British entry was supported by the other five EEC members and resisted only by Gaullist France, for whom Britain would be a trojan horse for American influence. In 1969 French President Pompidou finally agreed to British entry (along with those of Denmark and Ireland), which became effective in 1973 (Simonian, 1985). British entry was then welcomed as a counter-balance to a Federal Republic of Germany that had become far less accommodating under Willy Brandt's leadership. At each successive enlargement, vital French interests were initially felt to be threatened. In the case of Greece (1981) and Spain and Portugal (1986) the French feared the direct economic challenge to French farmers through increased competition for CAP resources. President Mitterrand was also originally hostile to opening up the EU to the former EFTA countries (Austria, Sweden, Norway, Finland) and even more so to those Central and Eastern European countries emerging from four decades of Communist rule. On each occasion, French attitudes shifted under the pressure of the Franco-German relationship itself; the role of Germany in ensuring French rallying to a wider Europe was evident on more than one occasion. The close personal relationship between Kohl and Mitterrand finally overcame early French resistance to expanding the EU to the northern rim (Sweden, Finland, Norway, Austria), nations that the French feared would look to Germany (or Britain) for leadership (Schild, 1994).

Underlying opposing stances on the enlargement of the Community lay diverging perceptions of national interest. France had traditionally preferred a compact Community, led by a Franco-German directorate within which it pretended to the leading political role (Haski, 1990a). This type of directorate had only ever existed during the Gaullist period, and was, arguably, rendered illusory by German unification, which altered durably the internal balance of the Franco-German relationship. Faced with this evidence, French attitudes to enlargement underwent an evolution; no longer opposed in principle to a wider Community/Union (which was inevitable), France now argued in favour of linking enlargement with the preservation of Community policies and the Community method. Through fear of a diluted, enlarged Community/Union, France came round to favour certain forms of flexible integration that would preserve its influence as a leading EC state and safeguard its privileged relationship with Germany. Hence, there was a direct linkage between issues of widening and deepening. Preserving a strong Community, and maintaining Community policies in areas of vital national interest such as agriculture, required inventing new forms of Community governance. Once it had made this intellectual leap, France became more favourable to a multi-speed Europe on its terms.

Germany felt no such conflict between a wider Community and the pursuit of essential national interests (Papcke, 1996). The Federal Republic drew from its collective memory the belief that she had a historic responsibility to promote the broadest possible historical reconciliation. More than any other country, Germany had a strong interest in regional stability after the dramatic processes occurring in Eastern and Central Europe from 1989 to 1991 (Garton-Ash, 1994). The new Germany bordered the countries of Central and Eastern Europe with which it had strong historic ties, and these countries looked to Germany for leadership. Any failure of democracy in the former Communist countries would create incalculable problems of economic and political dislocation on Germany's doorstep.

There was a gradual convergence of French and German views on enlargement. France came to admit the positive effects of widening on the stability of Central and Eastern Europe. Although Mitterrand remained reluctant, Jacques Chirac had supported widening to include the Eastern and Central European countries before his election as President in 1995. Germany became a rather less fervent partisan of enlargement at any price. In contrast to its predecessor, the Schröder administration (1998–) accepted the idea refuted at Amsterdam that institutional reform was an essential preliminary to future enlargement. In July 1997, the European Commission proposed to the European Union that it start negotiations for the admission of Poland, Hungary, the Czech Republic, Estonia and Slovenia (Blair, 1999). The Luxembourg summit of December 1997 retained these five countries plus Cyprus as candidates for EU membership, and negotiations started over accession in March 1998. The Helsinki summit of December 1999 invited six other countries to join in the negotiations (Romania, Bulgaria, Slovakia, Latvia, Lithuania, Malta) and offered the prospect of eventual Community membership to Turkey. The Helsinki summit also relaunched attempts to provide a solution for the institutional reforms that had stalled at Amsterdam (on more majority voting, limiting the number of commissioners, and a re-weighting of votes within the Council).

By the end of the decade, France and Germany had converged around support for the simultaneous processes of enlargement and institutional reform. The enlargement of the EU raised ever more pressing questions of flexible forms of integration and of Franco-German influence in an enlarged Community.

France, Germany and flexible integration

The debate over a European core has regularly resurfaced at critical junctures in the development of the European Union. Notions of a core/periphery divide had a particular pertinence during the 1990s, with which this book is chiefly concerned. The enlargement of the Community has ensured that the debate over flexible integration remains high on the political agenda. In the words of Samuel Brittan, 'despite the slogan there is no conflict between widening and deepening, we know that there is' (cited in O'Neill, 1996: 181). A Community of almost 30 states cannot function under the same rules as one of six, nine, twelve or even fifteen states. The unanimity rule for matters of vital national interest, which occasionally produced institutional gridlock in a Community of six members, would be a recipe for stagnation in a much wider community. Moves to more qualified majority voting in the Council of Ministers were recognised by most as an essential accompaniment to a wider community. There were several forms of flexible integration; these included the 'hard core', a Europe of 'concentric circles' and Europe à la carte. These three options were associated most closely with Germany, France and Britain respectively. These responses were embedded in more profound visions of legitimacy, European integration, republicanism and the nation state.

Proposals for flexible integration pose a challenge to the more simplistic neo-functionalist arguments. As the Community expanded, it became apparent that not all members would progress at the same pace. Spillover did not force the lowest members to keep pace with the fastest; rather it encouraged smaller groups of states to go it alone. In practice, the rate of integration appears dependent upon policy sectors and political choices. In specific sectors, a multi-speed Europe already exists, notably in monetary policy.

Unofficial German proposals for a 'hard core', published in September 1994, broke with the convention that German initiatives should be presented as joint Franco-German initiatives. The Schäuble–Lamers paper of 1994 (drawn up by Wolfgang Schäuble, a close aide of Helmut Kohl and now CDU chairman) was an explicit attempt to theorise a multi-speed Europe (Dubois, 1994). The CDU paper called for the adoption of a federal European constitution, an acceleration of EMU and the creation of a European defence community. At the heart of the proposals lay the creation of a hard core of five member states, consisting of Germany, France and the Benelux countries. The hard core would push ahead with a single currency and a single CFSP, allowing other states to catch up when and if they were able. The Schäuble–Lamers paper also advocated widening the Community to include the Central and Eastern European countries by the year 2000. Reconciling widening and deepening required the emergence of a hard core (Janning, 1996).

These proposals provoked a strong reaction in several European capitals, with excluded founding-member country Italy especially outraged. Not only the excluded countries objected to the naming in advance of candidates for the hard core. The French alternative of a Europe of 'concentric circles', outlined by Premier Balladur shortly afterwards, envisaged the eventuality – even desirability – of variable integration, but refrained from naming in advance those member countries apt to join in a hard core. The French contribution to the debate envisaged 'variable geometry'; the degree of integration should be dependent upon the qualities of the issue-area involved. The countries forming part of these 'circles' would vary on a case to case basis, though France and Germany would presumably be present in each of them. The French view was closer to the 'strengthened cooperation' procedure eventually adopted in the Amsterdam summit.

Reactions to the Schäuble–Lamers proposals demonstrated the difficulties for Germany of acting alone. A high degree of suspicion remained attached to unilateral German initiatives. The Schäuble–Lamers proposals, which did not follow any formal consultations between Bonn and Paris, caused much controversy. Critics argued that there were few democratic safeguards in this hard core, a form of renewed intergovernmentalism without the checks and balances of the actual EU institutions (Reeh, 1995). The French strongly opposed the idea of a two-speed EMU. With a changing balance of power, France sought ways to tie in Germany, but she feared being submerged in a Germanic sphere of influence, especially in the monetary domain (Giscard d'Estaing, 1996; Giret and Moatti, 1998). France had consistently espoused the cause of a broadly based economic and monetary union, a theme developed in Chapter 5. The hard core episode laid bare the ambiguities of the Franco-German relationship. Neither France nor

Germany wanted an exclusive Franco-German relationship. In one of the most important roles it performed within the EU, France continued to see itself as spokesperson for the Mediterranean rim countries, especially on matters of foreign policy and defence of the CAP. This role would be abandoned in a hard core.

Both Germany and France looked to Britain for protection in its dealings with the other. France feared being swallowed up in a 'hard core' entity, with Britain less able to play an intermediary role. Germany had forwarded the idea of a hard core in order to prevent a southern drift of the EU, perceived to benefit French interests. Germany perceived Britain to form part of the group of northern free trade states within the EU, against which France led a group of protectionist-inclined southern states. Unsurprisingly, the 'hard core' proposals were unacceptable to Britain.

The provisions for 'strengthened cooperation' in the Amsterdam Treaty were a timid move towards more flexible integration, jointly elaborated by French and German foreign ministers de Charette and Kinkel. But 'strengthened cooperation' fell far short of a hard core.

Conclusion

In Chapter 4, we have considered the operation of the Franco-German relationship at the level of the European Union itself. After setting out German and French perspectives on European integration, the chapter has concentrated on providing responses to the main intellectual question posed in the Introduction, namely does the Franco-German relationship exercise leadership, joint or otherwise, within the EU? The evidence is mixed and a fuller response is proposed in the conclusion (Chapter 8). Drawing upon the evidence presented in this chapter, we conclude provisionally that Franco-German brokerage is an important variable in constitutive politics, providing some support for the Moravscik version of the liberal intergovernmentalist realist argument. Inter-state bargaining is a powerful driving force during Treaty negotiations, where states remain by far the most powerful actors. As befits partners in a bilateral 'quasi-regime', France and Germany engage in mutual accommodations, and attempt to achieve above common denominator agreements. Germany in particular has demonstrated its willingness – to an extent – to compromise its own national objectives in order to satisfy French preoccupations. The Franco-German alliance has a dialectical quality that enables its contradictions to be surmounted – within limits. The importance placed upon agreement by both sides allows initially divergent positions to be bridged; we observed this in the fields of agriculture or international trade. Even when placed on the defensive, there is an inclination for France and Germany to attempt to reach agreement.

The contrasting evidence from the Maastricht and Amsterdam Treaty negotiations is that joint Franco-German stewardship is usually a necessary (but not a sufficient) condition for moves to further European integration. There is evidence to suggest that the classic role of the Franco-German relationship in policy impulsion has become less cogent with EU enlargement and with the broadening scope of EU intervention. The outcome of the Amsterdam summit in particular suggested the limits to Franco-German bilateralism in an EU of 15 member states determined to defend their national interest.

Outside of the specific case of history-making decisions, Franco-German dynamics were less important in the area of regulatory politics (Majone, 1996), such as research and technology or the environment, where patterns of governance are multilevel in character and where new actors (such as firms, interest groups and supranational actors) are more important. The dynamics of the EU policy process can legitimise new actors and produce unintended consequences beyond the control of any member state. France and Germany have both undergone constrained policy choices that conflict in important respects with their domestic political traditions.

The Franco-German relationship in the economic sphere: more than a hill of beans?

Nowhere is the Franco-German relationship more complex than in the economic and industrial spheres. Germany and France have traditionally subscribed to distinctive cultural and economic models. The post-war traditions of German ordoliberalism and French *dirigisme* cohabited uneasily, however close the political relations between de Gaulle, Adenauer and their successors. There were perceptibly different critiques of economic management, the role of the state and social partnership in France and Germany. But there is also a permanent process of exchange of ideas, policies and goods. Chapter 5 presents an overview of the Franco-German relationship in the economic, industrial and monetary spheres. After setting out the distinctive national economic paths in France and Germany, the main body of the chapter concentrates upon a detailed investigation of economic and monetary union, and the role of the Franco-German relationship therein.

Franco-German economic policy traditions and relations

The German – or Rhineland – model of regulated capitalism fell somewhere between Anglo-Saxon neo-liberalism and French *dirigisme*. The predominant economic policy beliefs shared by state and business interests alike were derived from the 'ordoliberal' school of regulated capitalism (Dyson, 1996). 'Ordoliberal' beliefs combined a liberal economic stance, anti-interventionist macroeconomics and a strong measure of state regulation. In the German ordoliberal tradition, the state has a duty to provide a stable framework of economic activity and business has a duty of social responsibility. More than Anglo-American liberalism, German ordoliberalism requires a strong state to regulate private industry; unlike French *dirigisme*, the state should avoid detailed meddling, or long-term planning. Germany never had an important state sector to compare with that of

France, the UK, Spain or Italy. The state's duty was to provide an economic constitution, a set of binding rules, not to intervene in a detailed manner in industrial policy. Above all, politicians should not intervene in the operation of markets. An impartial monetary authority – the *Bundesbank* – should ensure price stability, which would banish forever memories of inter-war hyper-inflation and the associated rise of political extremism. The *Bundesbank* and the strong Deutschmark were the institutional and monetary symbols of the ordoliberal tradition.

The political complements to this economic policy tradition were the social-market economy and social partnership. The social-market economy involved a commitment to basic welfare provisions financed by progressive taxation. Social partnership implied partnership in industrial relations, collective wage bargaining, detailed regulation and a redistributive taxation and social security system.

In France, there was no equivalent consensus behind basic economic objectives. There was a weaker tradition of social partnership in industrial relations, the consequence in part of late industrialisation and politically divided unions. To the German model of domestic consensus, traditional representations of French political culture emphasised a more sharply divided range of domestic interests, and model of interest articulation and aggregation (Cole, 1998a). One prevalent feature of the traditional French model of politics and policies was affirmative state activity in the economic and industrial sphere. Although the extent of post-war economic planning has been exaggerated, there was a widespread belief that the market needed to be regulated by a central state vested with an unchallenged political legitimacy. The state represented the general will of the people, over and above the particularistic interests of business, unions and voluntary groups. Moreover, in the economic sphere the state was vested with the duty of public service. The public sector was responsible for providing essential services (and ensuring essential investment) that private capital interests were unwilling (or incapable) of assuming. This produced a pattern of close interlocking relationships between the civil service, political elites and the boards of the leading French firms, which depended to some extent on public procurement policies.

Unlike the German ordoliberal tradition, French *dirigisme* overtly favoured indicative planning and state-level industrial policy aimed at producing national champions (Schmidt, 1996). French industrial policy was traditionally built upon the belief in the failure of perfect competition and the right to protect industries. In a *dirigiste* sense, governments should be able to direct market competition. Governments should protect their industries against disloyal competition and social dumping, and engineer industrial change in the long-term national strategic interest. Here we should sound a note of caution. The original features of French post-war economic management (such as planning) had faded in importance long before French governments attempted to harmonise economic policy with European Union partners in the 1980s and 1990s (Cohen, 1996).

Recent research has uncovered the existence of several distinct traditions of economic thought within and across France and Germany (Dyson and Featherstone, 1999; Howarth, 1999). Protectionist–*dirigiste* and orthodox–liberal schools of economic thought existed within each country, rather than being confined to France or Germany. While economic doctrines were fairly distinctive, industrial practices were not always so far apart. Although French governments were sometimes accused of neo-protectionist policies, German industrial practices were explicitly designed to forestall any hostile foreign takeovers of German companies (Joly, 1994). The insider pattern of German corporate governance, involving close bank–industry relations, employee co-management and cross-shareholdings amongst the leading firms, made German companies virtually takeover-proof. Consequently, foreign companies often found the German market even harder to crack than the 'protectionist' French one.

In the dominant German ordoliberal tradition, there were ingrained doubts about the credibility of France as an economic partner (Froehly and Schiller, 1999). French politicians interfered excessively in economic and industrial management, they pursued excessively loose monetary policies and they displayed imbued protectionist tendencies. Suspicions lingered long after these salient traits of French economic management had become less salient. France was viewed with no particular indulgence by the *Bundesbank*, the pivotal institution of German monetary management. To regain credibility, French governments were urged to import Germany's tested system as a benchmark.

There has been some convergence between French and German macroeconomic models. French economic policy has been driven since the Barre plan of the late 1970s by a determined effort to match Germany in terms of economic performance (Frears, 1981). The traditional French model – based on centralism, state intervention in economic management, high inflation, and growth – was progressively modified during the 1980s and 1990s by key elements of the German model, with its insistence on low inflation, high productivity, central bank independence and a strong currency. As the process of European integration gathered pace after the mid-1980s, French policy-makers emulated central features of the German economic model such as price stability and central bank independence. The single currency project (considered later in this chapter) embodies this process of policy transfer and emulation between Germany and its continental European partners.

The Franco-German bilateral economic relationship appears in most respects much weaker than the political one, notwithstanding the single currency project. Although France and Germany are each other's principal trading partners, their relationship has had to adapt to numerous tensions. This can be demonstrated in the pattern of commercial and industrial exchange.

Franco-German commercial and industrial relations

Franco-German economic relations can be understood in terms of asymmetrical interdependence, with the French economy more dependent on the German than vice versa. While Germany remained by far France's largest trading partner (18% of all trade in 1994), France was less important for overall German trade (12.5%) (Markovits and Reich, 1997). As the two countries are each other's most important trading partner, it is appropriate to think of the Franco-German relationship in terms of interdependence rather than hegemony (Joly, 1994). Inherent in the nature of the postwar Franco-German relationship is a complex trade-off between political prestige and economic power. While political prestige traditionally underpinned the French contribution to the partnership, economic power became an increasingly more powerful resource as memories of the Second World War faded.

Franco-German commercial exchanges have been rather unevenly weighted in favour of Germany. German power has been disseminated through its role as a *Handelsstaat* (trading state) and its structural primacy in the economic and monetary spheres (Hueglin, 1995; Kaelberer, 1997). Whether measured by economic growth, commercial balance, price stability or employment productivity, the post-war German model proved a paradigm for other Europeans to emulate (Dyson, 1996; Markovits and Reich, 1997). The permanent economic surpluses produced by the German model underpinned the economic consensus on the social-market economy.

Manufacturing exports were the driving force of German economic growth. Germany has been the machine tool supplier of Europe, and the main provider of high quality, heavy investment goods to other EU countries. Her export penetration of European and world markets outstrips that of her main EU rivals France, the UK and Italy. As a percentage of GDP, West German exports grew from 20% to 36% from 1970 to 1993. Other smaller EU states closely integrated to the German economy – such as the Netherlands, Belgium and Luxembourg – also increased their world market share, but France and Italy stagnated, in percentage share, over the period 1958–92 (Markovits and Reich, 1997). Germany has benefited far more than any other EU country from the opening up of European markets. Germany is by far the biggest exporter to other members of the EU. She accounts for one-quarter of all intra-EU exports (26.25% in 1992), compared with a steady second place for France with under one-sixth (16.3% in 1992). In 1993, the Germans were the best exporters within the EU, yet only 41% of their exports (in 1993) went on intra-EU trade. Most exports were global. Germany's dependence on EU markets has diminished at the same time as her control has increased. Other EU economies, including the French, were far more dependent on the EU regional economy.

The German model has faced powerful challenges during the 1990s (Welfens, 1993). As we observed in Chapter 4, German unification stretched Germany's traditional role in the EU, not least because it posed an increasing financial burden on the German state. Integrating the East German economy proved difficult; it was financed by massive financial transfers from West to East Germany. The transition costs of unification were, in part, responsible for an unemployment total of 4 million, well over 10% of the active population; a decline in average national individual wealth; and rising budget and current account deficits. There was also a vigorous debate on the *Standort Deutschland* about the attractiveness of Germany as an industrial location. High labour and welfare costs, onerous levels of taxation, labour inflexibilities, and the costs of social partnership were all presented as reasons for the delocalisation of leading German companies to sites in Eastern Europe or elsewhere in the EU, and for falling levels of inward investment (Parkes, 1997). As a general point, changes in the international political economy have challenged salient aspects of the German model. The moves to post-Fordist regulation and service-based economies have posed adaptability problems for an economy whose traditional strength lay in high-quality manufacturing exports. To take one example, the traditional model of house banks and close bank–industry relations has been challenged by the globalisation of equity finance. On the other hand, German firms have adapted themselves in a remarkable manner to the changing rules of the international game. German firms have emerged as highly effective international predators, as demonstrated in the sectors of automobiles, insurance, merchant banking, telecommunications and many others.

The French economy is the fourth largest in the world. Thirty years of spectacular economic growth from 1945 to 1974 – *les trente glorieuses* – placed France second in the ranking of European nations, trailing only the Federal Republic of Germany. Although France has maintained its ranking as Europe's second economic power, the 'thirty glorious years' were followed by over two decades of painful adjustment to depressed conditions in the world economy. The effects of the oil crises of 1973 and 1979, and of growing internationalisation and increased European integration during the 1980s and 1990s were to highlight the importance of the external constraints weighing upon the French economy, and the limited margins of manoeuvre of its governments in undertaking unilateral economic policies.

The French economy has performed particularly well in the agricultural and service sectors, with a more mixed manufacturing performance (Bensahel, 1998; INSEE, 1995, 1996, 1997, 1998). Its record in the agricultural sector has been the most spectacular. Buoyed by exceptional increases in agricultural productivity, and supported by the incentive structure of the CAP, France has become the world's second largest food exporter, behind the USA. The inbuilt French surplus in agricultural products is of great benefit for the French balance of trade account, counterbalancing the nation's energy deficit. France is the world's fourth largest exporter of manufacturing goods. Alongside its mixed record of success in the high technology activities such as information technology, computers and consumer electronics, the French economy has performed well in intermediate branches such as car manufacturing, glass, rubber and chemicals. These are sectors where long-term state investments facilitated economies of scale. As in Germany and other EU nations, a decline in the traditional manufacturing sector (textiles, steel, mining, shipbuilding) has occurred in France, but French performance in the service sector has more than compensated for its mixed industrial performance. France is one of the world's largest exporters of services, with particular strengths in tourism, retailing, transport, banking and insurance.

There has been a conventional complementarity between the French and German economies: 'a strong French surplus in the agricultural sector is offset by a strong German surplus in machine tools and industrial goods' (Froment-Maurice, 1997: 36). Traditionally running a current account deficit with Germany, the strong performance of the French economy in the 1990s reversed standard patterns. Buoyed by a record trade surplus, in 1997 France moved into commercial surplus with Germany. While Germany remained by far the largest supplier of French imported goods (259 billion francs) she exported even more to Germany (264 billion francs) (INSEE, 1998). The French current account was in surplus in 1998 for the sixth consecutive year, reaching 3.2% of domestic GDP in 1997. There is some suggestion that France's dynamic service-based economy is catching up with that of a Germany still digesting unification. French export successes in the past 15 years demonstrate that she has gained from the operation of more integrated European (and to some extent global) markets. The economic problems faced by French governments have been rather similar to those of Germany – how to tackle persistently high unemployment (over 11% in 1999) while combining economic growth with a tight control over inflation, limited budget deficits and a balance of trade surplus. As in Germany, French industry complains of high labour and welfare costs, excessive levels of taxation and rigid labour markets.

There is no real evidence to suggest a privileged Franco-German industrial alliance. The industrial and economic sphere is one that escapes increasingly from the political impulsion of Franco-German political relations. German and French firms sometimes cooperate, sometimes not. There are much closer relationships – such as between German and Austrian companies, for example. Only in sectors such as aerospace and defence, where public procurement policies are of primordial importance, have French and German companies responded to political pressures to merge or collaborate. Industrial mergers in sectors such as pharmaceuticals (Rhône Poulenc and Höechst) have followed an industrial, rather than a political logic. In areas of recent market liberalisation, France and Germany have often been at loggerheads. This is the case in telecommunications, where an early alliance between France Télécom and Deutsche Telekom (aimed essentially against BT) collapsed in 1999 amidst bitter recriminations, when Deutsche Telekom launched an unsuccessful takeover bid of the principal Italian operator. Even the limited Franco-German industrial collaboration in the joint US venture Sprint has disintegrated. A similar pattern can be observed in energy, where regionally based German energy firms have opposed the acquisitive tastes of the French energy conglomerate EDF-GDF. In the automobile sector, there was stiff industrial competition between Renault and Volkswagen, best illustrated by their rival bids to take over Skoda in the Czech Republic. In financial services, the creation of the London/Frankfurt *grand bürse* was perceived as a slight not just by the Paris stock exchange, but more generally by the French government. In transport, the rivalry between the Anglo-French Alcatel-Alsthom and the German Siemens for the realisation of high-speed train links spanned the globe.

There are counter-examples. Franco-German cooperation in the Airbus consortium was close and fruitful; the Airbus A320 emerged as a serious rival to the US Boeing's domination of the civil aviation market. Airbus was produced by a European consortium including Bae and the Spanish Casa. The creation of a Franco-German aerospace alliance (EADS) between French firm Aerospatiale/Matra and the German DASA/Chrysler-CASA in October 1999, produced a European realignment in line with the declared wishes of European politicians. The reluctance of the French to transform Airbus into a limited company for long set the French against the other (especially British and German) partners. Equally significant, the Eurofighter alliance (UK, Germany, Italy, Spain) and the French Rafale were in open competition for the production of the next generation of fighter aircraft. The divergence of military doctrines until 1996 prevented more fruitful Franco-German bilateral cooperation in the defence sector.

Policy styles spilled over into bilateral industrial relations. Although French governments (especially that of Jospin, 1997–) engaged in a programme of industrial and financial privatisations from 1986 onwards, the tendency of the French government to retain golden shares, and/or majority share-holdings in firms such as France Télécom, Aerospatiale and Air France, complicated Franco-German commercial relations. German private sector firms did not want to be engaged in alliances with French public or mixed sector concerns. They feared the covert influence of the French government in such joint ventures. Germany itself was rather inconsistent, however; the acquisitive behaviour of Deutsche Telekom openly raised concerns of a level playing field, given that the German state owned a majority of shares in the leading German telecommunications operator.

Thus, there is insufficient evidence to evoke a Franco-German axis in industrial and commercial affairs. Indeed, there was a blurred line between commercial and political rivalries. By 1994, Germany carried out six times more trade with the Eastern democracies than did France (Markovits and Reich, 1997: 174). The French feared not only that German investment in Central and Eastern Europe would provide a long-term market for German products – somewhat similar to the role performed by Japan in South-East Asia – but also that Germany's political alliances would follow its economic interest. As the balance of Germany's trading interests moved further east, so her political interests might also shift; if not at the expense of the EU, then at least in terms of cultivating alternative relations within an enlarged EU. These French fears were rather similar to those expressed in debates surrounding economic and monetary union, to which we now turn.

The Franco-German relationship and economic and monetary union

The Franco-German relationship was critical in understanding the process leading to the initiation and implementation of the single currency. Although the eventual consequences of the single currency were interpreted by many as an unprecedented leap into supranational integration, the negotiation of the single currency fell squarely into the realm of inter-state bargaining. The French and German governments were the principal players, though there were other significant actors. We do not propose to retrace in minute detail the history of the single currency project. There are several pertinent studies, most especially the authoritative *The Road to Maastricht* by Dyson and Featherstone (1999). Rather, we will consider the extent to which France and Germany – together or separately – initiated and implemented the single currency project before attempting to interpret EMU from the perspective of the Franco-German relationship.

In *The Road to Maastricht*, Dyson and Featherstone (1999) identify several critical junctures leading to economic and monetary union (EMU), from the Balladur memorandum of January 1988, through to the implementation of the single currency on 1 January 1999.[1] In reality, the debate over EMU went back a lot further. EMU had been advocated from various quarters as a policy solution to the problem of monetary instability since the late 1960s, a policy solution advocated notably by economic conservatives in the Trésor division of the French Finance Ministry and amongst the Financial Inspectorate (Dyson and Featherstone, 1999).

Throughout the first 25 years of the post-war period European currencies were tied to the US dollar in the system known as the Bretton Woods agreement. Transatlantic tensions were ignited by the US decision to suspend the Bretton Woods fixed parities agreement in 1971 and to allow the dollar to float freely (downwards) on international financial markets. This provided a boost for the USA, but posed a major threat to European economies.

The collapse of Bretton Woods and the oil crises of 1973–74 increased the pressure on European countries to adapt and coordinate their monetary policy instruments. The 'snake' (1972–76) and the European monetary system (1979–93) were both attempts to achieve greater European monetary coordination which stopped short of full currency union (Chang, 1999; Story, 1999). In 1969, European leaders meeting at the Hague summit issued the Hague declaration, co-initiated by Chancellor Brandt and President Pompidou, which called for eventual monetary union as a response to problems of monetary instability (Simonian, 1985). The Werner report arising from the Hague declaration envisaged a staged progression to economic and monetary union to be achieved by 1980 at the latest. Stage one, which began in 1972, involved the creation of a currency basket (the 'snake in the tunnel'), which allowed currency readjustments in a system of fixed parities between 15 participating European currencies. This system was asymmetrical, in that it was the responsibility of the central banks of weaker currency states (such as France) to defend their currencies. Later stages would only come about once the participating countries had achieved a higher degree of economic convergence; this required efforts to control inflation and to limit the use of economic policy instruments (such as devaluation and interest rate manipulation). No date was set for a transition to stage two, and on this occasion the European countries never got

---

[1] These critical junctures were: the Hanover summit of June 1988, which commissioned the Delors report; the Madrid summit of June 1989 (where commitment to EMU was reasserted); the fall of the Berlin wall leading to ultimate German unification; the launching of the Intergovernmental Conferences at the Rome summit (October 1990) and the Maastricht summit of December 1991. Once the EMU decision had been taken, there were other landmarks: the ratification and monetary crises of September 1992 and August 1993, the election of Chirac as French president in 1995, the French strike movement of December 1995, and the changes of government in France and Germany in 1997 and 1998.

beyond stage one of the proposed monetary union. This first experiment collapsed under the pressure of international economic crisis; governments were unable or unwilling to cope with the shock of the first oil crisis of 1973 and adopted contradictory national responses. Unable to control its inflationary targets, France quit the snake in 1974, and again in 1976 (Brodersen, 1991). The French departure from the snake convinced the Germans that the French were not capable of EMU.

The next effort to harmonise European monetary policies was the European monetary system (EMS), launched by Chancellor Schmidt and President Giscard d'Estaing in 1979. Although the EMS was presented as a joint Franco-German initiative, it was inspired largely by German Chancellor Schmidt, against the opposition of powerful domestic interests. The EMS was envisaged as a zone of monetary stability in the wake of the exchange rate fluctuations following the ending of the Bretton Woods agreement and the oil crises of 1973–74. The EMS served both French and German interests. The EMS gave France a share in monetary policy-making – one larger than its economic weight strictly justified. It also provided a convenient external scapegoat for internal economic reforms. For Germany, it provided a European cloak for its economic leadership ambitions. Rather like the snake, the exchange rate mechanism (ERM) provided for currency adjustments around a central target, the European currency unit (ecu), determined as the average value of participating currencies. Currencies were allowed to float in bands of ±2.5% of their agreed value. Once a currency fell to the bottom of the basket, it was the duty of the central banks of the strongest and weakest countries to purchase it; this arrangement was more equitable than the snake, because effort would be distributed between strong and weak currency countries. Currency rates were periodically realigned to take into account inflation differences in the participating countries. By joining the EMS (and especially ERM), countries pledged to adopt strong money policies designed to bear down on inflation, and to reduce the use of economic policy instruments (such as devaluation and budgetary deficits). Unlike the snake, the record of the EMS was a positive one: from an average of 11% in 1980, inflation was brought down to under 3% in 1987. Although there were 12 monetary realignments within the EMS during 1979–87, from 1987 onwards there were no further realignments until the system effectively collapsed in August 1993 (Chang, 1999).

The operation of the European monetary system from 1979 to 1993 demonstrated unambiguously *de facto* German economic primacy in Europe. The Deutschmark was confirmed as the European anchor currency against which all others had to measure themselves. German economic primacy was emphasised through its control over monetary policy; whether inside or outside of the EMS, other countries were forced to align interest rate policy with that of the *Bundesbank*, a body with a constitutional duty to favour price stability above all other economic objectives. Interest rates had to be kept higher in other EMS countries than in Germany itself. Such pressures became more intense after German unification, as the *Bundesbank* relied mainly on interest rate policy (rather than taxation) to control the inflationary pressures arising from the German currency union and the massive financial transfers to the former East German *Länder*. Through the ERM, Germany was able to control the macroeconomic performance of her partners without allowing them an influence in policy formulation. This asymmetrical dependency of other European economies on the German was perceived by France and others as a strong argument for currency union.

From the 1970s onwards, German norms in economic management were exported across Europe. In France, from the Barre plan of 1976 onwards (excepting the period 1981–83) the importance of France mirroring the performance of the German economy was repeatedly expressed. Hence the importance of the strong franc policy, engaged with vigour from 1984 onwards and only loosened under Jospin once France had qualified for single currency membership (Aeschimann and Riché, 1996). With the partial exception of the 1981–83 period, French governments had welcomed close relations with the German economy as a means of modernising their own. There was no alternative economic strategy. The devaluation of the franc on three occasions from 1981–83 highlighted the fallacies of a belief in national economic sovereignty and unilateral neo-Keynesian relaunch (Cameron, 1996). Tying the franc to the Deutschmark through the ERM produced substantial economic benefits. It allowed inflation to be mastered, the productivity gap with Germany to be narrowed, and even an improved commercial balance with Germany. On the other hand, persistently high unemployment was perceived as a legacy of this policy. Moreover, punitively high interest rates from 1990 onwards were imposed on Germany's partners by the *Bundesbank*, as the price to pay for German unification. In a reversal of the traditional dynamic, the French government – along with others – learnt the lesson that sovereignty could be recovered by the solution of Europeanisation. Since monetary sovereignty had already disappeared, a single currency would allow the French and others to recover elements of national sovereignty by promoting European solutions.

The Federal Republic was initially far more reluctant than its partners to entertain ideas of monetary union: a single currency would eliminate the two institutions of post-war German success, namely the *Bundesbank* and the Deutschmark. While the *Bundesbank* remained impervious to pressures from Germany's political partners, the attitudes of German politicians gradually shifted. Helmut Kohl, in particular, was sympathetic to the efforts made by France and other European countries to align their economies with the benchmark German economy. Strong political pressure from French President Mitterrand and Commission President Delors made an impact, but it is unclear whether monetary union could have materialised without the events of 1989. Most commentaries identify German unification as being a critical juncture. Although the principle of a single currency had been accepted before German unification (at the Hanover summit of June 1988, where the Delors report was commissioned), a firm German commitment to an intergovernmental conference and to a phased move to monetary union only came later, once the fall of the Berlin wall had drastically altered the European landscape. A German commitment at the Maastricht summit to a three-stage move to monetary union by 1999, at the latest, was a major French negotiating achievement (Sandholtz, 1993). In the nested game of high-level leadership bargaining, a phased progress to monetary union was agreed by Chancellor Kohl in order to reassure Germany's European allies (and especially France) of the future orientation of the unified German state. Kohl demonstrated great political vision and used the historic opportunity of the events of 1989–90 to further not only German, but European unification as well (Cole, 1998b). The linkage of German and European priorities also enabled Kohl to impose his views on a sceptical domestic advocacy coalition, represented by the *Bundesbank* and the Finance Ministry, with strong backing from German public opinion.

In their research on monetary union, Dyson and Featherstone (1999) identify two rival advocacy coalitions – the 'monetarists' and the 'economists' – divided on the proper relationship between economic convergence and monetary union. The dominant coalition was the 'economist' one. It was represented by German, British, Dutch and Danish governments and their central banks. This advocacy coalition envisaged monetary union as being the end result of a long process towards economic convergence. If it ever occurred, monetary union would crown a gradual process of political union. The Germans were reluctant to sacrifice control of the Deutschmark unless they received water-tight guarantees in exchange. For this reason, they insisted upon the tough economic convergence criteria as a preliminary for EMU. There remained much domestic German opposition to the prospect of creating a monetary union with countries with a weaker record of economic management.

The 'economist' coalition was opposed by the 'monetarist' one. This consisted of a group of states led by France (including Italy and Belgium) and supported by the Delors Commission. The monetarist coalition argued that the creation of a new monetary institution would itself force a process of economic convergence. This was consistent with the traditional Community method approach, based on elite socialisation into EC institutional structures, the assumption of passive approval and progress through tight deadlines. The preference of the monetarist coalition was for a large number of states to be able to progress to EMU, rather than a narrow core. A hard core EMU would be little more than a Deutschmark zone and would entrench German hegemony. From the French perspective, convergence should be encouraged by fiscal transfers from the richer to the poorer countries. The Edinburgh European Council meeting of December 1992 agreed to increase structural funds to ease the fiscal adjustment process for weaker countries. Germany feared this type of response; she would pay. From the German perspective, a lasting monetary union required determined convergence efforts on behalf of participating countries. This would provide a sounder basis upon which to found a monetary union than meeting politically driven deadlines. Hence, the German insistence on tough convergence criteria to accompany a phased progression towards monetary union (cf. below).

While the tensions between the economist and monetarist coalitions were real, by the early 1990s there had been a general convergence of domestic economic management styles across Europe, based on the pursuance of strong money policies and exchange rate stability. The *franc fort* policy was not imposed on France by Germany (though Germany undoubtedly acted as a model to imitate) but followed a distinctive domestic path, one of expanding the elite consensus in favour of a strong currency and structural economic reform.

Winners and losers of EMU

Most commentary depicted France as a probable winner of EMU. EMU had long been a French policy demand. It had been advocated since the late 1960s by French economic conservatives in the Trésor as a solution to the problem of asymmetrical interdependence. EMU would tie in the Germans to the European economy and harness German economic strength to European objectives. It would impose internal discipline on France and encourage long overdue structural reforms. It would allow France more influence over the definitions of economic policy priorities – largely dependent on the *Bundesbank* since the late 1960s. French leaders also favoured EMU as a means of increasing European autonomy from the USA. There was, in addition, a clear economic case for monetary union. EMU should lower production costs, thereby helping France to recover its share of the world market. Growth would create jobs. EMU would allow for lower interest rates. The principal political motivation, however, was that France would recover influence with EMU; it would be present in those institutions making monetary policy decisions. France was speaking for other countries in seeking to broaden and institutionalise EU monetary policy.

Germany is usually presented as the country with most to lose from a single currency. The ERM allowed Germany to exercise monetary hegemony without acknowledging any influence for Germany's partners (Sandholtz, 1993). Any other arrangement would be less favourable. While this point of view was widely shared within Germany, it underplays the political dynamics of European integration and the importance of nested bargaining games. By accepting a European monetary settlement, Kohl demonstrated the importance placed by Germany upon European integration. German and European unification were 'two sides of the same coin' (Paterson, 1998). Sacrificing the symbols of German post-war success – the Deutschmark and the *Bundesbank* – on the temple of European unification sent a powerful political message about the nature of the unified German state. The economic evidence was more mixed. Germany would share in lower transaction and production costs, but she would sacrifice the Deutschmark, the pivot of the EMS, and might run risks with inflation unless tight control was exercised at the implementation stage. There was also a strong economic argument – understated in most accounts – that EMU would principally benefit the German economy (Brodersen, 1991). The reduction of transaction costs and exchange rate stability would favour Germany by preventing an overvalued currency (a risk present within the EMS) and boosting exports. Indeed, the realist argument can be inverted; there was an important political imperative in presenting Germany as the country with the most to lose. As a counterpart to agreeing to EMU – for which a strong German economic case could be made – the Germans could insist on shaping the institutions and policies that would govern the future monetary union. The Germans were able to define the paradigm – that of an independent European Central Bank, with price stability as its principal objective. This *sine qua non* of German participation was conceded by Mitterrand in December 1988.

With a clear resonance of Putnam's two-level bargaining model, domestic German divisions proved a source of diplomatic strength during the Maastricht negotiations. German negotiators were able to use domestic opposition to sacrificing the Deutschmark as a negotiating card. Economic and monetary union was not a German policy issue. Indeed, it alarmed sections of German public opinion, and powerful interests within Germany remained opposed to EMU: notably, Kohl's finance minister, Theo Waigel, and the *Bundesbank*. The Franco-German relationship was a resource for German Chancellor Kohl, because it provided a framework for overcoming domestic opposition. The unification chancellor could use Germany's European commitments as a powerful argument to conquer domestic resistance. The two-level bargain thus worked in both directions. Given the nature of the sacrifice that Germany was being asked to make, Kohl could insist that Germany define the agenda and shape the institutions of the future monetary union. The 'German way of doing things' underpinned the EMU negotiations in the Maastricht pre-negotiations. An acceptance of Germany's primacy in monetary affairs was a precondition for even considering EMU. This explained the stout German resistance to the French advocacy of an 'economic government' to direct the operations of a future European Central Bank (ECB).

Within Germany itself, Kohl placed himself at the head of an advocacy coalition stressing the primacy of European integration as an article of faith, against a rival coalition (of the *Bundesbank* and the finance ministry) anxious lest the leap into the dark of EMU produce economic and political instability (Dyson and Featherstone, 1996). In Kohl's view, there was a necessary trade-off between European integration – which required sacrificing the Deutschmark and the *Bundesbank* – and economic stability, which demanded that the single currency be at least as strong as the German currency. The single currency was, after all, to be irreversible. The Delors committee, which drafted the EMU text, was dominated intellectually by Pöhl, president of the *Bundesbank*, and the Germans subsequently considered they gained over 80% of their objectives in the Delors report.

Germany gained in terms of the basic principles governing monetary policy in part because an international epistemic community of central bankers and professional economists believed the German model to be a benchmark (Sandholtz, 1993). The Maastricht Treaty provided for an independent central bank, modelled along the lines of the *Bundesbank*. The ECB would be run by a directorate of six full-time officials (the *Bundesbank* had between five and eight) and the presidents of the 11 European central banks, who would take an oath of independence. ECB members were to be nominated for eight years, exactly the same as the *Bundesbank*. The Council of Governors, which brings together the directorate and the heads of the national banks, is modelled on the *Bundesbank* central council.

Article 107 of the Maastricht Treaty explicitly proclaimed the principle of central bank independence. The ECB would not 'take instructions from Community institutions or bodies, from any government of a member-state or from any other body' (*Agence Europe*, 1992: 9). Article 107 reflected the victory of the German preconceptions over French plans for more political direction. The French had consistently attempted to associate a social counterpart to the monetarist thrust of EMU. Mitterrand's 'economic government' was an attempt to offset the financial logic of a future ECB. Delors' 'white paper' of 1994 was a much more explicit attempt to give a social dimension to EMU (Drake, 2000). Both failed. In his call for economic government, Mitterrand implied that the European central bank should be accountable to the political leadership of the European Union, the European Council and the Council of Finance Ministers (ECOFIN). This was anathema to most

German actors. For Germany, the bank had to have the maximum independence from political directives. The Maastricht Treaty did contain certain concessions to French positions on the single currency. The treaty confirmed that ECOFIN would 'determine the economic policy orientations of each member-state' and that the European Council would determine 'exchange rate policy' (Article 109). The significance of these clauses should not be minimised; control over exchange rate policy proved a major bone of contention between ECOFIN and the ECB after the introduction of the single currency in 1999 (Delhommais and Leparmentier, 1999).

The details of EMU appeared to bear the imprint of German rigour at every stage of policy implementation: from the location of the European central bank in Frankfurt, to the name of the currency (the Euro, rather than the ECU favoured by France), to the 'stability pact' accompanying its implementation (de Bresson, 1996). Above all, Germany was able to insist on tough convergence criteria accompanying the implementation of the single currency. The criteria outlined in the Maastricht Treaty included precise objectives for inflation (within 1.5% of the best performing state), budget deficits (no more than 3% of GDP) and public sector borrowing (below 60% of GDP). They also required central bank independence and the complete mobility of capital (Andrews, 1993). These criteria were designed to ensure a lasting convergence of economic performance before final moves to monetary union could take place.

If the basic institutional design of the new monetary institutions was imposed by Germany, the end game of monetary union revealed itself to be a process with unintended consequences. Since the introduction of the single currency in 1999, the Europeanisation of monetary policy institutions has reduced Germany to one voice amongst others. The possibility of the *Bundesbank* representative being placed in a minority in the ECB is a very real one. As we illustrate in Chapter 7, French and German finance ministers were able to influence the conduct of the ECB in some important respects, and there were new areas of tension between central bankers and politicians.

In the period after the Maastricht summit the German and French governments showed remarkable persistence in maintaining exchange rate stability, and in proclaiming monetary union to be on course. The Franco-German alliance emerged strengthened from the 1993 ERM crisis, which showed the strains that high German interest rates had on relations between the two countries (Smith and Sandholtz, 1995). The *de facto* priority given to the defence of the franc by the *Bundesbank* (by contrast with sterling or the lira) revealed that, on economic as well as political grounds, the solidity of the Franco-German alliance was regarded as crucial for the future of EMU. The Balladur government (1993–95) resisted the 'window of opportunity' opened by the collapse of the ERM to devalue the franc, or to relax its interest rate policy. After a period of initial hesitation from May to October 1995, President Chirac pledged full support for the single currency and the convergence criteria. The Euro also survived the changes of government in France and Germany in 1997 and 1998.

The official launch of the Euro on 1 January 1999 demonstrated strong political will, especially on behalf of France and Germany whose political investment in the single currency project was total. Once the initial decision had been taken, neither the French nor German governments could allow the project not to succeed. Although Germany had sought to control the implementation of the single currency – through the convergence criteria and the institutional design – the actual process escaped from the control of any national government. As established in the treaty, the Council determined (in May 1998) which countries had fulfilled the convergence criteria, but political criteria were at least as important as economic ones. Not only France (which excluded France Télécom's pensions funds from its public sector resources) but also Germany (which attempted an aborted revaluation of the *Bundesbank*'s gold reserves in 1998) manipulated the rules to reduce their own budget deficits to below the 60% ceiling. The Franco-German tandem was ill-placed to castigate countries such as Belgium and Italy, whose budget deficits remained well above the official criteria. Indeed, Germany's economic difficulties effectively ruled out proceeding to monetary union with only a 'hard core' of member states. Only Greece was deemed not to have achieved the criteria, while Britain, Sweden and Denmark chose to stay outside. Although casting itself as the guardian of the temple of monetary rigour, Germany was powerless to prevent a widely-based Euro. To this extent, the French calculation proved astute.

Interpreting monetary union

There are several, to some extent rival, interpretations of the Franco-German relationship and monetary union. These include explanations rooted in asymmetrical economic interdependence, in the convergence of domestic economic circumstances, in nested bargaining games and the importance of joint Franco-German leadership and in the role of technical communities of experts.

why did the EMU emerge?

The German dominance theses

Some of the most persuasive accounts contend that EMU arose as a response to the pattern of asymmetrical interdependence between Germany and other leading EU economies (Hueglin, 1995; Markovits and Reich, 1997; Kaelberer, 1997; Pedersen, 1998). Many writers have emphasised the centrality of German economic hegemony – and how to control this – as the central force driving closer European monetary integration. The changing internal equilibrium of the Franco-German relationship was firmly rooted in economic realities. By 1970, the German economy had become the locomotive of European growth. Germany resisted the economic crisis of the 1970s better than any of her neighbours, and, by the mid-1970s, most other European economies were tied to German monetary and economic performance.

The German dominance hypothesis can be sub-divided into two sub-categories: hegemony and standard setting. In the former version, Germany acts as a regional hegemon on account of its economic primacy, providing active leadership of regional monetary integration (Marsh, 1992; Lankowski, 1993; Hueglin, 1995). This appears difficult to substantiate. Germany did not seek monetary union, but had leadership thrust upon it (Sandholtz, 1993). In a more refined account, if Germany is a policy leader this is not through hegemonic design, but as a result of its standard setting role. The German policy model has proved irresistible for others to imitate. Strengthened by the expert beliefs of professional economists and central bankers, central bank independence has been held up as a panacea for inflation and other economic ills (Andrews, 1993). Countries sought to import monetary credibility by imitating Germany and breaking political control of monetary policy, a feature much less pronounced in France than in many other EU countries (Howarth, 1999). Germany was a model to be imitated, especially amongst the smaller EU states structurally tied to the German locomotive. Throughout the EMS episode, other EU states willingly yielded control of monetary policy-making to the *Bundesbank* – the independent central bank of a partner country. In the words of Kaelberer (1997: 45): 'through a process of tying hands, EMS countries sought to import German monetary credibility; in return, they were required to align their monetary behaviour alongside the policy model of the benchmark state, Germany'. This leadership role through standard setting is a more accurate representation of informal German economic policy leadership than is the problematical concept of hegemony. Germany has, by and large, been a model that others have followed, rather than an active leader.

2 Domestic policy convergence

Other observers emphasise the importance of gradual policy convergence from the late 1960s onwards (Andrews, 1993). International financial instability created strong pressures for closer convergence from the late 1960s onwards. France and Germany were united in accusing the US administration of irresponsible monetary management, and of using the dollar as a tool in pursuit of its own economic aims. Transatlantic relations were worsened by the US decision to suspend the Bretton Woods fixed parities agreement in 1971. French and German monetary interests moved closer in important respects. France had traditionally advocated closer international monetary coordination to challenge American economic primacy, while Germany – the post-war export locomotive of Europe – was detrimentally affected by an undervalued dollar. By the late 1960s, the Deutschmark was subject to specific exchange rate pressures; as an international reserve currency, it strengthened when the dollar weakened. The American dollar float thus encouraged a massive flow into the Deutschmark, in turn forcing other EC countries to impose higher interest rates in order to shadow the German currency.

The fundamental economic policy paths in France and Germany (and elsewhere) had narrowed long before the moves to monetary union. Significant policy change took place throughout the 1970s and 1980s in those countries seeking to join in EMU. Monetary union thus crowned a process of EC economic convergence that was already well engaged. The French case is indicative. The 'strong franc' policy pursued intermittently from 1976 onwards (and vigorously after 1983) had a domestic political origin. After the 1983 economic U-turn, the parties of the mainstream left and right were committed to orthodox economic policies and a monetary policy of shadowing the Deutschmark. Tying hands thus performed a valuable domestic politics function; it allowed French policy-makers to identify an external scapegoat for overdue internal reforms.

Nested bargaining games and joint Franco-German leadership

The German dominance accounts underplay or ignore the French contribution to EMU. In one account 'French leadership determined the speed of integration and its institutional design during the course of monetary integration over the last two decades' (Chang, 1999: 9). There was no reason for Germany to accept EMU, the argument runs, because it already benefited from monetary stability and a single market through the EMS. If Germany came round to EMU, this was essentially for political considerations. EMU was nested in the higher order game of German unification (Dyson and Featherstone, 1999). German opinion – elite and public – was divided over EMU. While Chancellor Kohl envisaged EMU for reasons of political solidarity with Germany's EU partners (even before unification) the *Bundesbank* was mainly hostile.

Kohl committed Germany to EMU at Maastricht in spite of opposition from powerful sections of Germany's political and business elites. France was able to exploit these inherent divisions within the German core executive to influence the institutional design of EMU. French preoccupations seeped into the Maastricht Treaty. Consistent with its 'monetarist' stance, France won a phased timetable for EMU. The German Chancellor Kohl argued against a firm date for EMU in a letter to Mitterrand days before the December 1989 Strasbourg summit. The French obtained the critical commitment to stage two (1 January 1994) at the Maastricht summit, against much opposition from within Germany. Under Article 109, it was the member states (meeting in the Council) and not the central bankers who decided which countries had fulfilled the convergence criteria and were permitted to join in the single currency (Arrowsmith, 1996). As candidates for EMU were selected by the European Council, the 'convergence criteria' were always likely to be interpreted liberally, as indeed was the case. Even the German-inspired Growth and Stability Pact was politically negotiated; the decision to incur penalties on a defaulting member state would be a political one.

Inter-state bargaining was the crucial dynamic in determining the single currency decision and its subsequent implementation. The single currency project was closely related to the internal dynamics of the Franco-German relationship. France used its special relationship to constrain Germany to go further along the road of monetary union than it initially deemed acceptable and ensured that the monetary policy institutions were not entirely shaped according to German wishes. French political support for German unification was the essential ingredient in obtaining the initial single currency decision.

Epistemic communities

Dyson and Featherstone (1999) identify an epistemic community of central bankers and monetary economists, united by shared beliefs in economic conservatism, that managed to place economic and monetary union on the European policy agenda. Political actors were not competent to make technical decisions as to the feasibility of a single currency. The advocacy of EMU as a technical policy solution by a coherent epistemic community was important in setting the single currency agenda. The epistemic community was based on three foundations: the importance of price stability; the belief that credibility could be borrowed by tying one's currency to an anchor currency; and the belief that the German model formed the basis around which negotiations should proceed. Central bankers formed the core of this epistemic community. As predicted in the Haas model (1992), their role went beyond one of diffusing technical information. Through their pivotal influence in the various institutional arenas established by the Delors committee, central bankers came to form a recognisable transnational group able to articulate its vision of a technically feasible single currency. Financial elites thus performed an essential role in promoting an external standard for the modernisation of European economies.

Conclusion

The various explanations considered above are appropriate for understanding different dimensions of the Franco-German relationship and EMU. The technical expertise of a cohesive epistemic community was important in an agenda setting sense, but technical expertise would have remained of secondary importance without the effort of determined (joint) political leadership and a measure of prior domestic economic convergence. A comparison of the mid-1970s (when the snake collapsed amidst Franco-German discord) and the late 1990s (when France and Germany jointly steered EMU) demonstrates the point. Indeed, the French and German styles of economic management had moved closer in many respects over the three decades separating the Hague summit from the end of the century.

While German economic primacy is not in doubt, the German hegemony thesis overlooks the fact that the French, not the Germans, were the driving force behind EMU. From the perspective of French policy-makers, monetary union was a means of diluting German economic hegemony, while tying Germany into the European economy for the benefit of its main trading partners (especially France) and reducing transaction costs for everybody. A variant of this argument stresses the security dimension. For Baun (1996) or Mazzucelli (1997) the single currency decision could be explained by changes in the geopolitical environment; monetary integration was propelled by the desire to tie Germany into Western institutions after the end of the cold war. In both accounts, the Franco-German relationship is central. In the nested game of high-level leadership bargaining, a phased progress to monetary union was agreed by Chancellor Kohl in order to reassure Germany's European allies (and especially France) of the future orientation of the unified German state. To this extent, binding Leviathan had a security dimension, as well as an economic and a political one.

The bilateral Franco-German relationship has always involved the exchange of policy ideas and institutions. The case study of EMU demonstrates not only the efficacy of Franco-German cooperation at its most effective, it also underlines the fact that the vital interests of the two nations are not set in stone. The process of learning and exchange itself can produce outcomes that correspond neither to French nor German initial visions.

The Franco-German relationship in the international arena

In Chapters 4 and 5, we investigated the role of the Franco-German relationship in driving moves to closer European integration. Defence and security issues have proved a source of past (and continuing) disagreement between the two nations, but also a source of rich initiatives to enhance European cooperation. Although France and Germany have two very different security cultures, one observer contends they have forged 'the closest bilateral security relationship in Europe' (Gordon, 1993: 139). Chapter 6 sets out the very different French and German security cultures. It examines the importance of the bilateral Franco-German relationship in security and defence affairs, and investigates moves to a European defence and security identity. It concludes that there is evidence of greater convergence in this sphere of public action. Because foreign and security policy lie at the heart of national sovereignty, however, there remain many underlying ambiguities in the development of a closer European defence and security policy.

National security cultures in France and Germany

Any policy convergence that has occurred between France and Germany has been predicated upon the narrowing of highly distinctive and divergent security cultures in the two countries. We start by considering these security cultures before moving on to an analysis of the relationship itself.

France: rank and greatness

The French security culture has stressed maximum national independence (Gordon, 1995). National security policy in the post-war period looked to restore France as a great – or significant – power, including in the military sphere. This predated Gaullism. France was determined to exploit its status as a victor in the Second World War. It insisted on creating a French occupation zone in Germany, as well as demanding a seat on the UN security council, and re-establishing its colonial possessions.

The vision of renewed French greatness achieved its fullest expression under President de Gaulle (1958–69). There were six principal features of the Gaullist foreign policy legacy. These were the primacy of national independence (over European or Atlantic solidarity) in foreign policy-making and defence; the belief that France was a first-rank, hence nuclear, power; the belief that France had a vocation to provide for European defence leadership separate from the Atlantic Alliance (France withdrew from the military command structure of NATO in 1966); the consequent pursuit of a priority security relationship with Germany within Europe; the maintenance of a special, neo-colonial relationship with francophone African states; and the concentration of foreign policy-making within the presidential sphere. By the late 1970s, Gaullist priorities formed part of a domestic French defence consensus, spanning the Communist left to the Gaullist right (Jenson, 1984). These traits in themselves made cooperation with Germany difficult, because they challenged the foundations of Germany's own Atlanticist foreign policy.

The guiding theme of classical Gallium was the primacy given to the pursuit of an independent foreign policy over and above a European defence identity. First and foremost, this required France to be an independent nuclear power. At the heart of Gaullist nuclear doctrine lay the idea of the nation as a unique protected sanctuary. The French nuclear weapon was only designed to protect France, not France's allies. The particular Gaullist doctrine of national independence – *la défense du faible au fort* (the weak's defence against the strong) – refuted any tactical use of nuclear weapons and prevented nuclear guarantees being extended to France's allies, such as Germany. Gaullist France preferred to concentrate on developing its nuclear capacity, rather than pledging troops to defend Germany on the cold war front line. President Giscard d'Estaing tentatively developed the doctrine of the extended sanctuary, whereby tactical nuclear, as well as conventional forces could be deployed to protect West Germany from a Soviet invasion. But even this limited innovation was abandoned after powerful opposition from within the ruling coalition (Frears, 1981). President Mitterrand refused Giscard d'Estaing's concept of the 'extended sanctuary' and reasserted de Gaulle's belief that it was impossible to extend the protection provided by the French *force de frappe* to Germany. In this and other respects, Mitterrand lay more squarely within the Gaullist tradition than his predecessor Giscard d'Estaing.

This French stance evolved somewhat during the 1990s. Shortly after his election as president in 1995, Chirac evoked the prospect of joint deterrence, whereby, although she would retain sole possession of her nuclear weapons, France could involve other EC countries, such as the UK, Germany and Spain, in a body to determine joint deterrence policies (Butcher, 1996).

This initiative should be read in the context of France's move closer to NATO, which we consider below. Chirac's proposal came to nothing. It ran contrary to the painfully negotiated nuclear non-proliferation treaty, and the Germans expressed little interest. But it demonstrated the paradox that the incumbent Fifth President of the Fifth Republic – elected as a Gaullist – had moved furthest to challenging the Gaullist foreign policy legacy.

Germany: partnership and interdependence

Germany's post-war strategic heritage was the antithesis of the French, in that it stressed the inseparable twinning of European integration and Atlanticism. Defeat and military occupation prevented the Germans from playing a prominent military role (Garton-Ash, 1994). Unlike France, Germany did not have the luxury of an independent foreign policy and was forced into dependency on the USA throughout the cold war period. Until unification, Germany performed a secondary role in the international arena, leading to Brandt's affirmation that Germany was an 'economic giant but a political pygmy'. Germany is neither a permanent member of the UN security council, nor a nuclear power, having abandoned in 1955 the idea of ever procuring nuclear weapons (Boniface, 1993). Germany did not exist as a sovereign state until 1949, and it had no army until 1955. Constitutionally, German troops were barred from operating outside of the Republic. The Federal Republic had good reasons for not adopting an expansive foreign policy. She could plead the division of the national territory, the situation in West Berlin, her status as a semi-sovereign state, and a particular historical legacy.

Although the Federal Republic of Germany did not seek to play a global role, it exercised foreign policy influence through its important role in multilateral structures. The status of Germany as a front line NATO state led to a special relationship with the USA. German influence in NATO was enhanced as a result of France's partial withdrawal, because the Federal Republic was the main continental US partner. As we observed in Chapter 1, tying Germany to the Western alliance was a precondition of any move to unification. No post-war German government could accept the promise of unification in exchange for neutrality.

Since 1989 Germany has enjoyed enhanced opportunities for a prominent international role (Grosser, 1991; Papcke, 1997). More than ever, Germany appears at the centre of gravity of the new European Union. After 1989 Germany became far less tied to a bloc logic and looked with greater serenity upon a European defence identity. The collapse of the USSR weakened Germany's dependence on the USA, but if anything increased her interest in regional stability. With EU enlargement firmly on the political agenda,

Germany is the major exterior influence on the new democracies of Central and Eastern Europe, an influence cemented by favourable trade flows (Friend, 1999). The 1994 decision of the Federal Constitutional Court to allow German troop deployment abroad was symbolically important as a demonstration that Germany was a 'nation like the others' (Trouille, 1994). The role of German troops in Bosnia and Kosovo was in this respect exemplary.

The Federal Republic was traditionally suspicious of French motives in security policy, especially during the Gaullist period. The role of the USA in particular divided France and Germany from the late 1950s onwards (Moisi, 1995). Germany suspected France of seeking to create distance between her and her American protector; after 1966 France suspected Germany of wanting to force her back into NATO structures. The end of the cold war gave German foreign policy new scope for influence, but Germany was also anxious that the EU and USA retain close relations. During the 1990s, France and Germany continued to differ on the appropriate role of the USA in Europe. This was illustrated in subjects as diverse as the 1992–94 GATT round, relations with the Central European democracies and the Balkans, or European defence (specifically Germany's insistence that the Eurocorps be compatible with NATO). But there was also an underlying convergence in favour of a more affirmative European security identity that became more apparent as the 1990s wore on.

A semi-sovereign Germany renounced all intention of being a nuclear power, and she confirmed her non-nuclear status at the moment of German unification. German public opinion has been steadfastly anti-nuclear, as demonstrated during the Euromissile crisis of the early 1980s. Germans feared being the theatre for any eventual tactical nuclear conflict; hence their majority opposition to the build-up of US Cruise and Soviet SS20s in the early 1980s, and their objection to French plans in the late 1980s to develop short-range tactical missiles (the HADES programme) which, if ever deployed, would land on East German or Czech territory.

From this brief overview, we are able to depict a pattern of contrasting security cultures. Conscious of wider European political imperatives, France and Germany have worked all the harder to build a constructive relationship.

The bilateral Franco-German relationship in security and defence

France and Germany have developed elaborate institutional structures to attempt to promote common policies on security and defence issues. As bilateral initiatives between France and Germany have been embedded in a broader European context, we propose in this chapter to examine the operation of the Franco-German relationship not just as a bilateral relationship, but also by reference to the ongoing debate on a European defence and security identity.

When observing the post-war European security debate, one is struck by the tension between national, bilateral and multilateral initiatives. The idea of a European defence identity goes back to the early days of European integration. The Dunkirk Treaty (1947), the Brussels Treaty (1948) and the Washington Treaty (1950) were all early attempts to define European defence identity (Tindemans, 1997). The Pleven Plan of 1950 created the impetus for a genuinely supranational European army; the failure of this initiative in 1954 led to the incorporation of Italy and Germany into the US-dominated NATO in 1955. With the supranational perspective abandoned, the Fouchet plan proposed by de Gaulle (1960–62) then failed in its attempt to create a common defence identity on an intergovernmental basis (Soutou, 1996). De Gaulle's plan proposed closer 'confederal' coordination between the French and German governments on issues of foreign policy and defence, along with a thoroughgoing reform of the NATO military command structure to enhance European autonomy. Under pressure from de Gaulle, on the one hand, but threatened with the withdrawal of US troops from continental Europe on the other, Adenauer finally sided with the Atlantic Alliance against the 'European' defence option. Disagreement over defence finally killed off the Fouchet plan in January 1962.

The rapprochement between de Gaulle and Adenauer during the Fouchet plan negotiations laid the groundwork for the 1963 Elysée Treaty (Soutou, 1996). The treaty contained provisions for intensive consultation in security policy and defence, with a view to harmonising military doctrines. It established a set of institutional structures designed to bind the two countries in close collaboration. The treaty provided for regular meetings between French and German defence ministers (every three months), the chiefs of staff (every two months) and heads of state or government (at least every six months). Each country accepted a duty of consultation with the partner before determining foreign policy decisions, and agreed to try and harmonise defence thinking. The nuclear issue was specifically excluded from bilateral negotiation, however, and the subsequent evolution of Gaullist foreign policy made effective collaboration even more difficult. Although Adenauer was more receptive to a Franco-German defence identity than subsequent German leaders, when faced with a security choice between France and the USA, West German governments reaffirmed their primary attachment to the Atlantic Alliance (Szabo, 1990; Garton-Ash, 1994). The *Bundestag*'s strongly pro-Atlanticist prelude to the 1963 treaty emptied the defence clauses of much of their content. The replacement of Adenauer in October 1963 by the Atlanticist Erhard effectively froze the Franco-German security relationship until it was revived by Mitterrand and Kohl in the 1980s.

Franco-German defence and security cooperation appeared moribund throughout the period of the Gaullist defence consensus, especially after France's withdrawal from the military command structure of NATO in 1966. Even under the Schmidt/Giscard d'Estaing partnership, military cooperation always lagged behind economic and financial cooperation (Gordon, 1993). Germany was suspicious of French unilateralism in foreign policy and defence; the two countries adopted opposing stances on nuclear policy, on the role of NATO, on the Soviet Union and on French activities in Africa. Imbued with a spirit of national independence, France was highly ambivalent about a more integrated Western European foreign and security policy. Thus, in April 1975, President Giscard d'Estaing opposed a common Western European security policy for fear of offending Moscow (Soutou, 1996). Supportive in principle of greater French-led pan-European autonomy in defence and security affairs, in practice France resisted any dilution of her military independence in favour of any extraneous body. At the EU level even the Political Cooperation (EPC) procedure in foreign policy coordination proved controversial and as late as June 1983 France opposed the creation of an EPC secretariat (Haywood, 1989).

Various forces drove closer Franco-German collaboration in the 1980s. First, the cold war atmosphere of the early 1980s forced European nations to close ranks against the threat of Soviet aggression. In a famous speech to the German lower chamber (the *Bundestag*) in January 1993, French President Mitterrand insisted that Germany hold firm against potential Soviet aggression and deploy US cruise and pershing missiles against Soviet SS20s (Mitterrand, 1996). President Mitterrand's speech confirmed the importance of security issues to the Franco-German relationship and laid the basis for a close personal entente with Kohl. This resolutely pro-Atlanticist position contrasted with the pacifist neutralism of many German social democrats (Ehrhart, 1991). Second, there were uncertainties about the long-term US commitment to European defence. Even Atlanticist Germany questioned the US commitment to remain within Europe in the light of reductions in short-range nuclear weapons from the mid-1980s onwards. Third, closer Franco-German cooperation in other domains – especially after the French Socialists' U-turn of 1983 – created pressures for political 'spillover'; the security and defence sphere was caught up in the general enthusiasm for closer European integration from the mid-1980s onwards.

The Mitterrand–Kohl partnership produced closer security collaboration than at any period since 1945. From their first meeting, Mitterrand and Kohl agreed to implement the dormant clauses of the 1963 treaty. A Franco-German commission on security and defence was created in 1982, which brought together defence and foreign ministers and their officials at least twice a year. On Mitterrand's insistence, in 1984 France and Germany agreed to relaunch the West European Union (WEU), providing a possible institutional basis for a European defence identity. Created in 1949 as a European defence arm, the WEU had been moribund almost since its inception. Since its self-exclusion from the NATO military command structure in 1966, France had attempted to revive the WEU as an embryonic European defence organisation and as a forum from which the Americans were absent. At the Maastricht summit of 1991, France and Germany proposed making the WEU accountable to the EC heads of state meeting in the European Council. Faced with stiff British resistance, the Maastricht Treaty was deliberately ambiguous on whether the WEU was the defence arm of the EC, or the European pillar of the NATO alliance.

Other initiatives testified to a much closer bilateral Franco-German security relationship. These included the conduct of joint military manoeuvres (Operation Bold Sparrow in 1986), a French commitment to consult with the Germans before using tactical nuclear weapons in Germany, the creation of the Franco-German Defence and Security Council in 1988, and the creation of the Franco-German brigade in 1990 (Gordon, 1995). The last two initiatives were symbolically highly important. The Defence and Security Council brought together the French president and German chancellor, the foreign ministers, the defence ministers, and the French and German chiefs of staff. The Franco-German brigade – composed initially of some 4200 troops – was envisaged by Mitterrand and Kohl as the nucleus of a future European army corps (Feld, 1989).

Germany was the driving force behind moves to Europeanise – or at least bilateralise – foreign and security policy. What did Germany want from a greater French engagement? Germany had traditionally criticised French nuclear strategy as excessively national in orientation; instead, it sought a conventional French commitment to the defence of the German front line. The creation of the French Rapid Reaction force (FAR) in 1983 (a 47 000 crack unit of the French army) was a welcome development from the German perspective, but only served to emphasise the imbalance between French nuclear and conventional forces. Later on, with the changing security situation created by unification and the collapse of communism, Germany sought French support for its initiatives in Eastern and Central Europe. Germany looked to Europeanisation as a solution for its particular strategic dilemma – how to perform a normal foreign policy role without causing undue alarm to her neighbours. German involvement in foreign policy would be facilitated by a genuinely supranational common foreign and security policy (CFSP), because this would provide a multilateral framework for policy action. From the German perspective, a European foreign and security policy could be used as a tool to improve relations with the Central and

Eastern democracies and to define a coherent policy to Russia. A strong CFSP would also allow Germany to escape from its foreign policy dilemma: either to take a low profile (the 'political pygmy'), or conduct a 'Gaullist' foreign policy itself and revive old memories.

Support for greater Europeanisation in the sphere of security policy was provisional upon certain safeguards. The most important of these was that European CFSP measures must not be incompatible with Germany's role in NATO. There was a strong ambivalence on the part of the USA to the developing CFSP; this theme emerges throughout this chapter. The USA expressed support for wider European burden sharing but was wary of European defence autonomy and the possible undermining of NATO. The Germans sought to reassure the Americans that the CFSP would fall under the Atlantic umbrella. Indeed, some German officials argued privately that the Maastricht CFSP agreement had brought France closer to NATO; it provided a means of binding the French into a European pillar of the Atlantic Alliance.

There is common agreement that the Mitterrand–Kohl partnership was critical in driving moves to more integrated decision-making. The Kohl–Chirac relationship, on the other hand, was initially fraught with tension. One of Chirac's first acts on being elected president in 1995 was to resume French nuclear testing in the South Pacific, a decision deplored by the German government, the rest of the EU and international public opinion. Then, in February 1996, President Chirac announced a series of far-reaching defence reforms with damaging consequences for the Franco-German relationship. These included the end of French conscription, the dissolution of regiments on German territory and the calling into question of certain common arms programmes. Although they made little reference to Franco-German friendship, the substance of Chirac's reforms was coherent (Debouzy, 1996). The French reforms were inspired by the need for closer European cooperation, for building a European defence and security identity that took into account the realities of the post-cold war period. In the new security environment, the large conscript armies required to face a Soviet onslaught appear redundant. There has been a move towards smaller, better equipped and more effective armed forces, capable of a rapid reaction to regional crises such as in Bosnia or Kosovo. In deference to the security concerns of Germany and her other European partners, moreover, Chirac went further than any other French president in accepting that European defence and security reforms could not ignore the role of the Atlantic Alliance. Before considering the evolution of the Franco-German relationship in relation to NATO reform, it is appropriate next to consider the role of the Franco-German relationship in promoting a more integrated European defence and security identity.

The Franco-German security relationship and the European Union

After 1989 pressures intensified for a stronger external dimension to the European Union and for a more affirmative European presence in international affairs, consistent with the economic weight of the EU. Converging conclusions were drawn – by French and German leaders amongst others – from a changing security environment. The end of the cold war had uncovered new dangers to European security, in the form of conflicts based on ethnicity, nationalism and religion. Events such as the break-up of former Yugoslavia forced security issues to the top of the political agenda (Stark, 1992; Vernet, 1995b). The changing and unstable situation in Russia gave cause for particular concern; Germany and France sought to associate Russia with pan-European security developments, notably via the CFSP and the NATO Partnership for Peace of 1996 (Truscott, 1997). Throughout the decade, France and Germany attempted to bring Russia into the negotiation of regional conflicts in the Balkans and elsewhere. European interest in regional stability was overwhelming and immediate. The disintegration of the Russian federation would pose a major threat to regional stability, with economically damaging and theoretically catastrophic nuclear consequences. Moreover, the expansion of the EU and NATO depended upon Russian benevolence, neutrality and eventually self-interest (via economic side-payments). The imperious necessity to prop up democratic politics and the market economy in Russia mobilised Western powers and financial institutions (especially German banks and the IMF) to the full.

The belief that the EU needed a more coordinated and cohesive presence in international affairs (especially in areas of immediate concern within the European continent) was in part predicated upon a record of policy failure and institutional absence during the 1990s. The EU's record during the 1990s could be read as a catalogue of foreign policy failures. The Gulf War of 1990–91 illustrated unambiguously the failure of Europe as a coordinated foreign policy unit; subsequent events in Yugoslavia, Bosnia and Kosovo confirmed the shortcomings of CFSP and European foreign policy coordination.

By the end of the decade, France and Germany had converged in the belief that Europe needed to develop a distinctive European perspective and capacity in the field of defence and security. Rather like EMU, the CFSP became part of the European political project. In the following section, we consider first the Maastricht CFSP agreement and the role of France and Germany in driving through this initiative; second, the disunited European response to the conflict in former Yugoslavia; and, third, the continued faith placed by French and German leaders in institution building in the form of the Eurocorps.

The Maastricht agreement

As we observed in Chapter 4, France and Germany performed a critical role in pre-shaping the Maastricht negotiations. This was as true for CFSP as it was for monetary policy. Close Franco-German bilateral collaboration underpinned the Mitterrand–Kohl plan of October 1991, the central tenets of which were written into the Maastricht Treaty, finally ratified in 1993. For the first time, the Maastricht Treaty attributed a treaty-based role to the European Union in security policy. The Maastricht Treaty officially contained provision for a CFSP as a second 'pillar' of the European Union. Article J.1 of the Maastricht Treaty affirms 'The Union and its member-states shall define and implement a common foreign and security policy' (cited in de Guistino, 1996: 271). Although the Maastricht Treaty also referred to 'the eventual framing of a common defence policy, which might in time lead to a common defence', there were no concrete provisions for a common defence policy.

The Maastricht agreement represented the culmination of moves to closer Franco-German security cooperation since the relaunch of the early 1980s. But important disagreements persisted between France and Germany. France favoured the intergovernmental European Council as the arena for determining foreign and security policies, rather than the Commission; a CFSP must be defined by heads of state, rather than by unelected Commissioners. The French president was determined to continue to exercise the primordial influence in foreign policy. France was also insistent on the need to safeguard the unanimity rule; she could not envisage being placed in a minority in this sphere of core sovereignty. This was a point of agreement with the UK. Consistent with her integrationist policy, Germany ideally favoured a greater involvement of the Commission and a general move to majority voting – including in the sphere of CFSP. As in many other provisions of the Maastricht Treaty, French positions prevailed over German ones. In the Maastricht Treaty, though the Commission retained its generic right to propose (the 'monopoly of initiative'), the European Council was recognised as having the pre-eminent role in defining 'the principles and general orientations of the CFSP'. Some majority voting would be introduced, but only with regard to the implementation of decisions of principle adopted unanimously by the Council.

Beneath these institutional preferences lay different political choices. While Germany called for a Europeanisation of defence policies consistent with the framework of the Atlantic Alliance, French officials preferred to reason in terms of a common security policy, leaving far greater reign for independent national defence arrangements.

The Yugoslav conflict

Following their tenuous relationship during the Gulf War, declarations of privileged Franco-German partnership rang hollow faced with their disunited response to the Yugoslavian crisis (Stark, 1992; Vernet, 1995b). The events in former Yugoslavia in the course of 1991–96 can be open to several interpretations, the most common of which was that the Yugoslavian conflict tested the reality of European foreign policy concord as formulated at Maastricht. The inability of the European Community to formulate a coherent response to the disintegration of Yugoslavia augured ill for an effective common foreign and security policy. Franco-German dissent was manifest. Under pressure from Chancellor Kohl, the EU recognised Croatian, Slovenian and Bosnian independence in January and April 1992. Convinced that the preservation of the Yugoslavian federation was the only alternative to civil war, the French president for long refused to designate Serbia (traditionally a French ally) as the main protagonist. Mitterrand's belief that the EC, under German pressure, had recognised Croatian and Bosnian sovereignty too soon was widely shared in other European capitals, including London. The European nations were incapable either of stopping the conflict, or of preventing ethnic cleansing in Croatia and Bosnia. For four years EU nations were unable to secure implementation of signed declarations, and their 'joint actions' were limited to sending humanitarian aid and peacekeeping troops under United Nations – and not EU – auspices (UNPROFOR). Only after the Srebenica massacre in 1995, which sparked the US and NATO into military intervention, was a solution to the Bosnian conflict found.

Against this harsh verdict another reading is possible (Juppé, 1995a; Delors, 1999). The existence of the EU, and of the Franco-German relationship in particular, arguably mitigated the effects of European divisions. In the absence of their special relationship, Franco-German divergences might have had more dramatic effects. After their initial disunity, EU member states gradually demonstrated greater cohesion. Franco-British military cooperation in Bosnia pointed the way to closer defence ties, and Germany eventually sent troops to help in the war effort. Franco-German cooperation was especially important in bridging community divisions. The Juppé–Kinkel plan was agreed by the EU after 18 months of the Bosnian conflict, and then supported by the Contact Group. The creation of the informal Contact Group, which brought together the USA, Russia and Europe (France, the

UK, Germany and Italy) provided a form of *ad hoc* pan-European defence cooperation. France and Germany were particularly insistent on the need to bring Russia into the Contact Group, and into any eventual Balkans peace agreement. The failure of the European Union's CFSP should be placed in perspective; the USA delayed settlement of the Bosnian conflict by its initial refusal to commit US forces.

Eurocorps and beyond

Alongside moves to a European Union security policy – driven by France and Germany – bilateral Franco-German cooperation continued throughout the Kohl–Mitterrand period. In their joint letter of 14 October 1991, Mitterrand and Kohl announced their intention to transform the Franco-German brigade, created in 1987, into a full European army corps. More details emerged at the Franco-German bilateral summit of La Rochelle in 1992, and the terms of engagement were agreed with NATO in 1993. Operational in 1995, the Eurocorps consisted of around 45 000 troops, drawn from France, Germany, Belgium, Spain and Luxembourg (Gordon, 1995).

Eurocorps is sometimes presented as a successful Franco-German bilateral initiative which subsequently dictated the norm of EU action. Its birth was celebrated by Mitterrand as evidence of France and Germany acting as the 'motor' of European integration in the sphere of security and defence. This perspective was not unanimously shared. Although Belgium, Spain and Luxembourg associated themselves with the Eurocorps, French and German attempts to multilateralise this bilateral initiative met with stiff resistance from the UK, Italy and the Netherlands and much ambivalence from the USA.

The Eurocorps initiative could not conceal traditional Franco-German preferences. While French leaders portrayed the Eurocorps as an embryonic European army, German policy-makers were careful not to set Eurocorps against the Atlantic Alliance. Germany announced early on that troops it attributed to Eurocorps would be 'double-hatted', serving simultaneously as German regiments within NATO. German policy-makers presented Eurocorps as part and parcel of a Europeanisation of NATO, as a means of pulling France back into the NATO orbit while promoting a more autonomous European defence capacity. Under German pressure, France eventually accepted that the corps could come under NATO command, not only for European defence, but also for peacekeeping missions. For the first time since 1958, France accepted, via the Eurocorps, the concept of multinational military integration. This was a prelude to moving closer to NATO. Important as a symbol of closer Franco-German collaboration, in practice Eurocorps performed a marginal role in security debate in the 1990s, its durability called into question by the EU itself at the 1999 Cologne and Helsinki summits. Eurocorps never performed any security, peacekeeping or peacemaking missions. The creation of the European Rapid Reaction Force at the December 1999 Helsinki summit witnessed a broader acceptance across the EU of the need for highly trained and mobile troops to be placed at the disposal of the EU. The political success (but military failure) of Eurocorps was the signal for its transformation into a better equipped, more professional and more operational European Rapid Reaction Force.

The Franco-German relationship and NATO reform

A legacy of the Gaullist consensus, French governments traditionally envisaged an independent European defence identity as being separate from NATO. In French Gaullist strategic thinking, an independent European defence would be based either on French leadership or upon a Franco-German directorate. The ultimate logic of the French position was that Germany would eventually decide to liberate itself from the Atlantic Alliance and would turn to France for a new defence arrangement.

The unswerving pro-NATO sentiment of the Federal Republic limited French propositions for a genuinely independent European defence pole. For the Germans, a European defence identity had to be developed in cooperation with the USA, and in parallel with reforms to NATO. Germany was convinced that the USA wanted the emergence of a European defence identity, a view initially contested by France. The strengthening of NATO after the events of 1989 made it less likely to disappear, even if a European defence pillar took shape. By the mid-1990s, NATO was the only real organisation of collective security in Europe. Several reasons explained the survival and strengthening of NATO. Its rivals were weak. The Organisation for Security and Cooperation in Europe (OSCE) had been paralysed by its unanimity rule and the diversity of interests represented therein. The EU itself had been divided over security and defence issues: the CFSP began as a fiasco, with national rivalries laid bare by the Yugoslavian conflict. President Clinton proved an adept defender of US interests. There was a belief within the Atlanticist capitals (especially London) that only NATO could ensure the continuing presence of the USA on European territory.

One sure sign of the good health of NATO was the successful process of NATO enlargement. The opening up of NATO to Poland, the Czech Republic and Hungary in 1997 preceded that of the European Union itself, a fact that France in particular could not ignore. There was a close relationship between the expansion of NATO and the debate on EU enlargement. EU enlargement and NATO expansion were both envisaged as a means of preventing insecurity in Europe. Although France and Germany advocated an extension of NATO (and the EU) to the new democracies of Eastern and Central Europe, they both endeavoured to reassure the Russians that NATO expansion in particular was not aimed against her. Managing the delicate expansions of NATO and the EU to the Eastern and Central European countries required holding forth prospect of future political and economic collaboration with the Russian giant. The extension of NATO brought its own contradictions: its expansion arguably took place at the expense of the foreign policy capability of the EU and the OSCE.

There was fundamental ambivalence surrounding the debate over a European security and defence identity (ESDI). From the Brussels NATO summit of 1994 onwards, President Clinton called upon the Europeans to shoulder a greater burden of defence responsibility (Delattre and Vernet, 1996a). Many European countries, including France and Germany, agreed that Europe must address the causes of its own international weakness and even plan for an eventual US withdrawal from the European continent. The NATO Berlin council (June 1996) was a critical juncture in this respect. The USA agreed at Berlin that the European NATO states should be encouraged to develop their own European security and defence identity (ESDI) within NATO. The summit initiated the Combined Joint Task Force (CJTF) procedure, whereby European states, operating through the WEU, could use NATO military resources – satellites, troops, intelligence – without US participation, but with US support. It was also agreed that the WEU could be called upon to carry out a military role in purely European conflicts. This was a major concession to the French, who argued the WEU should be allowed access to NATO equipment for carrying out European peace operations. As the USA had argued for burden sharing, it could only support these measures. There was much ambivalence, however. While the Americans called for greater burden sharing, they looked askance at anything resembling an autonomous European policy. It was unclear whether the European countries could call upon NATO military means in the face of US opposition; in practice, this would be impossible. The political decision to intervene anywhere in the world would be taken by the NATO council, dominated by the USA. This led critics to argue that the Europeans were inviting the Atlantic Alliance to exercise a greater oversight role in European security policy (Quilès, 1996).

The key to unravelling the events of 1994–97 lay in the evolution of the French position. France's move towards the Atlantic Alliance, timidly engaged under Mitterrand, began in earnest under the Balladur government. The 1994 Defence White Paper advocated the participation of the defence ministry and Chief of Staff in NATO meetings (Vernet, 1996b). The first of these meetings took place in Spain in October 1994. Under President Chirac, France made a more determined effort still to move closer to her European partners within NATO. In December 1995, Chirac announced France's intention to rejoin the military command structure of NATO once certain conditions had been met. These were that NATO should be genuinely 'Europeanised', with European officials taking over control of NATO military commands and that NATO forces should be available for European action without US approval. In the eyes of the French (supported by the Germans), moving closer to NATO had to be counterbalanced by a Europeanisation of NATO structures. By going so far, Chirac broke the last taboos of Gaullism. Mitterrand had never believed that France might re-enter the military command structure of NATO; the European defence identity was an alternative to Atlanticism. Chirac reversed this order of priorities; because her European allies remained attached to the Atlantic link, a European defence identity could only be built from within NATO, albeit one reformed to take account of new geo-political realities. Chirac calculated that the French would be able to play a major role in a NATO Directory, alongside the UK, USA, and Germany – somewhat like under de Gaulle's earlier vision.

The promise of a French re-entry into the NATO military command was based on the faith that the Americans would loosen their control over European operations of the Atlantic Alliance. To many, such an understanding was misguided. French moves might have been interpreted by the USA as signifying that the Europeans were not yet ready for their own foreign and security policy (interviews). At the Madrid summit of 1997, the Americans refused to agree to the two central French demands – that NATO enlargement include Romania and Bulgaria, and that the NATO southern command in Naples (SACEUR) be assumed by a European. Negotiations between Paris and Washington were interrupted by the left's victory in the April 1997 elections. The French Socialists in opposition had harshly criticised Chirac's overtures to NATO. On 2 July 1997 a joint statement from the French presidential and prime ministerial offices declared that the circumstances were not right for a full return of France to NATO (Rosenzweig, 1997). As the Bosnian and Kosovan examples demonstrated, full membership of NATO was not a precondition for participating in NATO-led military operations. France would resort to a 'case by case' approach in its dealings with NATO.

Towards Franco-German convergence?

The NATO reform episode revealed new areas of emerging Franco-German consensus. France and Germany both agreed that NATO must not become a tool of US security policy to dominate Europe. Germany had become progressively more autonomous in outlook since the end of the cold war, which had lessened dependency on the USA. France and Germany cooperated closely in relation to NATO enlargement and Russia. Both accepted that NATO had to expand after the July 1997 Madrid summit, but also that Russia must be reassured over NATO's intentions. Chirac and Kohl cooperated closely to ensure that Russia was associated in the European security debate. Germany looked to closer collaboration with France as a means of diminishing her reliance on the USA and of enhancing the process of European unification. Both France and Germany were in agreement on the need to create a European pillar within the Atlantic Alliance. The Germans supported the French – against the Americans – over bestowing the southern command of NATO to a European officer. The duty for solidarity and for mutual support was observed to a greater degree in the 1990s than in the 1960s. The momentum for a European defence policy received fresh impetus from the incomplete process of NATO reform. Germany became increasingly convinced that the only German foreign policy could be a European one. A common European foreign policy would be another milestone on the road to political union.

As in the Maastricht pre-negotiations, France and Germany defended commonly defined positions in the inter-governmental conference launched in Turin in March 1996. French and German negotiating positions in the sphere of foreign and security policy were based on an agreement between Chirac and Kohl made public on 27 February 1996 (negotiated by the defence and European affairs ministers) only days after Chirac's announcement of major defence reforms (Delattre, 1996). These provisions were remarkably similar to those eventually agreed in the Amsterdam summit. The Franco-German accord was made formal in the defence agreement of December 1996. This agreement bore the imprint of French ideas, notably the insistence that CFSP decisions must continue to be taken on the basis of consensus between European governments (Delattre, 1996). The agreement drew a distinction between matters of principle, which required unanimous support in the Council, and matters of implementation, which could be approved by qualified majority vote. Any state would have the chance to opt out of CFSP decisions, but would have to justify their refusal (the principle of constructive abstention). This fell far short of German preferences for a communautarisation of foreign policy, with more qualified majority votes in the Council and a strengthening of the Commission.

The greatest innovation of these Franco-German proposals concerned the creation of a 'Mr or Mrs PESC': the nomination of an individual to coordinate CFSP, and to represent the EU in international negotiations. The French insisted that such an individual must be accountable to the Council, thereby retaining essential foreign policy-making power in the hands of heads of government. Germany had preferred the role to be conferred to a civil servant attached to the Commission. The Franco-German agreement also envisaged the creation of a 'forecasting and planning unit' attached to the Council (which reappeared in the Amsterdam Treaty) and advocated the fusion of the WEU into the EU (which was shelved after British opposition at Amsterdam). Finally, the Franco-German text called for 'strengthened cooperation' in the area of CFSP; states should be able to use EU resources to engage in common actions supported by qualified majority votes. States not participating in common actions might be required to display financial solidarity with other members.

The Chirac/Kohl agreement of February 1996 was followed later that year by the publication of the 'common strategic concept' adopted by the Franco-German Nuremberg summit of 9 December 1996 (Soutou, 1997). The Franco-German Nuremberg joint concept was, in its way, ground-breaking. For the first time Germany and France jointly defined the objectives of a common defence policy. At the heart of their strategic thinking was the notion of 'parity' between France and Germany. The French and German armies were called upon to cooperate closely in their 'indissociable' common interests. This cooperation was to occur within NATO and the EU. The common text included an agreement 'to discuss the role of nuclear deterrence within a European defence policy'. The text also advocated closer defence cooperation. The EU should initiate a common defence policy, to be determined by the European Council. The WEU should be fully integrated into the EU. In return for Germany's backing of these French objectives, France would support Germany's claim for a permanent seat on the UN Security Council.

The 'common strategic concept' represented a new level of Franco-German defence collaboration. A similar concept had been suggested by Guy Mollet to Konrad Adenauer back in 1956, but it had then been rejected by the German chancellor (Vernet, 1997). This notion of a common strategic concept went further in the direction of Franco-German collaboration than either de Gaulle and Adenauer (in the defence clauses of the Elysée treaty) or Mitterrand and Kohl (in the Franco-German Security and Defence Council) had managed. Several obstacles had always prevented France and Germany agreeing on common strategic aims: the role of nuclear weapons and the *force de frappe*; the role of NATO in a European defence system; German military intervention outside of the NATO area. By agreeing to 'parity', France abandoned a claim to military leadership. Although driven by Franco-German bilateral negotiation, this evolution specifically parted ways with earlier, bilateral accords. The limits to purely bilateral action were recognised; the agreement envisaged closer Franco-German cooperation within multilateral structures such as the EU and NATO. The agreement would facilitate closer Franco-German cooperation across the range of international security organisations within which both countries collaborated.

The Amsterdam Treaty

The Amsterdam Treaty bore many similarities to the Franco-German agreement published in February 1996. Directly inspired by this agreement, the Treaty established an Early Warning and Planning Unit to enhance EU intelligence gathering, crisis management and forecasting (Dolan, 1997). It called for the appointment of a 'Mr or Mrs PESC', as spokesperson for the EU's common foreign and security policy. The treaty also formally included the 'Petersburg tasks' (international peacekeeping/peacemaking missions) as part of the EU's remit. The Amsterdam Treaty included a 'mutual solidarity' clause, as a first step towards a common defence policy. The treaty also included the provision that the European Council alone could decide whether or not the Amsterdam Treaty should lead to a common defence policy. There would be no need for a new treaty were the council to decide to go ahead with a common defence policy. In certain respects, the Amsterdam Treaty fell far short of integrationist expectations. Faced with resistance from Britain, the Amsterdam IGC did not ratify provisions for strengthened cooperation in the CFSP sphere. Moreover, the treaty gave no mandate for peace enforcement, such as the intervention of NATO which brought the Bosnian crisis to an end. On the other hand, the treaty did refer to the possible incorporation of the WEU into the EU, and made the development of the WEU into an integral part of the development of the Union's foreign and security policy. For all the strategic rethinking the European Parliament's *rapporteur* concluded that 'defence remains the last bastion of national traditions' (Tindemans, 1997).

Un ménage à trois?
Britain and the Franco-German relationship

The victory of the left in Britain and France in 1997 and in Germany in 1998 was heralded by optimists as the dawn of a new era of progressive international cooperation. The relationship between these three centre-left governments and their principal protagonists is considered in some detail in Chapter 7. One area of particular innovation appeared to be that of defence and security. In the concluding section we address the ongoing debate about European defence and security in the light of the eruption of Blairism on the international scene.

The Franco-German bilateral relationship is by no means the only significant European relationship in foreign policy and defence. As a nuclear power and a leading member of NATO, Britain engages in regular top-level bilateral contact with both France and Germany. Relationships with France have steadily improved since the early 1990s, when relations were soured over the abortive long-range ASPL missile, and over Britain's decision to buy US helicopters rather than the Eurocopter Tiger (Guisnel, 1995). Bilateral talks between Britain and France had been taking place since 1992 over the evolution of nuclear doctrine and possible synergy between British and French nuclear weapons systems (Butcher, 1996). Franco-British defence collaboration had made great strides since Chirac's election in 1995. In July 1995, France and Britain had created the European Air Group, to plan aeriel cooperation. This was not a fully formed unit, such as Eurocorps, but it testified to Franco-British cooperation after a decade of mutual recriminations. Close cooperation occurred between French and British troops first in Bosnia, later in Kosovo. The two armies worked well together. Chirac's defence reforms were to some extent modelled on the British professional army, rather than the continental conscript force.

Britain also traditionally exercised a close relationship with Germany, its major European NATO ally. Long regarded as the two Atlanticist capitals, London could rely on Bonn to moderate French anti-Atlanticism. Close collaboration between Britain and Germany within NATO had produced a community of vision over four decades. Britain was also locked into European armaments programmes with Germany (Eurofighter) and France (missiles [Bae/Matra] and the military version of Airbus). In spite of their adversarial traditions, Britain and France shared many common interests in debates over CFSP. The Germans were genuinely in favour of a communautarianisation of foreign policy; this involved QMV and the strengthening of supranational structures. Britain and France both opposed any moves to qualified majority voting in CFSP (except on details of implementation) and favoured the Council over the Commission. From a German perspective, the Anglo-French partnership was much closer in the defence sphere than either the Franco-German, or the Anglo-German relationship (interview).

Blair's defence initiatives forced France and Germany to take stock of new developments. Determined to place the UK at the centre of Europe, and aware of the discomfort of self-exclusion from the first round of Euro membership, Blair reversed Britain's traditional antipathy to CFSP. In a joint declaration with President Chirac at the Anglo-French Saint Malo summit (November 1998), the British premier called for 'the full and rapid implementation of the Amsterdam provisions of the CFSP' (Reuters, 1998). The Saint Malo declaration affirmed that NATO remained 'the foundation of the collective defence of its members', but it also urged the strengthening of the EU's 'appropriate structures', to facilitate decision-making when NATO was not directly involved (a reference to the Combined Joint Task Force procedure). 'Suitable military means' should be placed at the disposal of the EU. These would consist either of European capabilities pre-designated within NATO's European pillar, or national/multinational means outside of NATO. The EU must be given a capacity for strategic planning 'without unnecessary duplication' (Reuters, 1998).

There were ambiguities in the new British position. At the Portschach summit (October 1998), Blair only referred to options for the future of ESDI, and was careful not to commit the government to any of these. The Saint Malo declaration, which affirmed that the Atlantic Alliance was the foundation of the collective defence of its members, could be open to an Atlanticist reading. Blair's call to avoid duplication could be read as a disapproval of the EU developing its own intelligence and satellite resources, in opposition to French and German pressure. These remarks notwithstanding, in this instance the British government acted as the motor of European integration. Blair went much further than any other British leader in admitting that the EU could have a defence identity within the Atlantic Alliance. Blair also supported 'appropriate structures' accountable to the European Council to take decisions on Europe-only operations. This meant rapid reaction forces able to respond to European challenges. Proposals to create a European Rapid Reaction Force, of between 40 000 and 60 000 troops, were approved by the European Council meeting in Helsinki in December 1999.

The German presidency of the EU, January–June 1999

The German presidency of the EU (January–June 1999) was determined to move fast on the European defence dossier. In its discussion paper presented to the Reinhartshausen meeting of foreign ministers (dated 8 March 1999), the German presidency stressed that 'the Alliance remains the foundation of the collective defence of its members'. But NATO could not be the only conduit for a European defence policy. Non-NATO EU members (such as Ireland) should also be guaranteed the possibility of joining European operations; as should non-EU NATO members (such as Turkey). The Germans recommended that the EU should be able to lead operations, and call upon NATO military assets; indeed there should be 'a presumption of access to NATO assets and capabilities for European-led operations'. Moreover, the EU should be able to lead its own operations without recourse to NATO assets; few experts believe in the short-term feasibility of this. The EU must have political control of EU-led operations, whether under the aegis of NATO or not. This required the EU to develop its own intelligence resources, and EU nations to develop forces that are suited for crisis management operations. The Germans made their own the Franco-British Saint Malo declaration that the EU must be able to use 'suitable military means' to carry out its policies.

The Cologne summit of June 1999 represented the first move on common defence since Maastricht. All EU countries adopted as their own the Franco-British–German initiative. Javier Solana (the former NATO Secretary General) was appointed to the post of Mr PESC. In the Council declaration, the summit called for the EU 'to possess a capacity for autonomous action supported by credible military forces' (Lemaître, 1999d). The EU must be able to call on such forces and be able to commit troops to react to international crises. There remained much doubt about the EU's ability to call on NATO troops in the event of US opposition. It was unclear what would happen if the European Union wanted to use NATO forces, but the US refused. It was envisaged that a common defence policy would above all allow the EU to carry out 'Petersburg tasks', but it was inherent in the summit's conclusions that a common defence policy might eventually go beyond peacekeeping missions. In a separate development, France and Germany proposed to transform the Eurocorps into a rapid reaction force available for European or NATO actions. While the Franco-German brigade and the Eurocorps had been major advances in their time, French Foreign Minister Védrine concluded that they had outgrown their usefulness (Védrine, 1996). This was achieved at the Helsinki European Council in December 1999.

The Kosovo crisis

The outbreak of the Kosovo crisis into full-scale military conflagration in March 1999 highlighted the failure of EU efforts (led by Britain and France) at diplomatic mediation. The conflict underlined the vast technological superiority of the USA in operational military affairs. But it also demonstrated much closer cooperation between the leading European nations than during the Bosnian episode. In alliance with the USA and coordinated by NATO, the cohesion of the leading EU players (Germany, France and Britain) was noteworthy (although Kosovo strengthened NATO even more than the EU). Even Italy held firm to the alliance strategy, notwithstanding intense domestic pressures. Within the anti-Serbian alliance, however, it became possible to discern a Franco-German position that was subtly different from the Anglo-American one, more insistent on the need to involve Russia in the solution of the Kosovo conflict. Bringing Russia into the resolution of the conflict offered the prospect of a longer-term guarantee of maintaining European peace and security and of safeguarding future EU–Russian relations. Managing relations with Russia also spilled over into preserving prospects for a peaceful expansion of the EU to the Central and Eastern European countries. This was of especial interest for Germany, but also reflected the evolution of French attitudes over how to deal with Russia.

The German presidency of the EU – especially Foreign Minister Fischer – made a particular effort to promote peace in Kosovo. Supported by France, Germany was in part responsible for bringing the Russians into the resolution of the conflict, and strongly advocated involving the United Nations. The Kosovo crisis provided ample evidence of Germany acting as a 'normal' international player. Germany was the third military power on the ground and had its own occupation zone (along with the USA, France, Britain and Russia) after the Serb defeat. In this instance, international engagement strengthened the domestic standing of the beleaguered Schröder government. For once, 'coalition dependency' did not prevent effective action; although the Greens were completely split on the issue, the Green Foreign Minister Fischer held firm in favour of military engagement. Indeed, international obligations produced some surprising domestic consequences – the SPD and CDU unanimously supported the intervention in the *Bundestag* vote of April 1999. This put paid to the SPD's traditional opposition to all forms of military engagement. In Kosovo, for the first time since the end of World War Two, the Germans joined in as equal partners of France and Britain. The German *Bundestag* vote supporting the purchase of the Eurofighter also demonstrated German commitment to joint military procurement and pan-European security (this was supported by the SPD and the CDU). The new German polity had come of age.

Conclusion

Measured in the absolute, the above discussion demonstrates the limits of Europeanisation in the sphere of security and defence. If the European Union has gradually refined its security tools, the post-cold war decade strengthened US security influence over the European continent as a whole. NATO – and US military technology – appeared as the great victor. NATO enlargement preceded that of the European Union itself. In the Gulf War (1990–91), in Bosnia (1992–95) and in Kosovo (1999), European efforts were secondary to US global leadership. In the sphere of European defence and security, there was much ambivalence. The CFSP had difficulty recovering from the Yugoslav debacle. In practice, the ESDI procedure defined at the NATO Berlin summit was dependent for its military credibility on US logistical support and political approval. The European defence agreement defined at the EU Cologne and Helsinki summits left many questions unanswered, notably those relating to EU/US relations (specifically could the EU call on NATO military resources if the US refused, or engage rapid reaction troops against American opposition?). The European defence and security project remains fundamentally ambivalent.

As with the case of monetary policy investigated in Chapter 5, the sphere of foreign policy goes to the heart of state sovereignty. In contrast with monetary policy, however, the control of national state actors – acting in precise alliance contexts – has not been seriously challenged. The Franco-German security relationship can best be explained in terms of state-centric policy processes. Political leaders, alone or in concert, preside and decide. There was little evidence of supranational European Union influence in this sphere; the EU (and its CFSP) remained subordinated to national political processes and conceptions of sovereignty. In this sphere at least, French preferences prevailed over German ones.

As demonstrated by the Adenauer–de Gaulle and Mitterrand–Kohl partnerships, the dynamics of relationships between French and German leaders are an important facet of the Franco-German security relationship. Alongside this pattern of core executive domination, there are relatively few societal constraints; foreign policy does not generally mobilise domestic interest groups or advocacy coalitions to the same extent as trade or agricultural issues. Although personal inputs are important, the sphere of foreign policy is an interdependent one by definition. French presidents and German chancellors operate within inherited alliance structures and face well-defined strategic choices. In this sphere, as in others, the bilateral Franco-German relationship must take into account its surrounding environment. French and German leaders converged in the 1990s in favour of embedding their bilateral relationship in multilateral structures, whether in NATO, the EU or other international organisations. They recognised the inherent limits of Franco-German bilateralism.

During the cold war period, there was a manifest imbalance between French and German resources of military prestige and international rank. To the French vision of national greatness, Germany long responded with a vision of smallness. There is no equivalent German benchmark in this sphere to that of the Deutschmark, as a model for other countries to emulate. Indeed, in foreign policy and defence matters, Germany appears still as a rather junior partner, alongside France and the UK. Within the Franco-German relationship itself, however, there has been a redistribution of resources during the decade in question. The French claim to foreign policy primacy – that of political influence through military prestige and nuclear weapons – has been rather devalued since the end of the cold war. While France has come to recognise the need to operate through multilateral structures, Germany has in certain respects adopted a more autonomous foreign policy.

The result of these opposing movements has been a convergence in favour of a greater European security and defence identity. The French strategic culture of maximum national independence has gradually ebbed, to the extent that France for a while envisaged re-entering the military command structure of NATO, and 'Europeanising' the sacrosanct nuclear deterrent. In contrast, Germany has been less tied to the American protector, and more anxious to define its own security interests in Central and Eastern Europe in particular. The Franco-German relationship has facilitated this movement; it allowed France to move rather closer to NATO, while providing broader support for a more autonomous stance in German foreign policy. France and Germany were undoubtedly much closer on defence and security in the late 1990s than in the late 1960s. Germany and France managed to define increasingly coherent European positions – on Russia, on rapid reaction forces, on military procurement, on NATO reform, and on ESDI. Close contact has produced policy learning and a gradual convergence of previously highly distinctive national positions.

CHAPTER 7

Franco-German relations and the social democratic dawn, 1997–2000

The return to office of centre-left governments in Britain and France in 1997, and in Germany in 1998, promised a unique experience of social democratic political supremacy in Europe. Social democratic governments were in power simultaneously in Bonn/Berlin, Paris and London for the first time in the history of the European Union. Although the election of Schröder was the critical event in this European political realignment, the comparison between new Labour and the new Parti Socialiste has occupied more attention. Not only do the Blair and Jospin governments have the advantage of greater longevity, but both have presented more coherent political visions that to some extent are in competition for the heart and soul of the European socialist movement. There are obvious comparisons and contrasts between the two. While the new Labour enterprise was intended to demarcate the party from the perceived defeats and bankruptcy of traditional social democracy, the French Socialist administration is in the process of discovering and refining a familiar social democratic political style. While Blair looks to the international centre-left (to Clinton and the new Democrats in particular), and advocates reforming the policy environment to adapt to globalisation, Jospin's activity has been focused more firmly on reorienting the European centre-left towards a new equilibrium less favourable to globalised international exchanges and more resolutely favourable to EU-level and state public policy intervention (Cole, 1998b, 1999a). While the landmark reforms of the Jospin premiership were implemented in the face of fierce business opposition (notably the 35 hour week), Blair appeared more wary of espousing anti-business policies for fear of damaging a sustained effort at repositioning and repackaging an old party.

Strengthening the European arena as a level of concerted public policy action has been an important aspect of the Jospin government's effort to 'positivise' the European debate (Cole and Drake, 2000). From the perspective of the Jospin government, European integration provides a political arena whereby European governments (those led by social democratic parties in particular) can combine their governance capacity to create (or strengthen) a European political, social and economic model. The European arena is the only arena where politics can reinvent new forms of political regulation faced with economic globalisation. This belief sustains the pan-European activism of the French plural left government, which has called for a Keynesian relaunch at the European level and a concerted European effort against unemployment. It underpins the efforts of the Jospin government to strengthen social and employment policies at the European level. It explains developments such as Jospin's proposals for EU borrowing for capital investment purposes and the re-emergence on the political agenda of the withholding tax.

The British and French governments have been perceived to be competing for the political favour of the German social democratic government elected in September 1998. In this penultimate chapter, we consider whether the Franco-German relationship has had to reinvent or adapt itself in the light of this new European political reality. We begin by examining the shock to Franco-German relations occasioned by the election of the Jospin government in June 1997.

Franco-German dissension and the Amsterdam summit

The Jospin government elected in June 1997 had to make immediate choices. A new European Treaty (negotiated by Juppé and Chirac) was to be finalised at the Amsterdam summit only three weeks after Jospin's election. During the 1997 election campaign, the left had insisted on four new conditions before agreeing to join the single currency. These conditions were a broad membership, including Spain, Italy and the UK; a renegotiation of the Stability Pact; the creation of a European economic government to oversee the future European central bank; and a competitively priced Euro against the dollar and the yen. These conditions were tantamount to a renegotiation of the Maastricht Treaty. On 9 June 1997, the new finance minister Strauss-Kahn warned that the French intended to delay signing the Amsterdam Treaty, unless the treaty included provisions for an Employment Pact and measures to enhance economic policy coordination (Lemaître, 1997a).

In its next move the French government sent a 'memorandum' to Bonn on its proposals for a 'Stability, Growth and Employment Pact' (de Bresson, 1997b). The memorandum was formally presented to the Franco-German summit meeting of Poitiers on 12 June 1997, the first such summit attended by the Jospin government. The French text was very specific in its recommendations. It called for EU finance ministers (meeting in ECOFIN) to define employment policies, in close collaboration with the Council of Social

Affairs, the Commission and the social partners. It demanded the creation of an EU employment policy competence, with the definition of common national rules and enforceable guidelines. It advocated increased economic policy coordination in the areas of exchange rate policy, budgetary policy, structural reforms and tax harmonisation. It called for a 'dialogue' to take place between the ECB and the Council, with the aim of promoting sustainable growth. This initiative was coldly rejected by the Germans, and its most contentious provisions (such as the detailed measures of economic policy coordination or the European Growth Fund) did not appear in the Amsterdam Treaty. Worse, the Amsterdam Treaty incorporated Blair's call for an 'adaptable' workforce, although upon France's insistence it did not refer to flexibility. British positions won through, as they did in the eventual Employment Pact. The change of government in France in June laid bare the best prepared plans for close Franco-German collaboration.

Notwithstanding the PS election campaign, the new French government did not have any real possibility of unravelling the single currency, or of changing the conditions of engagement. On the main issues, the French were isolated and public divisions emerged between the plural left government and President Chirac, who insisted that France sign the Amsterdam Treaty and respect its international engagements. There was little support in Amsterdam for a renegotiation of the Stability Pact, and traditional French demands for an 'economic government' were resisted by Germany. But the new French government saved face at Amsterdam by obtaining the creation of an economic committee (later known as Euro-11) to monitor the work of the European Central Bank. While it bowed to the inevitable at the Amsterdam summit, the Jospin government laid a powerful marker for the future: to balance the French commitment to EMU with a push for a more social Europe, one more ideologically attuned to French conceptions of public service, social regulation and state economic interventionism. Such a vision lay outside of the realms of possibility for as long as Kohl remained chancellor. The French Socialist-led government thus looked forward to the German Federal elections of September 1998 with eager anticipation.

A new dawn for Franco-German relations?

Chancellor Kohl will go down in history as a leader who worked hard to promote close Franco-German collaboration (Pruys, 1996; Macé-Scaron, 1997). By the end of his long period in office, however, his relations with French leaders across the political spectrum had become strained. The Stability Pact had caused a serious rift. This was expressed openly in a dispute between Chirac and Kohl at the Dublin summit of December 1996 and the issue continued to sour relations between French and German negotiators at the Amsterdam summit of June 1997. Moreover, faced with the prospect of electoral defeat in the 1998 Federal elections, Kohl adopted a tougher position based on defending national German interests over and above the formalities of Franco-German concord. Thus, the carefully sculpted Franco-German position paper was thrown into confusion at the Amsterdam summit itself, when Kohl came out against plans for more EU competence in the sphere of social policy. Matters reached a new low point with the Brussels summit of March 1998, when Kohl and Chirac openly collided over the presidency of the European Central Bank (de Bresson, 1998a). Although isolated, the French insisted that their candidate for president of the Central Bank – Jean-Claude Trichet – should replace the Dutchman Wim Duisenberg after four years. A non-binding compromise was eventually formulated by the British presidency that appeared to satisfy the French, confirming that obstinate obstruction by a single member state could still hold the Community to ransom.

Anticipation of a change of government in Bonn produced a spate of diplomatic activity. Bilateral political party channels proved to be the most effective means of communication between French Socialists and German Social Democrats. A close relationship had developed between the French PS and the German SPD since Oskar Lafontaine took over as German SPD leader in December 1995. Joint PS/SPD working groups were created to discuss social, economic and security issues (de Bresson, 1998a). There was close personal contact between Lafontaine and Strauss-Kahn, later to become German and French finance ministers. While prominent new Labour strategists were closely involved in the German SPD election campaign, the first act of Gerhard Schröder as the new chancellor was to visit Paris for meetings with President Chirac and Premier Jospin. The forms of the Franco-German relationship had to be respected. There was immediate contact between the new German and French governments. The French and German finance ministers, Strauss-Kahn and Lafontaine, held a joint press conference in Saarbruken (Germany) even before the latter was officially nominated (de Peretti, 1998). Within days, the German and French foreign ministers, Fischer and Védrine, had held four hours of meetings, and two high ranking Chancellery officials, Michael Steiner (diplomatic advisor) and Wilhelm Schönfelder (European affairs advisor), had met with their counterparts in the French prime minister's office in order to prepare the working groups announced by Chirac and Schröder in their first meeting on 30 September (de Bresson, 1998a).

On the other hand, there was little personal warmth between Schröder and either Jospin or Chirac. While Kohl had come from the Rhineland-Palatinate, a state bordering France, Schröder was from lower Saxony in northern Germany. Schröder was universally portrayed by the international media as having natural sympathies with Blair and New Labour; his reference to the *neue mitte* on the evening of his election as chancellor appeared to send out a very clear political message in this respect. And if Schröder visited Paris before London, his first official visit was to the UK.

Chancellor Schröder's governing style appeared to pose a direct challenge to traditional symbols of the Franco-German relationship. In his declaration of general policy (10 November 1998) Schröder referred to the 'new consciousness of an adult nation' and appeared to favour national objectives over European ones (Gougeon, 1999). Although there were many areas of agreement between the new French and German governments, there were also serious divergences. The future of nuclear energy was one of these; the mismanagement of the nuclear dossier by the new German government created serious tensions with France and the UK (Millot, 1999). The interests of the two countries with regard to the CAP were at opposite ends of the spectrum. But, coming after the late Kohl years, optimism was expressed on both sides that a new era of Franco-German cooperation was about to begin. This atmosphere soon gave way to one of mutual recrimination.

We can observe the shift in Franco-German relations during the first year of the Schröder government by comparing the Potsdam and Toulouse Franco-German summits of December 1998 and June 1999 (Haski and Millot, 1998; de Bresson, 1999). The Potsdam bilateral summit of December 1998 was announced as the summit of the Franco-German relaunch. France and Germany appeared much closer on certain issues than during the late Kohl period, particularly on social, employment and economic policies. Both countries were determined that the Euro should be successfully launched. Both made a commitment to EU-level employment and social policy. The Potsdam summit proposed 'constraining and verifiable targets' in employment policy. It called for social, economic and fiscal harmonisation across the European Union and set ambitious deadlines to achieve these objectives. Moreover, Germany moved much closer to the French position on enlargement: in a speech to the French National Assembly Foreign Affairs Committee, the Green Foreign Minister Joscka Fischer intimated that EU enlargement would require a profound reform of EC institutions (Dauvergne, 1999). This had been the French position at Amsterdam. For once the new spirit of Franco-German cooperation was symbolised not by French and German leaders – President Chirac, Chancellor Schröder or Prime Minister Jospin – but by the close relationship between the two finance ministers, Lafontaine and Strauss-Kahn.

By the Toulouse summit six months later, relations had cooled. The German presidency of the European Union – considered below – was declared a disappointment by sources close to the French government.

Schröder resented being criticised by Jospin's advisors on the eve of the Toulouse and Cologne summits, and basked in the 'special relationship' with British premier Blair. Sources close to the German Permanent Representation in Brussels volunteered the information that there was a major problem in dealing with the French on a daily basis. The political fall-out from the Agenda 2000 negotiations spilled over into other areas of Franco-German relations. While at Potsdam Schröder appeared to agree with Jospin on the need for 'constraining objectives' in employment policy, there was no mention of this after the Toulouse summit – prefiguring the tone of the Cologne EU summit meeting days later. In two spheres of public action, however, France and Germany appeared to have recovered a role as motor of the European construction. These were economic policy coordination and employment policy.

The Franco-German relationship and economic policy coordination

For a short period after Schröder's election, the logic of politics and economics appeared to be on a collision course. The new German finance minister, Lafontaine, was determined to exercise close political supervision over the management of the single currency, to some extent challenging the model of central bank independence inherited from the *Bundesbank*. On more than one occasion Lafontaine called on central banks to lower their interest rates and promote economic growth: the French, German and other banks refused. At the informal Portschach summit in October 1998, the EU finance ministers declared themselves committed to a new growth agenda (Dyson, 1999b). The summit declaration referred to Article 103 of the Maastricht Treaty to encourage EU governments to exercise closer coordination over economic policies. The summit agreed that the forth-coming German presidency would draft an Employment Pact to be presented to the Cologne summit in June 1999.

These initiatives were driven by a strong alliance between French Finance Minister Strauss-Kahn and his German counterpart Lafontaine. In January 1999, the two ministers published a joint memorandum calling for a more coordinated response to macroeconomic policy, and the use of budgetary policy to promote growth and favour employment (Lemaître, 1999a). In a challenge to Blair's doctrine of employability, the memorandum affirmed that high growth (rather than structural reform) was 'the principal means of fighting unemployment'. Both men advocated a measure of governmental direction over the European Central Bank. Moreover, the finance ministers insisted on their right to set exchange rate guidelines that the central bank had to respect. This initiative was strongly contested by Wim Duisenberg,

President of the ECB, who had declared his opposition to any attempt to limit 'the independence of monetary policy' (Delattre, 1998). Moreover, there was some opposition from other member states at this renewed attempt at Franco-German leadership. Franco-German calls for economic relaunch were accepted coolly by the Netherlands, Spain and Portugal, countries that had made many sacrifices to join in the Euro. There were many ambiguities in the French stance. Although Jospin called for EU-level policies, the French government was anxious that nation states should guard the primary responsibility for budgetary and employment policies; the French were, after all, engaged in an original and untypical domestic policy experiment in the 35 hour week reform.

Proposals for closer economic policy coordination took the form of two precise policy proposals: the French push to make Euro-11 into an effective economic government, and the Franco-German proposals for closer tax harmonisation.

The Euro-11 committee was presented by the international media as a concession to the French at the Amsterdam summit, although many other EU finance ministers were receptive to the idea (Ladrech, 2000). In the eyes of French decision-makers, the Euro-11 committee created at Amsterdam should become an economic government, wherein politicians would determine economic priorities to be implemented by the system of central banks. The French view of Euro-11 as an economic government had been strongly contested by the previous German administration. Kohl's finance minister, Theo Waigel, was insistent that the Euro-11 would be a simple working group, without any specific secretariat – and without a formal statute. The early meetings of Euro-11 were beset by continuing disagreements over its role. At the first meeting of Euro-11 on 4 June 1998, it was agreed that the committee would meet immediately prior to the monthly meeting of ECOFIN, but that its role would be advisory (Lemaître, 1998). The meeting would be attended only by the finance ministers of the Euro-zone. The change of government in Germany appeared to bring the Euro-11 closer to French conceptions, with Lafontaine convinced of the need for political direction to the single currency project. The formal launch of the Euro in January 1999 coincided with a strong push from EU finance ministers for a redefinition of the role of the central bank. This political challenge to the central bank ended abruptly with the resignation of Lafontaine as finance minister in February 1999. Although Strauss-Kahn continued to argue (for instance at the Euro-11 meeting in Dresden, 16–17 April 1999) for a swifter move to economic coordination, and to advocate a flexible implementation of the Stability Pact, Lafontaine's departure from office in February 1999 signalled the end of attempts to ensure close political control of the ECB (Quatremar, 1999b).

While results in the sphere of economic policy coordination were mixed, the Strauss-Kahn/Lafontaine partnership spilled over into other areas. The tax harmonisation dossier was a good example of how close Franco-German cooperation could be enhanced by support from EU institutions. The Commission itself used a neo-functionalist style argument to advocate the creation of an integrated fiscal policy. Following the Commission logic, a dynamic process had begun. The single market had produced the demand for a single currency. A single currency had already accelerated economic convergence between EU states. The Stability Pact was essential to ensure that convergence was lasting. Eventually, a common fiscal policy would be essential for the smooth functioning of the single market, removing the ability of member states to 'distort' the market by competitive taxation policies. As early as January 1997, the Commission had floated the possibility of harmonisation of future tax policy inside the Euro-zone. The Commission openly evoked using the 'strengthened cooperation' procedure in order to facilitate such fiscal cooperation between member states within the Euro-zone.

France, Germany and the Commission represented a powerful advocacy coalition in favour of closer tax harmonisation. Tax harmonisation had long been a French Socialist demand, and it had featured in the governmental programme upon which the SPD and the Greens had fought the Federal elections of October 1998. At the Portschach summit of October 1998 the 15 finance ministers agreed to undertake measures to combat 'harmful tax competition' (Dyson, 1999b). Tax competition led to a diminution of tax receipts for everybody. The Commission – and a working group of member states – was entrusted to work out a code of good behaviour for tax breaks to industry. There was intense pressure to introduce a 20% withholding tax on all EU revenues. The UK was the principal opponent of proposals for tax harmonisation, and in particular the proposals for a 20% withholding tax, highly detrimental to the interests of the City of London. Tough British opposition succeeded in delaying proposals for a withholding tax, which were eventually placed on the agenda of the Finnish presidency, only to be further postponed due to stiff British resistance.

Franco-German efforts to introduce tighter political direction over macroeconomic policy were sharply called into question by the resignation of Lafontaine as German finance minister in February 1999 and the diminishing stature of the German administration. Both Strauss-Kahn and Lafontaine met with determined domestic policy resistance. German business opposition was so overwhelming that the Frankfurt bourse rose by 5% on the day of Lafontaine's resignation. Lafontaine's resignation had a negative symbolic impact on the Franco-German relationship. Lafontaine had been the architect of a pro-French orientation within the Schröder administration.

He had been presented as the guarantor of the relaunch of the Franco-German relationship after the end of the Kohl period, and the damaging disputes over the ECB (from the Dublin summit onwards). In his capacity as president of the SPD, Lafontaine had developed very close relations with the French socialists. Lafontaine shared certain ideas rather untypical of the German political class: that the management of the Euro-zone should not be left to central bankers; that a political authority should accompany the creation of the ECB; and that there needed to be much greater coordination of economic, social and environmental policies across Europe. The sacrifice of the messenger weakened the force of these ideas. The resignation of Strauss-Kahn in November 1999, after suspicions of financial misdeeds, removed from office the other member of this particular Franco-German couple.

The Franco-German relationship and employment policy coordination

At the heart of the new Franco-German entente in late 1998 was the priority given to employment throughout the European Union. The French plural left alliance had been elected in part to address the problem of unemployment. From his election as premier, Jospin made clear that fighting unemployment was the number one European and domestic priority. The domestic political priority of employment policy was demonstrated by a series of audacious measures, of which the 35 hour week and the Youth Employment plan were the most ambitious (Cole, 1999a). Likewise, the German SPD made reducing unemployment, and the proposed Partnership for Jobs, into the centrepiece of its successful electoral campaign in 1998. Employment policy was also the showpiece of the Blair administration in the UK, though the policy solutions advocated there were noticeably different than in France or Germany. In employment policy, as in macroeconomic policy, the real intellectual and political debate took place between Blair and Jospin, with the Germans adjusting their conceptual lenses according to personality and convenience.

Although unable to alter the Stability Pact at the Amsterdam summit of June 1997, the French managed to secure the convening of a special employment summit later that year. Countries were invited to address position papers to the Luxembourg presidency in advance of the conference; the French text demonstrated the gulf separating the French and German governments. The French position paper to the Luxembourg conference was specific in its recommendations (Biffaud and de Bresson, 1997). It called for the creation of 12 million jobs throughout the Union in the next five years. It argued that national economic plans should include precise, quantifiable employment targets. It called for employment policy to be coordinated and regulated at the EU level. In particular, France argued that industrial layoffs and closures should be approved by the Commission. This appeared to look back to past French practices of administrative authorisation of unemployment; it stood far apart from new Labour theses.

The Luxembourg summit of November 1997 formally placed the idea of an Employment and Growth Pact on the EU agenda. The summit decided upon a 'coordinated employment strategy', though this fell far short of imposing the rigorous employment criteria that Prime Minister Jospin had been seeking. The Luxembourg summit obliged states to produce employment plans and to enhance training opportunities, but there was no real parallel between these documents, and the deficit reduction plans that Euroland countries were obliged to produce under the Stability Pact (Moscovici, 1998). The text approved by the Luxembourg conference was closer to the British Labour government's theses on labour flexibility than the French government's interventionist approach.

The idea of employability permeated the Luxembourg text; the unemployed needed to be made more employable. This was a supply-side definition of employment that emphasised stimulating market potentialities, making labour markets more flexible, and providing incentives to reduce structural unemployment. The Luxembourg resolution reaffirmed that social policy was a matter of national sovereignty, with only limited scope for European oversight. While the Luxembourg text was coolly received in Germany and Spain (both against too much state intervention in social policy) it was seen as much too timid in France and about right in Britain (*Le Monde*, 1997).

While Kohl had been reluctant to embrace a European dimension for employment policy, the new German government declared social and employment policy to be one of the priorities of the German EU presidency. The French and German governments converged around the belief that while employment policy was a critical responsibility for national governments, the EU should also have a role to play. As we observed above, the spirit of Portschach gave a new impulsion to EU-level action. The Vienna summit (December 1998) contained the pledge that the European Union would draw up an Employment Pact, with verifiable objectives (de Bresson, 1998b).

The German government was determined to achieve the objective of an Employment Pact by the end of its EU presidency. This pact was formally adopted at the Cologne summit of June 1999 (Sauron and Asseraf, 1999). While Lafontaine and Strauss-Kahn had agreed on quantifiable employment targets, the force of the joint Franco-German approach was weakened by the departure from office of Lafontaine in early 1999, and by the public rapprochement between Chancellor Schröder and British premier Blair. On 6 June 1999, Blair and Schröder published a joint manifesto calling for a

'Flexible and Competitive Europe' (Bouvet, 1999). This document advocated greater labour flexibility as a response to structural unemployment, called for more support for business, praised the discipline of the market and defended equality of opportunity rather than equality of outcomes. To achieve these aims, the Blair–Schröder document called for lower taxes on labour, lower public expenditure and improved training. Although the signatories called for other parties to collaborate – the French and the Scandinavians in particular – the document was drafted by Peter Mandelson and Bobo Hombach, the *eminences grises* of Blair and Schröder respectively.

The EU Employment Pact was officially adopted at the Cologne summit of June 1999. The Employment Pact called for 'an increasingly close co-operation in order to favour employment and economic reform throughout Europe'. The Pact established an 'ongoing macroeconomic dialogue' over budgetary, wage and fiscal policies, to involve national governments, the Commission and the social partners. Although paying due deference to economic policy coordination, however, this was not a social democratic coordinated policy, at least not as understood by the French Socialists. Consistent with Blair's preoccupations, the problem of employment was defined primarily as an economic, rather than a political one. French-backed ideas, such as public works or coordinated reductions in the working week, did not appear in the Employment Pact. There were to be no constraining measures in favour of quantifiable employment targets, and Jospin's call for an official EU growth target of 3% to stimulate employment was opposed openly by Schröder and his finance minister, Eichel. The measures adopted in the Employment Pact were essentially supply-side oriented – encouraging training, adopting business-friendly policies, and enhancing employability. The Employment Pact represented the first occasion that EU governments had agreed to coordinate their employment policies. Given the political sensitivity of unemployment as an issue across the EU, most governments remained reluctant to accept cross-border transfers to finance employment growth in other countries. Germany and France did not provide convincing leadership in the sphere of coordinated employment policy.

Franco-German relations and the German presidency

Although the Austrian presidency had made little headway on unfinished business (institutional reform, Agenda 2000), the Portschach and Vienna summits had given an indication of the new spirit infusing European capitals. Helmut Kohl's departure as German chancellor and the arrival of a European social democratic majority had created an atmosphere of progressive optimism. A powerful Franco-German axis based on a new centre-left political majority appeared to reconstitute itself around the charismatic

figures of Lafontaine and Strauss-Kahn. As we observed above, the departure of Helmut Kohl rendered credible new EU initiatives in the sphere of
employment and macroeconomic policies.

This renewed spirit of Euro-optimism was fuelled by the forthcoming
launch of the single currency on 1 January 1999. This successful launch
attenuated somewhat the memory of the 1998 Federal election campaign
when Schröder had dismissed the Euro as a 'premature abortion' that would
increase unemployment (Quatremar, 1999a). Since his election, the tone
had changed. The Euro, Schröder insisted in December 1998, was 'the begin-
ning of our collective future', and Europe had to be more social, closer to
the citizen. At the same time, Schröder made it clear that Germany 'could
not resolve the problems of its neighbours with a German cheque-book'
(Quatremar, 1999a). This populist side to Schröder worried Germany's
neighbours.

The German presidency witnessed important symbolic advances in
European integration. The presidency started with the inauguration of the
European Central Bank in Frankfurt and the official launch of the Euro, a
project whose implementation owed as much to German stewardship as to
anything else. It rapidly became clear, however, that the Schröder government had no experience of European affairs. The confrontational style
adopted by Schröder proved irksome to other EU partners and the results
were meagre. The threatening tone adopted to promote budgetary reform
was counterproductive; it contravened the accepted European policy style of
building compromise and seeming to engage in above common denominator
decision-making. Sources close to the German government concluded that
managing European policy proved to be a difficult learning process for the
new administration.

On occasions the German government appeared overwhelmed by the presidency. There was an obvious lack of coordination in German negotiating
positions. While economics minister Lafontaine called for a stabilisation
of expenditure, the agriculture minister Funke argued for an increase in
agricultural spending (Deger, 1999). While foreign minister Fischer called
for national co-financing of the CAP, Funke advocated leaving the existing system intact. The negotiation of the CAP dossier in particular was
amateurish. The German agriculture minister insisted on holding bilateral
meetings with his counterparts; on no occasion prior to the Petersburg
summit (February 1999) had there been a plenary agriculture council
(Deger, 1999). The Germans admitted to inexperience; Schröder's comments
on German money being burnt in Brussels (December 1998) were typical of
this. Schröder had created domestic expectations that the German contribution could be reduced, but these proved unrealistic. Schröder and Fischer
gradually learned that German interests were interdependent with those of

its partners. More than other countries, Germany needed to get its neighbours on board in pursuit of its long-term aim of European unification.

The difficulties of coordinating German responses extended more generally to relations with Germany's EU partners, first and foremost France. This can be demonstrated by considering the two linked but entrenched policy dilemmas addressed by the German presidency: budgetary reform and the Common Agricultural Policy.

'Agenda 2000' was the name of the programme drawn up by the European Commission in July 1997 to prepare for EU enlargement. Agenda 2000 was also a package of detailed measures to reform the 2000–2006 EU budget. It contained over 1300 pages. Its central tenet was that enlargement must be accompanied by budgetary retrenchment and institutional reform. A cap on expenditure was vital if new members were to be admitted to the EU club. Institutional reform was primordial, to prevent institutional gridlock once the new entrants had joined the EU. With the enlargement process officially launched at the December 1997 Luxembourg summit, Agenda 2000 moved to the centre of the EU stage.

As Agenda 2000 covered all EU expenditure, every aspect of EU finance was laid on the table: member state contributions, common policies (such as the CAP) and structural and cohesion funds. For the first time in the history of the EU, it was proposed to freeze total spending at 1999 levels (1.27% of EU GNP), signalling budgetary retrenchment in real terms across the board (Paolini, 1998). At the same time, the German presidency made known its determination to reduce its budgetary contribution, inviting comparisons with Margaret Thatcher's 1984 'I want my money back'. Reform of the EU budget was closely tied in with reducing the German budgetary contribution. Kohl had demanded that the German contribution be reduced by 30% – some 11 billion Euro (*The Economist*, 1998). Schröder followed in his predecessor's footsteps, but gave no precise figure. Pruning the German contribution was essential – in German eyes – to assuage a domestic public opinion hostile to the abandoning of the Deutschmark. The Germans were determined to reduce their contribution, which accounted for 60% of the EU total: the German net contribution to the EU budget in 1998 was 10.9 billion Euro, against 0.8 billion for France (Gougeon, 1999).

Agenda 2000 was the first major occasion on which the EU had declared an economy drive. It was accepted by all that budgetary discipline was an imperative, not least in the context of the launch of the Euro (which required a tight control over public finances) and the prospect of future enlargement (and the demands on Community resources this implied). Steering the Agenda 2000 discussions was a thankless task; it was testament to German influence that other member states considered Germany to be best equipped to deal with the painful choices imposed by budgetary retrenchment. The British presidency had studiously avoided the issue of budgetary reform, and the Austrian presidency had lacked sufficient political authority to engage any meaningful discussion. The Germans were determined to use their presidency to bring the negotiations on Agenda 2000 to successful fruition, but also to reduce their budgetary contribution. From the outset, Schröder announced that it was imperative to conclude Agenda 2000 by the Berlin summit of March 1999.

Apart from reducing its own contribution, the German negotiating positions centred around the need to freeze expenditure on the cohesion and structural funds, to challenge the UK rebate and to reform the CAP. The structural funds and regional aid budgets had climbed from 17.5% to 35% of the EU total in ten years (Callé, 1999). In spite of several reforms of the CAP (notably in 1986 and 1992), agriculture continued to be the most important budgetary item, accounting for around half of EU expenditure. Germany was supported by the Netherlands, Sweden and Austria, all countries seeking a new funding formula in order to reduce their contributions. Most other member states argued for various degrees of national exceptionalism: Britain refused to lay its rebate on the table, Spain refuted any diminution of cohesion and structural funds, and France defended a position favourable to its farming interests over the CAP.

Reform of the CAP

In Chapter 4, we examined the paradoxical operation of the Franco-German relationship in the sphere of agriculture. Bilateral contacts were intense partly because disagreements were deeply embedded. The regime-like quality of the Franco-German relationship was demonstrated by Germany's striving to come to an agreement with France even when its own national interests appeared in doubt. As the CAP was part of the initial Franco-German bargain, Germany went to great lengths to protect France from isolation in the early 1960s and again in the early 1990s (Webber, 1999b). However, the Schröder government was far less favourable to the farm lobby than Kohl had been. While German (and especially Bavarian) farmers were politically aligned with the CDU-CSU, the Schröder government was linked to the trade unions and industrial labour. The new social democratic administration considered it an anomaly that half of the EU budget should go on agriculture.

As on many occasions in the past, the complex nexus of agricultural and trade issues revealed divergences of national interest between France and Germany in 1999. The need for CAP reform in 1999 stemmed in part from the decline in consumption of beef (the mad cow crisis). Overproduction and under-consumption had again produced mountains of beef. The EU had agreed in the GATT Uruguay round to limit the subsidy of exports onto third markets; hence excess beef could not be off-loaded onto third markets. To prevent overproduction, the Commission proposed another round of price cuts. These were in the order of 20% for cereals, 30% for beef and 20% for milk. The originality of the proposed reform was to compensate the proposed cuts only partially; direct grants would provide 50% of the difference for cereals, 80% for beef and 60% for milk (Lemaître, 1999b). There was an additional reason for these cuts – lower farm prices would favour the integration of the central and eastern democracies into the EU.

Germany and France both wanted to protect their vital national interests. The Germans addressed the problem of budgetary retrenchment by insisting that national governments should take over part of farm expenditure. France was willing to accept some cuts in guaranteed prices, but fiercely resisted the German/Commission proposals for 'co-financing' the CAP budget. This would involve national governments taking charge of farm aids once a given threshold had been reached. As the chief beneficiary of CAP, this was anathema to the French. The French argued strongly that CAP was the longest established common policy, and would be threatened by a partial nationalisation. The French position on CAP reform was a complex one; determined to resist co-financing at any price, the French demonstrated themselves to be innovative in other respects. France thus proposed a sliding scale system of grants (*dégressivité*); direct grants to farmers should be reduced according to the scale of production. This would affect large farms, with smaller producers being safeguarded. Extra finance would go into general preservation of the countryside; environmental aims would be taken into account. This marked a shift away from the traditional producer position. The really essential point for France was the principle of the CAP as a Community policy (Lemaître, 1999b).

As in the past, the French government stoutly defended its national interest, testament to the permanent pressure of the powerful domestic farming lobby. French resistance paid off; the Council of agriculture ministers of 22 March 1999 failed to come to agreement and the German presidency shelved its plans for 'co-financing'. Once again, the French revealed themselves to be expert defenders of their narrow self-interest. In the opinion of sources close to the negotiations, Agenda 2000 demonstrated the efficacy of French networks throughout the European institutions and the rapid learning process forced upon the German government.

Germany failed once again to translate its structural power into political effectiveness. Although Chancellor Schröder triumphantly announced an agreement at the Berlin summit in March 1999, this appeared as a hollow victory. The four main contributor nations (Germany, the Netherlands, Sweden and Austria) did not 'get their money back'. The new rules were only marginally more favourable to the contributor nations, but Germany remained by far the largest net contributor. Germany's partners had more satisfaction. France held firm on the CAP. Although she had to make some concessions (price decreases in milk would not be fully reimbursed), France obtained guarantees that there would be no national co-financing of the CAP, or other community policies. The survival of the CAP was not in doubt. Other countries also had reasons to be satisfied. The 'cohesion fund' countries (Spain, Portugal, Greece and Ireland) had to accept only a small decline in the structural funds, and the UK rebate was virtually unchanged. The economic giant continued to have difficulty in pulling its political punches. In spite of its structural power, Germany was incapable of arbitrating between rival national interests, or of using its influence to force through a solution. This was not the behaviour of a regional hegemon. On the other hand, the EU had a budget until 2006, enlargement negotiations could begin in earnest, and the Berlin summit also announced the reopening of the institutional reform chapter of the Amsterdam Treaty.

Conclusion

While the ideological sympathies amongst French and German social democratic led governments were marked in certain respects, there was no overriding, countervailing logic apt and able to challenge the influence of the prevailing economic orthodoxy, or to reshape well-trodden national paths. Differences between France and Germany – for instance, on the management of the central bank – continued to weigh heavily, and were only marginally affected (if at all) by the partisan affiliation of the French and German governments. The case studies of employment policy and economic policy coordination demonstrated both the distinctiveness of national solutions, as well as the real degree of policy convergence that had occurred. There was a wide acceptance of the need to counterbalance the tough economic convergence achieved with political and social advances. There remained a measure of conflict over the financing of any new arrangements.

The obduracy of state interests was best demonstrated by the Agenda 2000 negotiations. The Agenda 2000 crisis in the Franco-German relationship was a real one. The French negotiators in the Agenda 2000 budget discussions proved particularly tenacious, forcing the German presidency to accept a compromise over the CAP that fell far short of its initial intentions. When required to do so, the Jospin government demonstrated itself to be a stubborn advocate of French national interests. This firmness was revealed in spite of a common social democratic identity and a ritualistic celebration of the solidity of Franco-German relations in the aftermath of

Schröder's election. In line with realist precepts, national self-interest prevailed over party and ideology. The Agenda 2000 episode also illustrated that, in the absence of a coordinated Franco-German agreement, there was no alternative source of political leadership. The discredit of the Commission had left a vacuum, and the German chancellor alone lacked sufficient authority to bang heads together. In our final, concluding chapter, we shall now revisit the intellectual questions posed in the framework of analysis presented in Chapter 2, with a view to elucidating further the Franco-German relationship.

CHAPTER 8

Conclusion

In Chapter 2, we raised a series of research questions, and a range of accompanying, and to an extent, rival conceptual explanations for understanding the Franco-German relationship. In this chapter we will offer our preferred answers to the precise research questions we posed in Chapter 2: on the role of Franco-German leadership in the process of European integration; on the internal equilibrium and characterisation of the relationship itself; and upon the evolution of Franco-German policy processes. Before engaging this discussion, however, we address briefly the theoretical literatures elucidated in Chapter 2. Meta-theoretical debates between Institutionalists and Intergovernmentalists are of limited relevance in understanding the complexity of the Franco-German relationship. By selecting to study a bilateral relationship, we are driven to prefer a state-centric theoretical focus over a supranational one, but the questions posed by supranational integration theorists account for many of the policy dilemmas which France and Germany – together or separately – are forced to confront. In line with a move to more syncretic theories of integration, our starting point is that these approaches are all useful for explaining different dimensions of the Franco-German relationship. The theoretical frames are more or less appropriate in explaining the dynamics at play at any given time in any particular issue-area. Franco-German bargains are one important variable for understanding EU constitutive politics; our analysis of the Maastricht and Amsterdam Treaty negotiations highlighted the powerful agenda-setting role of France and Germany. Critics of the liberal intergovernmentalist approach have argued that concentrating on history-making decisions distorts the real picture. Most EU decision-making is not concerned with questions of grand strategy, but with the details of policy implementation where supranational actors – the Commission and the European Court of Justice especially – have a determining role to play. To some extent, the distinction between history-making and normal decisions is artificial. If we accept that France and Germany have exercised more influence than other states in shaping the former, their influence logically spills over into the latter.

France and Germany occupy a more distinctive role in state-centric than in supranational explanations of European integration. State-centric explanations are more convincing in certain issue-areas (such as security and defence and agriculture) than in others (such as competition policy). Franco-German dynamics were less pertinent in areas of regulatory politics and in new policy spheres where supranational actors have developed their competencies. It appears fanciful, for example, to explain the regulatory politics of the post-Single European Act period in terms of an overarching Franco-German relationship, a theme we insisted upon in Chapter 4. Rather than assuming a leadership role, the Franco-German alliance appeared on occasions as a defensive one, aimed at protecting national conceptions of public service, social policy or legitimate state economic activity against the reforming drive of policy entrepreneurs within the European Commission.

Particular case studies are also best explained by syncretic explanatory tools. In the case of EMU, for instance, the technical expertise of a cohesive epistemic community was important in an agenda-setting sense, but technical expertise would have remained of secondary importance without the effort of determined (joint) political leadership and a measure of preliminary domestic convergence. Consistent with state-centric models, France and Germany appear as the two leading EU nations (by most criteria) and exercise a strong a priori claim for joint leadership, a claim we consider below. In line with historical institutionalist explanations, however, policy evolutions are to some extent dependent upon the unintended consequences of past decisions. Even if it were conclusively demonstrated that France and Germany, acting together, pre-shaped most essential decisions, this would not be sufficient to 'prove' the intergovernmentalist case. France and Germany, together with other EU states, have to adapt to the consequences of decisions they could not have foreseen in advance. This invests the EU policy process with a dynamic quality that is beyond the control of individual member states, or even of the powerful Franco-German relationship.

Franco-German leadership and the European integration project

Our first series of research questions concerned core issues of the leadership of the European integration process. They combined the insights of intergovernmental and supranational paradigms of European integration. Have France and Germany traditionally exercised joint leadership (or 'hegemony' in the realist lexicon) within the European Union? Is this still the case?

From the evidence presented in the main body of the book, the Franco-German relationship appears as the principal relationship within the European Union. It can lay a stronger claim to leadership than any other coalition of member states, or, arguably, than any other coalition of interests within the EU. The Franco-German relationship has more resources at its disposal than alternative groupings. The first resource is that of symbolism. As the most significant founding fathers of the EU, France and Germany arguably count more than others. Their union symbolises reconciliation, solidarity and peace – these are precious qualities within the context of European history. Other member states look to France and Germany to bridge their differences and reach agreements precisely because of their symbolic leadership role. The second resource is that of economic influence. Germany and France are the leading EU economies. For many smaller member states, it is difficult to envisage adopting policy positions that openly defy Paris and (especially) Berlin. The close interdependence of European economies thus increases the political leadership potentialities of France and (especially) Germany. France and Germany also act as political and geographical brokers. France has often emerged as spokesperson for southern European interests, notably in agriculture, though this role has been increasingly contested by Spain. We observed in Chapter 5 how France was closely aligned with the southern European states in advocating a broadly-based Euro. Germany has tended to be aligned with the northern free trade states. France and Germany usually speak for broader coalitions of interest throughout the EU, hence their strong incentive to reach agreement.

If France and Germany exercise a leadership role, this is also because (many) other member states look to the Franco-German relationship to perform such a role. Other member states are particularly sensitive to the need for Franco-German agreement. When cooperation between France and Germany breaks down, deadlock is the feared consequence. If France and Germany manage to reach agreement on contentious issues, most other member states will fall into line. This explains why an agreed Franco-German position is usually supported in the Council, but unilateral German or French positions often are not (Webber, 1999a).

The image of the hegemon overstates the influence and misrepresents the nature of the modern German polity. Although Germany is the most significant European economic power, its lead over its main competitors and neighbours is not that great, and in most respects the 'economic giant' remains a military pygmy. Germany has substantial political leverage, but its influence within the EU depends upon coalition building. Herein lies the vital importance of the Franco-German relationship for Germany. There was a strong convention – breached somewhat during the 1990s but not abandoned completely – that French and German initiatives should be presented as joint Franco-German ones. Unilateral German proposals still raise suspicions of hegemony amongst Germany's European neighbours. Germany is anxious to maintain France as a friendly ally to its west and to allay the latter's security concerns. As demonstrated on repeated occasions in the 1990s, Germany went to great lengths to avoid French isolation within the EU and other international organisations. The Franco-German relationship operates as a mechanism to prevent the isolation of one or the other partner within the EU. As over the GATT agreement, over EMU, and over Agenda 2000, German solidarity has traditionally extended to avoid the isolation of its French ally. In return, in important areas of common interest such as monetary policy, France has been prepared to adopt the German benchmark as its standard.

The case for Franco-German leadership is strong, but should not go unanswered. The governance of the EU is inherently complicated and militates against the emergence of clear leadership structures such as an overarching Franco-German alliance. Close Franco-German relationships on one level can be counterbalanced by conflictual relations on another (as in the case of the parliament against the Council). The strengthening of the European Parliament has complicated further the Franco-German relationship, as demonstrated in the episode of the Santer Commission's resignation.

Franco-German relations have always been highly complex. Neither French nor German leaders have felt comfortable in an exclusive face-to-face relationship. Apart, perhaps, from the Gaullist period, they have preferred to develop their bilateral relations within a wider European context. A bilateral Franco-German relationship would be a very narrow conception of European unification, especially for Germany (Garton-Ash, 1994). Germany's interests extend well beyond those of its bilateral relationship with France, especially since unification. Germany has improved her bilateral relations with many countries since 1989, most notably the Netherlands, and is the obvious beacon for the new democracies of Central and Eastern Europe. France traditionally feared being submerged in a Deutschmark zone if left alone with Germany. This explained her negative reaction to immediate economic and monetary union with Germany (as suggested by the then president of the *Bundesbank*, Pöhl, in 1990) or to the Lamers–Schäuble proposals for a hard-core Europe in 1994. Both countries looked to other EC countries (such as Britain and Italy) or to the USA for mediation in their dealings with one another.

The metaphor of the Franco-German motor underplays the complexities of European integration. There are too many other bilateral and multilateral relationships. Helen Wallace (1990) argued a decade ago that EU coalitions are variable, according to the issue-area and institutions involved. If anything, EU policy-making became even more complex during the 1990s, as a result of enlargement and increased supranational activism. As the community has expanded, coalitions have become more diverse and more complex. The blocking role of the Franco-German alliance has also been weakened. Since the mid-1980s (and the passage of the Single European Act), France and Germany have been less able to resist the activism of the European Commission, at least in those areas where the latter has clear legal competencies. As demonstrated at Amsterdam, the Franco-German relationship could not forestall the determined defence of established interests on behalf of other EU coalitions, such as the 'cohesion group' countries or the Benelux states. The Franco-German relationship has never exercised a hegemonic role, and in some respects its role has diminished with time. The Franco-German directory model underplays the dynamic qualities of the EU policy process and the changes wrought on the EU as a result of successive enlargements. Future enlargements make it even less likely that the Franco-German relationship – as a directorate – will be able to impose its views.

The Franco-German relationship can perform a powerful agenda-setting role in the right circumstances. Its leadership is most effective when it is encouraged by other states to be proactive. When France and Germany have attempted to impose their leadership without the agreement of other states, however, they have generally failed (Soutou, 1996). Other EU member states are important. Spain has emerged as a powerful and ambitious spokesperson for the 'cohesion fund' countries; this was demonstrated both at the Amsterdam summit and during the Agenda 2000 negotiations. British influence remains strong, especially since the election of the Blair government in 1997. In certain spheres such as defence and security policy Britain cannot be ignored. A more constructive British attitude has challenged the Franco-German relationship in several important respects, not least by sowing the seeds of division between Jospin and Schröder. The Benelux states have always been influential, not least because of their activism within the Commission and their over-representation in the Council (on a population basis). Even a small country such as Denmark can place obstacles in the way of Franco-German grand strategy; this was the lesson to be drawn from the 1992 Danish referendum on the Maastricht Treaty. On the other hand, amongst the big countries the Italians could privately regret that the Franco-German 'axis' appeared so dominant (interviews), but they generally fell in behind Franco-German centrality. There was no Anglo-Italian alternative to the Franco-German relationship. France and Germany remain the most important alliance grouping within the EU, but their leadership potential depends upon the specific qualities of the policy sector, and the agreement of the other principal players. On balance, this pattern falls rather short of hegemony – single or joint. The direction of change is towards a rather weaker steering role for the Franco-German relationship across the whole dimension of EU policy.

Asymmetry and the Franco-German relationship

Our second series of research questions related to the internal operation and the changing equilibrium within the Franco-German relationship during the period since German unification. We argued in Chapter 3 that the Franco-German relationship could best be understood as a bilateral 'quasi-regime'. Rather than in its degree of institutionalisation, the effectiveness of the Franco-German relationship lies in its flexibility and its informality. The Franco-German relationship works best as an informal, often invisible compact, driven by networks of officials sharing common understandings and engaged in inter-elite bargaining and policy learning. The Franco-German relationship is an elite-driven project; there is little evidence of collaboration at the level of societal policy networks or interest groups. French and German leaders have figured prominently as the driving force of the Franco-German relationship. There is an understanding that French and German leaders will attempt to reach agreement where possible, even against their initial preferences. The regime-like quality of the Franco-German relationship is essential because France and Germany often represent distinctive viewpoints within the EU. In the absence of determined joint leadership, the Franco-German relationship falters, though the interests at stake are such that it rarely fails altogether. Although relations between leaders are heavily routinised, personal factors do make a difference. The fruitful relationship between the French President Mitterrand – elected as a socialist in 1981 – and the Christian Democratic German Chancellor Kohl demonstrated that personal understandings and common strategic visions were far more important than party political affiliations.

Franco-German relations in the post-war period have been based on hard-headed realism (McCarthy, 1993a). Before 1989, it was commonly argued that the relationship enabled one power to control itself (Germany) and to accept that a traditional enemy (France) had a right to exercise a partial control over its destiny. Until German unification, Franco-German relations had prospered under the theme of the reconciliation of hereditary enemies. The historical circumstances of the Second World War, combined with the legacy of Gaullist foreign policy, created a subtle equilibrium, where French diplomatic, military and political prestige counterbalanced growing German economic primacy. The symbolic claims to legitimacy became less powerful as memories of the Second World War faded and especially as German unification challenged the post-war European equilibrium.

Neo-realist arguments emphasise the changes in the power distribution that accompanied the end of the cold war (Baun, 1996). While the ensuing decade did not proceed entirely according to realist predictions, the internal equilibrium of the Franco-German relationship has shifted. French fears of being a junior partner in a relationship within which it had long pretended to seniority appeared to materialise. The French response to German unification and its aftermath was to advocate binding Leviathan. From the French perspective Europeanisation and the Franco-German relationship were both ways of ensuring that a unified and confident Germany would be embedded in constraining multilateral institutions. During the early years of the decade, French politicians repeatedly called for the 'tying in' of Germany on account of its monetary primacy, its geostrategic location and its political centrality. EMU, CFSP and the institutional reforms accompanying enlargement could be read as French strategic responses to the new European balance of power. That France managed to achieve so many of its goals was testament to the regime-like quality of the bilateral Franco-German relationship. However this did not obviate the changing internal balance of the relationship.

France and Germany each have their own reasons for affirming the solidity of the Franco-German relationship, but these are not identical. French support was a critical commodity during the period of German unification and its immediate aftermath (1989–91). The importance of the nested bargaining game over German unification and monetary union has been repeatedly stressed throughout this book. After unification Germany needed France in order to consolidate its role as facilitator of Central and Eastern Europe and to present a traditional bilateral Franco-German front for specifically German policy initiatives. These were important roles, but, after 1989–91, French accompaniment of Germany was less vital on balance than before 1989. The Franco-German alliance remained the cornerstone of German European policy, but it was not Germany's only option. To some extent she could look to alternative configurations within the European Union, especially as the EU enlarged to take in the new democracies of Northern, Central and Eastern Europe. More than 50 years after the end of the Second World War Germany no longer needed France in the same manner to demonstrate its commitment to Europe and liberal democracy. France had only its European policy and needed Germany more than ever. In order to preserve the myth of the Franco-German motor, France set its standard by that of Germany.

The asymmetrical character of the Franco-German relationship has been aggravated since German unification and enlargement. Within the Franco-German relationship itself, there has been a redistribution of resources during the decade in question. The French contribution to the relationship – that of political influence through military, especially nuclear, prestige – has been rather devalued since the end of the cold war. The German contribution – that of setting the monetary and economic standard – has risen in value. While notions of German hegemony are unsatisfactory for reasons discussed in Chapter 5, the Franco-German relationship in the year 2000 can best be described as one of asymmetrical interdependence.

The Franco-German relationship has adapted to changing circumstances and withstood the test of time. Its internal equilibrium has shifted, and yet it has become more genuinely convergent as the economic and security dilemmas of post-cold war Europe become apparent. There is an expectation from others that France and Germany will work to overcome differences and reach above common denominator agreements. Although the Franco-German relationship does not consistently offer leadership of the European Union (and even less so of other international organisations), it does constitute a recognisable bilateral quasi-regime that is likely to remain a central force of EU governance for the foreseeable future.

National paths and policy convergence

Our third research question concerned the degree of policy convergence over the period observed. Post-war Franco-German relations have built upon a measure of convergence of ideas and interests, a joint management of political projects and an institutionally embedded existence. But the assumption of inherent coherence so often made in journalistic accounts is misplaced. As we have observed throughout this book – particularly in relation to economic policy paradigms and security cultures – French and German positions are often highly distinctive. The effect of the relationship can be strongest on bridging diverse traditions and reconciling contrasting ideas.

Since the events of 1989–90, the Franco-German partnership has suffered severe strains and new challenges. One astute observer contends that French and German interests have diverged remorselessly since 1989 (Soutou, 1999). German unification was a zero-sum game, played out at the expense of France. The collapse of the Communist threat, moreover, damaged the underlying cohesion of the Franco-German alliance, which had functioned most effectively as a cold war Atlantic outpost against the Soviet threat. Superficially attractive, this argument underplays the growing policy convergence between France and Germany since the 1960s.

Certainly, France and Germany start from opposing positions on many of the issues facing contemporary Europe. French and German interests have diverged across a broad range of the policy sectors surveyed in this book. These have included the GATT negotiations, CAP reform, the Atlantic Alliance, Yugoslavia, Bosnia, enlargement, and relations with the new democracies of Eastern and Central Europe. The Franco-German relationship is frequently undermined by its own internal tensions. While the Franco-German alliance has a dialectical quality that enables its contradictions to be surmounted, this does not obviate the internal contradictions themselves.

French and German positions are often opposed. As Kolboom and Picht (cited in Webber, 1999a: 11) observe, 'there is hardly a single area in which the world views, concepts and approaches of the two countries could provide a solid base for joint European action'. Bilateral channels are used, they contend, as much to put a brake on reforms objectionable to one side as they are to produce new initiatives. As we observed in Chapters Five and Six, disagreements had often prevailed within the Franco-German committees on defence and security, and on economics and finance.

This image of the unalterable character of nationally distinctive positions is rather misleading. In essential areas of public policy, there has been a narrowing of nationally distinctive positions over time. We agree with Moravscik (1991) that the relaunch of European integration in the mid-1980s stemmed as much from a domestic policy convergence in France and Germany as from anything else. On many issues, France and Germany instinctively agree and there is evidence of increased convergence during the past decade. This was demonstrated in Chapters 4, 5 and 6 with respect to enlargement, EU institutional reform, the single currency, economic policy paradigms and defence and security policy. This process of policy convergence was most remarkable with respect to the two issue-areas where national distinctiveness was previously most marked: monetary policy and defence and security.

To some extent, EMU was predicated upon a prior domestic economic convergence. By the early 1990s there had been a general convergence of domestic economic management styles across Europe, based on the pursuance of strong money policies and exchange rate stability. As the process of European integration gathered pace after the mid-1980s, French policymakers emulated central features of the German economic model such as price stability and central bank independence. More than any other, the single currency project embodied this process of policy transfer and emulation between Germany and her continental European partners. We identify the role of epistemic communities (in an agenda-setting capacity) and political leadership (in a decision-making and mobilisation capacity) as the critical variables in explaining the EMU decision.

The evidence is rather different in the case of security and defence, but we uncovered firm evidence in Chapter 6 of a narrowing of highly distinctive national models in this domain. There was an underlying convergence in favour of a more affirmative European security identity that became apparent as the 1990s wore on.

There was a narrowing of the distinctiveness of national security cultures. The French strategic culture of maximum national independence gradually ebbed, with France moving much closer to defining a common strategic alliance with Germany and other European allies within NATO and the European Union. The official recognition of Franco-German 'parity' in the 1996 common strategic concept was an important milestone in burying the Gaullist defence paradigm. France no longer explicitly claimed a leadership role in this quintessential sphere of national rank. If France moved closer to the Atlantic Alliance, Germany became less tied to the American protector and more anxious to define its own security interests, particularly in Central and Eastern Europe and in Russia. The Franco-German relationship facilitated this movement; it allowed France to move rather closer to NATO, while providing broader support for a more autonomous stance in German foreign policy. France and Germany were undoubtedly much closer on defence and security in the late 1990s than in the late 1960s. The bilateral Franco-German relationship has always involved the exchange of policy ideas. Close contact has produced policy learning and a gradual convergence of many previously highly distinctive national positions. In response to our third series of research questions, France and Germany were much closer on most substantive policy issues at the end of the 1990s than they were at the end of the 1960s. A process of policy emulation had occurred between the two countries, encouraged by the dynamics of the Franco-German relationship itself.

The final question concerns convergence to which standard. The changing equilibrium within the Franco-German alliance is emphasised by the fact that convergence has tended, on balance, to be towards German rather than French standards. This is most obviously the case in monetary policy standard-setting, as investigated in Chapter 5. Although French policy positions have prevailed in certain instances (for example on the broad membership of the Euro) and though France has proved adept in defence of its vital national interests (such as in agriculture), German standard-setting was the norm, at least in this primordial sphere of monetary policy. Along with the other member states of the Euro-zone, France agreed to import a monetary policy model and set of institutions initially designed in Germany. Given the importance of monetary policy, and the management of the single currency, future political spillover is likely to produce outcomes consistent with this paradigmatic choice. The counterpart to this is the rather paradoxical observation that Germany will be forced to continue to offer important side-payments as a direct consequence of encouraging other EU countries to adapt to its standard-setting role. Given its economic resources, political ambitions and strategic location, Germany will not escape lightly from its role as underwriter of Community finances. Upon this, as on many other but not all issues, it can rely on France for support.

Bibliography

Ackermann, U. (1996) France-Allemagne: aller-retour. Réponses à une enquête, *Esprit*, 5, 24–43.

Aeschimann, E. and Riché, P. (1996) *La Guerre de sept ans – histoire secrète du franc fort*, Paris: Calmann-Lévy.

Agence Europe (1992) *Treaty on European Union*, Agence Europe, 1759/60, 1–57.

L'Allemagne, la France et l'Union européenne ou comment relancer l'Europe, *Cahiers de la fondation*, 334–5, July–December 1994, p. 139.

Allin, D. (1993) Germany looks at France, in P. McCarthy (ed.) *France–Germany, 1983–1993. The Struggle to Co-operate*, Basingstoke: Macmillan, pp. 27–50.

Allison, M. and Heathcote, O. (1999) (eds) *Forty Years of the Fifth Republic. Actions, Dialogues and Discourses*, Bern: Peter Lang.

Andersen, S. (1999) *The Amsterdam CFSP components: a lowest common denominator agreement?* Paper presented to the European Community Studies Association conference, Pittsburgh, United States, June. 57 pp.

Andrews, D. (1993) The Global Origins of the Maastricht Treaty on EMU: Closing the Window of Opportunity, in A. Cafruny and G. Rosenthal (eds) *The State of the European Community, Volume 2*, Harlow: Longman, pp. 107–23.

Armand, F. (1993) La Relation avec l'Allemagne en matière de politique étrangère et de securité, 1988–1992, *Relations Internationales et Stratégiques*, 9, 147–59.

Armstrong, K. and Bulmer, S. (1998) *The Governance of the Single European Market*, Manchester: Manchester University Press.

Arrowsmith, J. (1996) *Is EMU riding for a fall?* Paper presented to the Research Seminar of Bradford University, 8 November. 14 pp.

Assembly of Western European Union (1999) *Time for Defence. A Plan for Action Proposed by the WEU Assembly*. Adopted by the Assembly's Standing Committee, 16 March.

Attali, J. (1993) *Verbatim. Tome 1. Chronique des années 1981–1986*, Paris: Fayard.

Baltas, N. (1999) *The Common Agricultural Policy: Past, Present and Future*. Paper presented to the European Community Studies Association conference, Pittsburgh, United States, June. 17 pp.

Banchoff, T. (1999) National identity and EU legitimacy in France and Germany, in T. Banchoff and M. P. Smith (eds) *Legitimacy and the European Union. The Contested Polity*, London: Routledge. pp. 180–98.

Baun, M. (1996) *An Imperfect Union. The Maastricht Treaty and the New Politics of European Integration*, Boulder, CO: Westview.

Beckinridge, R. (1997) Reassessing Regimes: The International Regime Aspects of the European Union, *Journal of Common Market Studies*, 35, 173–87.

Beilmeier, J. (1999) Bilan de la présidence allemande de l'union européenne, *Documents. Revue des Questions Allemandes*, **54**, 46–9.

Bender, P. (1994) La Politique Etrangère de l'Allemagne, *Revue des Deux Mondes*, **10**, 22–30.

Bennett, C. (1991) What is Policy Convergence and What Causes it?, *British Journal of Political Science*, **21**, 215–33.

Bennett, C. and Howell, M. (1992) The lessons of learning: Reconciling theories of policy learning and policy change, *Policy Sciences*, **25**, 275–94.

Bensahel, L. (1998) (ed.) *L'Economie de la France face aux defis du 21ème siècle*, Grenoble: Presses Universitaires de Grenoble.

Biffaud, O. and de Bresson, H. (1997) A Luxembourg, les Européens tentent de jeter les bases d'une Union sociale, *Le Monde*, 12 November.

Blaauw, M. (1997) *WEU's role in the organisation of European Security after the decisions taken by the European Union in Amsterdam and by NATO in Madrid.* Report to the 43rd session of the Assembly of Western European Union, 16 October. Document 1581. 13 pp.

Blair, A. (1999) *The European Union Since 1945*, London: Longman.

Bloch-Lainé, A. (1999) Franco-German Co-operation in Foreign Affairs, Security and Defence: a Case Study, in D. Webber (ed.) *The Franco-German Relationship in the European Union*, London: Routledge, pp. 149–59.

Bocquet, D. (1996) La France et L'Allemagne. Un couple en panne d'idées, *Notes de la Fondation Saint-Simon*, February–March, 7–60.

Boniface, P. (1993) La dissuasion nucléaire dans la relation franco-allemande, *Relations Internationales et Strategiques*, **10**, 19–25.

Bonnefous, E. (1995) L'Europe et la Reconciliation Franco-Allemande, *Revue des Deux Mondes*, **2**, 22–30.

Bourlanges, J.-L. (1997) Les trois erreurs d'Amsterdam, *Libération*, 2–3 August.

Bouvet, L. (1999) (ed.) Blair–Schröder. Le texte du manifeste. Les analyses critiques, *Les Notes de la Fondation Jean-Jaurès*, **13**, 1–120.

Bouvet, L., Delors, J., Kluxen-Pyta, D., Lamers, K. and Rovan, J. (1998) *France–Allemagne: le bond en avant*, Paris: Odile Jacob.

Boyer, Y. (1996) France and Germany, in B. Heurlin (ed.) *Germany in Europe in the Nineties*, Basingstoke: Macmillan, pp. 241–6.

Bozzi, J. (1995) L'Allemagne et la France sur le chemin de l'Union économique et monetaire, *Bulletin de la Banque de France*, **14**, 139–45.

Brigouleix, B. (1995) La France et la défense de l'Europe, *L'Année Européenne*, pp. 56–60.

Brodersen, H. (1991) L'Allemagne et la France face à l'Union économique et monétaire européenne, *Allemagne Aujourd'hui*, **116**, 15–50.

Brodersen, H. (1995) L'Allemagne et la France face à la réforme européenne de 1996, *Allemagne Aujourd'hui*, **133**, 42–73.

Bruno, C. (1995) L'Allemagne joue-t-elle le role de locomotive vis-à-vis de la France? *Revue de l'OFCE*, **53**, 165–94.

Bulmer, S. (1983) The European Council's first decade: between interdependence and domestic politics, *Journal of Common Market Studies*, **24**, 91–8.

Bulmer, S. (1994) The Governance of the European Union: A New Institutionalist Approach, *Journal of Public Policy*, **13**, 351–80.

Bulmer, S. and Paterson, W. (1996) Germany in the European Union: Gentle Giant or Emergent Leader? *International Affairs*, **72**, 9–32.

Bulmer, S. and Paterson, W. (1987) *The Federal Republic of Germany and the European Community*, London: Allen and Unwin.

Butcher, M. (1996) Nuclear Weapons in the European Union, *Issues in European Security*, **5**, 1–22.

Cafruny, A. and Lankowski, C. (1995) (eds) *Europe's Ambiguous Unity. Conflict and Consensus in the Post-Maastricht Era*, London: Lynne Reiner.

Callé, M.-F. (1999) Budget des Quinze: Schröder veut imposer son rythme, *Le Figaro-Economie*, 12 January.

Cameron, D. R. (1996) Exchange Rate Politics in France, 1981–1983: The Regime-Defining Choices of the Mitterrand Presidency, in A. Daley (ed.) *The Mitterrand Era. Policy Alternatives and Political Mobilization in France*, Basingstoke: Macmillan, pp. 56–82.

Centre for European Security and Disarmament (1996a) Summary of CFSP and Defence Issues in the IGC Negotiations, *ISIS Europe*, **1**, 1–6.

Centre for European Security and Disarmament (1996b) Summary of CFSP and Defence Issues in the IGC Negotiations, *ISIS Europe*, **3**, 1–4.

Chang, M. (1999) *Dual hegemony: France, Germany and the Making of Monetary Union in Europe*. Paper presented to the European Community Studies Association conference, Pittsburgh, USA, June. 33 pp.

Chaulieu-Bonneau, C. (1998) La coopération militaire franco-allemande, *Défense nationale*, **54**, 62–8.

Chevènement, J.-P. (1996) *France–Allemagne. Parlons Franc*, Paris: Plon.

Clemens, C. and Paterson, W. (1998) *The Kohl Chancellorship*, London: Frank Cass.

Cohen, E. (1996) *La Tentation Hexagonale. La Souveraineté à l'épreuve de la mondialisation*, Paris: Fayard.

Cohen, S. (1986) *La Monarchie Nucleaire*, Paris: Hachette.

Colard, D. (1991) L'Allemagne Unie et le Couple Franco-Allemand, *Defence nationale*, **47**, 99–114.

Cole, A. (1993) Looking on: France and the New Germany, *German Politics*, **2**, 358–76.

Cole, A. (1997) *François Mitterrand. A Study in Political Leadership*, 2nd edn, London: Routledge.

Cole, A. (1998a) *French Politics and Society*, Hemel Hempstead: Prentice Hall.

Cole, A. (1998b) Political Leadership in Western Europe: Kohl's Leadership in Comparative Perspective, *German Politics*, **7**, 120–42.

Cole, A. (1999a) French Socialism in Office: Lessons from Mitterrand and Jospin, *Modern and Contemporary France*, **7**, 71–88.

Cole, A. (1999b) The *Service Public* under Stress, *West European Politics*, **22**, 166–84.

Cole, A. and Drake, H. (2000) The Europeanisation of French Politics? *Journal of European Public Policy*, **7**, 26–43.

Cornut-Gentille, F. and Rozes, S. (1991) La reunification vue de l'Héxagone; les Français engourdis, in O. Duhamel and J. Jaffré (eds) *SOFRES: l'Etat de l'opinion*, Paris: SOFRES, pp. 75–91.

Costigliola, F. (1994) An arm around the shoulder: The United States, NATO and German unification, *Contemporary European History*, 3, 87–110.

Cottey, A. (1998) The European Union and conflict prevention: The role of the High Representative and the Policy Planning and Early Warning Unit, *International Alert*, December. 29 pp.

Crouigneau, F., *et al.* (1994) L'Allemagne, la France et l'Union européenne ou comment relancer l'Europe, *Les Cahiers de la Fondation*, 34–35, 1–109.

Dauvergne, A. (1999) Paris–Bonn: l'heure de doute, *Le Point*, 30 January.

David, D. (1995) Paris, Bonn Moscou: un triangle pour l'Europe, in H. Stark (ed.) *Agir pour l'Europe*, Paris: Masson, pp. 34–44.

de Bresson, H. (1996) Le fonctionnement de l'Union monétaire fait l'objet de difficiles tractations entre les Quinze, *Le Monde*, 3 December.

de Bresson, H. (1997a) Les principaux points du Traité d'Amsterdam, *Le Monde*, 19 June.

de Bresson, H. (1997b) La France a proposé en vain aux Quinze la création d'un fonds européen de croissance, *Le Monde*, 21 June.

de Bresson, H. (1998a) Vers une relance du couple franco-allemand, *Le Monde*, 25 October.

de Bresson, H. (1998b) L'Allemagne assume la présidence de l'Union à un moment charnière pour l'Europe, *Le Monde*, 30 December.

de Bresson, H. (1999) Le sommet de Toulouse n'a pas décrispé la relation franco-allemande, *Le Monde*, 1 June.

de Guistino, D. (1996) *A Reader in European Integration*, Harlow: Addison Wesley Longman.

De la Serre, F. (1990) Le couple franco-allemand et la politique étrangère européenne, in R. Picht and W. Wessels (eds) *Motor für Europa. Deutsch–französischer Bilateralismus und europäische Integration*, Bonn: Institut fur Europäische Politik, pp. 211–24.

de Peretti, B. (1998) Paris et Bonn retrouvent le discours orthodoxe des banques centrales, *La Tribune*, 17 November.

Debouzy, O. (1996) France–OTAN: la fin de l'autre guerre froide, *Commentaire*, 74, 349–52.

Dedman, M.-J. (1996) *The Origins and Development of the European Union, 1945–95*, London: Routledge.

Deger, M. (1999) Les ratés de la présidence allemande, *La Tribune*, 25 February.

Delattre, L. (1996) Paris et Bonn s'entendent sur l'un des chapitres de la réforme de l'Europe, *Le Monde*, 29 February.

Delattre, L. (1997) Le doute s'installe en Allemagne sur l'euro, *Le Monde*, 8 March.

Delattre, L. (1998) Les ministres des finances sociaux-démocrates européens élaborent un projet économique commun, *Le Monde*, 22 November.

Delattre, L. and Tréan, C. (1996) MM Chirac et Kohl adressent à leurs partenaires des propositions communes pour la réforme de l'UE, *Le Monde*, 11 December.

Delattre, L. and Vernet, D. (1996a) La Defence française entre l'Europe et l'Atlantique, *Le Monde*, 23 March.

Delattre, L. and Vernet, D. (1996b) L'Alliance atlantique se donne une dimension européenne, *Le Monde*, 5 June.

Delhommais, P.-A. and Leparmentier, A. (1999) Paris conteste les propositions allemandes en matière de communication sur l'euro, *Le Monde*, 9 June.

Delors, J. (1999) Speech to the students of ESSEC, March 1999, Cergy-Pontoise: ESSEC.

Deporte, A. (1991) The Foreign Policy of the Fifth Republic, in J. Hollifield (ed.) *Searching for the New France*, London: Routledge, pp. 250–74.

Documents: Revue des Questions Allemandes (1996) L'Europe à l'épreuve de la conférence intergouvernementale. Special Issue.

Documents: Revue des Questions Allemandes (1999) France–Allemagne, passions et raison. Special Issue.

Dolan, A. (1997) The European Union's Common Foreign and Security Policy: the Planning Dimension, *ISIS Europe*. Briefing Paper no. 14. November. 12 pp.

Drake, H. (1994) François Mitterrand, France and European Integration, in G. Raymond (ed.) *France During the Socialist Years*, Aldershot: Dartmouth, pp. 32–63.

Drake, H. (2000) *Jacques Delors*, London: Routledge.

Dreyfus, F.-G. (1997) Les relations Franco-Allemandes de l'échec de la CED (1954) au protocole Kohl–Chirac (1996) *Regard Européen*, 1, 13–17.

Dubois, N. (1994) Karl Lamers tente de vendre le 'noyau dur' européen à ses interlocuteurs français, *Libération*, 9 November.

Duverger, M. (1991) L'Héritage européen, *Le Monde*, 26 April.

Dyson, K. (1996) The Economic Order: Still Modell Deutschland? in G. Smith, W. E. Paterson and S. Padgett (eds) *Developments in German Politics: 2*, London: Macmillan, pp. 194–210.

Dyson, K. (1998) Chancellor Kohl as Strategic Leader: the Case of Economic and Monetary Union, in C. Clemens and W. Paterson (eds) *The Kohl Chancellorship*, London: Frank Cass, pp. 37–63.

Dyson, K. (1999a) The Franco-German Relationship and Economic and Monetary Union: Using Europe to 'Bind Leviathan', *West European Politics*, 22, 25–44.

Dyson, K. (1999b) Benign or Malevolent Leviathan? Social-Democratic Governments in a Neo-Liberal 'Euro-Area', *Political Quarterly*, 70, 195–209.

Dyson, K. (1999c) EMU, Political Discourse and the Fifth French Republic: Historical Institutionalism, Path Dependency and 'Craftsmen' of Discourse, *Modern and Contemporary France*, 7, 179–96.

Dyson, K. and Featherstone, K. (1996) EMU and Economic Governance in Germany, *German Politics*, 5, 325–55.

Dyson, K. and Featherstone, K. (1999) *The Road to Maastricht*, Oxford, OUP.

Eberlein, B. and Edgar, G. (1999) Integration with a Spluttering Engine. The Franco-German Relationship in Research and Technology Policy, in D. Webber (ed.) *The Franco-German Relationship in the European Union*, London: Routledge, pp. 93–110.

Eberlein, B. and Grande, E. (1999) Integration with a spluttering engine. The Franco-German relationship in European research and technology policy, in D. Webber (ed.) *The Franco-German Relationship in the European Union*, London: Routledge, pp. 93–110.

Ehrhart, H.-G. (1991) La securité européenne vue par le PS et la SPD, *Documents. Revue des Questions Allemandes*, 5, 25–31.

Epstein, P. (1997) The Uruguay round of GATT negotiations: limitations on government control of trade policy, *Modern and Contemporary France*, 5, 167–80.

Featherstone, K. and Ginsberg, R. H. (1996) (eds) *The United States and the European Union in the 1990s: Partners in Transition*, Basingstoke: Macmillan.

Feld, W. (1989) Franco-German military cooperation and European unification, *Revue d'integration europeenne*, 12, 1–14.

Fischer, J. (1999) Speech to the European Parliament, 11 January 1999. Auswartiges Amt: Bonn. 11 pp.

Fontaine, A. (1991) Diplomatie Française: un modèle Gaullien? *Politique Internationale*, 52, 57–67.

François, E. (1998) Le Couple Franco-Allemand: Exigence d'une ambition, d'imagination et de modestie, *Documents. Revue des Questions Allemandes*, 53, 26–9.

Fransen, F. (1999) *On the incongruities of Monnet's Europe*. Paper presented to the European Community Studies Association conference, Pittsburgh, USA, June, 19 pp.

Frears, J. (1981) *France in the Giscard Presidency*, London: Hurst.

Friend, J. (1999) *French–German Relations and the EU at the century's end: the economic aspects*. Paper presented to the European Community Studies Association conference, Pittsburgh, USA, June. 18 pp.

Friend, J. W. (1998) *The Long Presidency. France in the Mitterrand Years, 1981–1995*, Boulder, CO: Westview.

Frisch, A. (1999) Sur le chemin d'une défense commune, *Documents. Revue des Questions Allemandes*, 54, 53–8.

Froehly, J.-P. and Schiller, T. (1999) Comment penser les relations franco-allemandes? Pour un véritable renouveau dans les débats, *Allemagne Aujourd'hui*, 150, 71–84.

Froment-Maurice, H. (1997) Les relations économiques franco-allemandes, *Défence nationale*, 53, 30–43.

Gaffney, J. (1996) (ed.) *Political Parties in the European Union*, London: Routledge.

Gaffney, J. and Kolinsky, E. (1991) (eds) *Political Culture in France and West Germany*, London: Routledge.

Garrett, G. (1992) International co-operation and institutional choice: the European Community's internal market, *International Organization*, 46, 533–60.

Garton-Ash, T. (1994) *In Europe's Name. Germany and the Divided Continent*, London: Vintage.

George, S. (1996) The European Union. Approaches from International Relations, in H. Kassim and A. Menon (eds) *The European Union and National Industrial Policy*, London: Routledge, pp. 11–25.

Gerbet, P. (1993) Le rôle du couple Franco-Allemand dans la création et le développement des communautés européennes, in H. Ménudier (ed.) Le Couple Franco-Allemand en Europe, Paris: Publications de l'Institut d'Allemand d'Asnières, pp. 27–58.

Giret, V. and Moatti, G. (1998) Chirac, Jospin et l'Euro. L'histoire secrète d'une conversion, *L'Expansion*, **572**, 50–62.

Giscard d'Estaing, V. (1996) Veiller à maintenir la parité entre France et Allemagne, *L'Express*, 18 April.

Gordon, P. (1993) The Franco-German Security Partnership, in P. McCarthy (ed.) *France–Germany 1983–1993. The Struggle to Cooperate*, Basingstoke: Macmillan, pp. 139–60.

Gordon, P. (1995) *France, Germany and the Western Alliance*, Boulder, CO: Westview.

Gougeon, J.-P. (1999) Les raisons d'une crispation, *Libération*, 10 March.

Grosser, A. (1988) La politique européenne de général de Gaulle, *Espoir*, **62**, 18–28.

Grosser, A. (1991) L'Allemagne élargie dans l'Europe élargie, *Politique Etrangère*, **56**, 825–31.

Guisnel, J. (1995) Embryon de coopération militaire franco-britannique dans les airs, *Libération*, 31 October.

Guy-Peters, B. (1994) Agenda-setting in the European Union, *Journal of European Public Policy*, **1**, 9–26.

Haas, E. B. (1958) *The Uniting of Europe. Political, Social and Economic Forces 1950–1957*, Stanford, CA: Stanford University Press.

Haas, P. (1992) Introduction: epistemic communities and international policy coordination, *International Organization*, **46**, 1–35.

Haine, J.-Y. (1995) Eurocorps: de la dimension symbolique à la réalité opérationnelle, *L'Année Européenne*, 68–73.

Haski, P. (1990a) Pour le meilleur et pour le pire, *Libération*, 30 March.

Haski, P. (1990b) Le tandem se veut toujours le moteur de l'Europe, *Libération*, 27 April.

Haski, P. and Millot, L. (1998) Paris et Bonn: une même ambition pour l'UE, *Libération*, 2 December.

Hayward, J. (1997) Changing partnerships: firms and the French state, *Modern and Contemporary France*, **5**, 155–66.

Haywood, E. Z. (1989) The French socialists and institutional reform, *Journal of European Integration*, **12**, 121–49.

Henig, S. (1997) *The Uniting of Europe. From Discord to Concord*, London: Routledge.

Heurlin, B. (1995) (ed.) *Germany in Europe in the Nineties*, Basingstoke: Macmillan.

Hirst, P. and Thompson, G. (1995) Globalisation and the future of the nation-state, *Economics and Society*, **24**, 408–22.

Hix, S. (1994) The Study of the European Community: The Challenge to Comparative Politics, *West European Politics*, **17**, 1–30.

Hix, S. and Lord, C. (1997) *Political Parties in the European Union*, Basingstoke: Macmillan.

Hoffmann, S. (1989) The European Community and 1992, *Foreign Affairs*, **69**, 27–47.

Hoffmann, S. (1995) *The European Sisyphus. Essays on Europe 1964–1994*, Boulder, CO: Westview Press.

Hooghe, L. and Marks, G. (1995) Contending Models of Governance in the European Union, in A. Cafruny and C. Lankowski (eds) *Europe's Ambiguous Unity. Conflict and Consensus in the Post-Maastricht Era*, London: Lynne Reiner, pp. 21–43.

Howarth, D. (1999) *French aversion to independent monetary authority and the development of French policy on the EMU project*. Paper presented to the Political Studies Association conference, Nottingham University, March. 26 pp.

Howorth, J. (1992) Franco-German defence cooperation: the ambivalent entente, *Modern and Contemporary France*, **49**, 20–8.

Howorth, J. (1994) Foreign and Defence Policy: from Independence to Interdependence, in P. Hall, J. Hayward and H. Machin (eds) *Developments in French Politics*, Basingstoke: Macmillan, pp. 201–17.

Hueglin, T. (1995) Europe's Ambiguous Federalism: A Conceptual and Analytical Critique, in A. W. Cafruny and C. Landowski (eds) *Europe's Ambiguous Unity. Conflict and Consensus in the Post-Maastricht Era*, London: Lynne Reiner, pp. 45–67.

INSEE (1995, 1996, 1997, 1998) *Tableaux de l'Economie Française*, Paris: INSEE.

International Affairs (1994) Europe post-Maastricht and the run-up to the 1996 intergovernmental conference of the European Union. Special issue.

Interview with Pierre Moscovici (1998) *L'Humanité*, 8 December.

Interview with Hubert Védrine (1998) *Libération*, 24 November.

ISIS Europe (1999) The Informal Foreign Affairs meeting at Reinhartshausen, 13–14 March 1999: The German Presidency's text. *ISIS Europe*, 17 March. 6 pp.

Israelewicz, E. (1997) L'Allemagne, le Mark et nous, *Sociétal*, **4**, 27–32.

Izraelewicz, E. (1996) L'Allemagne imprime sa marque sur l'euro, *Le Monde*, 25 September.

Janning, J. (1996) A German Europe – a European Germany? On the debate over Germany's foreign policy, *International Affairs*, **72**, 33–41.

Jeffery, C. (1995) The Changing Framework of German Politics since Unification, in D. Lewis and J. R. P. McKenzie (eds) *The New Germany: Social, Political and Cultural Challenges of Unification*, Exeter: University of Exeter Press, pp. 101–26.

Jenson, J. (1984) How the French Left learned to love the bomb, *New Left Review*, **146**, 5–36.

Johnson, D. (1990) Strains in the Euro axis, *The Times*, 13 December.

Joly, H. (1994) Les limites d'une européanisation du pouvoir économique. Le cas de la France et de l'Allemagne, *Revue de l'IRES*, **16**, 39–73.

Joly, H. (1996) France–Allemagne: le résistible déclin des modèles nationaux, *Revue Française de Gestion*, **111**, 185–98.

Joxe, A. (1997) Noyau dur Franco-allemand autonome ou pilier euro-atlantiste? *Le Monde*, 7 February.

Juppé, A. (1995a) Bilan et Avenir de la Politique Etrangère et securité commune, *L'Année Européenne*, pp. 46–51.

Juppé, A. (1995b) La France et la securité européenne, *Défense nationale*, 51, 5–15.

Jurt, J. (1996) Les Français vus d'Allemagne, *Commentaire*, 74, 335–9.

Kaelberer, M. (1997) Hegemony, Dominance or Leadership? Explaining Germany's Role ·in European Monetary Cooperation, *European Journal of International Relations*, 3, 35–60.

Kassim, H. (1994) Policy Networks, Networks and European Union Policy-Making. A Sceptical View, *West European Politics*, 17, 15–27.

Kassim, H. (1997) French autonomy and the European Union, *Modern and Contemporary France*, 5, 167–80.

Keohane, R. O. and Hoffmann, S. (1991) Institutional Change in Europe in the 1980s, in R. O. Keohane and S. Hoffmann (eds) *The New European Community. Decision-making and Institutional Change*, Boulder, CO: Westview Press, pp. 1–39.

Keohane, R. O. (1984) *After Hegemony: Cooperation and Discord in the World Political Economy*, Princeton: Princeton University Press.

Kergoat, J. (1991) Le Long combat des socialistes français, *Le Monde*, 8–9 November.

Kielinger, T. (1990) Waking up to the new Europe – with a headache, *International Affairs*, 66, 249–63.

Klein, J. and Schutze, W. (1991) La question allemande, *Ramses*, 52–69.

Kolboom, I. (1993) Pensées hérétiques sur la polititique étrangère et européenne de la France, *Documents. Revue des Questions Allemandes*, 48, 32–7.

Krasner, S. (1983) (ed.) *International Regimes*, Ithaca: Cornell University Press.

Krause, J. (1994) The illusion of French exceptionalism in European security, *Contemporary French Civilisation*, 18, 134–50.

Kuisel, R.-F. (1991) De Gaulle, le défi Américain et la Communauté européenne, *Espoir*, 76, 73–85.

Ladrech, R. (1994) Europeanization of domestic politics and institutions: the case of France, *Journal of Common Market Studies*, 32, 69–88.

Ladrech, R. (2000) *Social Democracy and the Challenge of the European Union*, London: Lynne Reiner.

Lalliement, R. (1995) La politique commerciale, pomme de discorde entre l'Allemagne et la France? in H. Stark (ed.) *Agir pour l'Europe. Les Relations Franco-allemandes dans l'après-guerre froide*, Paris: Masson, pp. 118–34.

Langguth, G. (1993) Le role de l'Allemagne en Europe, *Belles Feuilles*, 3, 18–28.

Lankowski, C. (1993) (ed.) *Germany and the European Community: Beyond Hegemony and Containment*, New York: St. Martins Press.

Leblond, L. (1997) *Le Couple Franco-Allemand depuis 1945*, Paris: Le Monde Editions.

Le Gloannec, A.-M. (1990) Nouvelle Allemagne: ni tout à fait la même, ni tout à fait différent, *Politique Internationale*, 49, 319–36.

Le Gloannec, A.-M. (1993a) *France, Germany and the New Europe*, Boulder, CO: Westview Press.

Le Gloannec, A.-M. (1993b) (ed.) *L'Allemagne après la guerre froide*, Paris: Editions Complèxe.

Le Gloannec, A.-M. (1996) L'Allemagne, l'Europe et la securité, *Defence Nationale*, **52**, 37–42.

Le Gloannec, A.-M. and Hassner, P. (1996) L'Allemagne et la France: deux cultures politiques? *Esprit*, **5**, 44–52.

Le Gloannec, A. (1996) L'Allemagne, l'Europe et la Securité, *Défense nationale*, **52**, 37–42.

Le Monde (1997) Le sommet de Tony Blair, 23–24 November.

Leenhardt, J. and Picht, R. (1997) (eds) *Au Jardin des Malentendus. Le Commerce Franco-Allemand des Idées*, Paris: Actes Sud.

Lees, C. (1999) *The Red–Green Model*, Die Neue Mitte *and Europeanisation: Conflicting Trends within German Social Democracy*. Paper presented to the European Community Studies Association conference, Pittsburgh, USA, June. 21 pp.

Leimbacher, U. (1995) La cooperation franco-allemande dans le cadre de la Politique étrangère et de securité commune de l'Union européenne, in H. Stark (ed.) *Agir pour l'Europe*, Paris: Masson, pp. 2–24.

Lemaire-Prosche, G. (1990) *Le PS et l'Europe*, Paris: Editions Universitaires.

Lemaître, P. (1992) La France dans le collimateur, *Le Monde*, 7 November.

Lemaître, P. (1997a) L'examen européen de Lionel Jospin, *Le Monde*, 17 June.

Lemaître, P. (1997b) Le 'moteur' Franco-Allemand de l'Europe connaît des ratés, *Le Monde*, 19 June.

Lemaître, P. (1998) Escarmouches franco-allemandes lors de la première réunion de l'Euro 11, *Le Monde*, 6 June.

Lemaître, P. (1999a) Les ministres européens des finances se retrouvent pour evoquer l'après-euro, *Le Monde*, 17 January.

Lemaître, P. (1999b) La réforme des aides agricoles proposée par la France laisse ses partenaires dubitatifs, *Le Monde*, 21 January.

Lemaître, P. (1999c) Parvenir à un nouvel équilibre des productions et du financement, *Le Monde*, 23 February.

Lemaître, P. (1999d) La naissance officielle de l'Europe de la défense a été proclamée à Cologne, *Le Monde*, June 5.

Lequesne, C. (1990) Formulation des politiques communautaires et procédures de consultation avec la RFA en France, in R. Picht and W. Wessels (eds) *Motor für Europa. Deutsch–französischer Bilateralismus und europäische Integration*, Bonn: Institut fur Europäische Politik, pp. 123–44.

Lequesne, C. (1993) *Paris–Bruxelles*, Paris: Presses de la FNSP.

Lequesne, C. (1996) French central government and the European political system: change and adaptation since the Single Act, in Y. Mény, P. Muller and J.-L. Quermonne (eds) *Adjusting to Europe: the Impact of the European Union on National Institutions and Policies*, London: Routledge, pp. 110–22.

Lewis, D. and McKenzie, J. R. P. (1995) *The New Germany. Social, Political and Cultural Challenges of Unification*, Exeter: University of Exeter Press.

Macé-Scaron, J. (1997) Kohl: Grand Electeur Français, *Revue des Deux Mondes*, **1**, 11–18.

Majone, G. (1996) (ed.) *Regulating Europe*, London: Routledge.

Malnes, R. (1995) 'Leader' and 'Entrepreneur' in International Negotiations: A Conceptual Analysis, *European Journal of International Relations*, 1, 87–112.

March, J.-G. and Olsen, J.-P. (1989) *Rediscovering Institutions. The Organizational Basis of Politics*, New York: The Free Press.

Markovits, A. and Reich, S. (1997) *The German Predicament*, Ithaca and London: Cornell University Press.

Marks, G., Hooghe, L. and Blank, K. (1996) European integration from the 1980s: state-centric versus multi-level governance, *Journal of Common Market Studies*, 34, 341–78.

Marsh, D. (1992) *The Bundesbank: the Bank that Rules Europe*, London: Heinemann.

Martin, G. (1996) *The Member-states of the European Union and the Inter-Governmental Conference. Briefing Paper*, UKREP: HMSO.

Marzal, L. (1997) L'Office Franco-Allemand de la Jeunesse, *Regard Européen*, 1, 38–9.

Mathieux, J. (1993) Les rapports franco-allemands, *Le Trimestre du Monde*, 23, 121–32.

Maurice, M. (1993) La Formation professionnelle en France, en Allemagne et au Japon, *Entreprises et Histoire*, 3, 47–59.

Mazzucelli, C. (1997) *France and Germany at Maastricht. Politics and Negotiations to Create the European Union*, New York: Garland.

McCarthy, P. (ed.) (1993a) *France–Germany, 1983–93. The Struggle to Cooperate*, Basingstoke: Macmillan.

McCarthy, P. (1993b) France Looks at Germany: How to Become German (and European) while Remaining French, in P. McCarthy (ed.) *France–Germany, 1983–1993. The Struggle to Cooperate*, Basingstoke: Macmillan, pp. 51–72.

McClean, M. (1994) *France and GATT: the Economic Implications of the New World Order*. Paper presented to the Association for the Study of Modern and Contemporary France conference, University of Portsmouth, 2–4 September, 18 pp.

Mentré, P. (1993) France et Allemagne face à la division internationale du travail, *Commentaire*, 63, 507–12.

Ménudier, H. (1993) (ed.) *Le Couple Franco-Allemand en Europe*, Paris: Publications de l'Institut d'Allemand d'Asnières.

Millot, L. (1999) Les dégressifs contre les cofinanceurs, *Libération*, 26 February.

Milner, H. (1991) The Assumption of Anarchy in International Relations Theory: a Critique, *Review of International Studies*, 17, 67–85.

Milward, A. (1979) Fascism and the Economy, in W. Laqueur (ed.) *Fascism. A Reader's Guide*, London: Pelican Books, pp. 409–53.

Milward, A. (1984) *The Reconstruction of Western Europe 1945–51*, London: Routledge.

Mitterrand, F. (1996) *De l'Allemagne, de la France*, Paris: Odile Jacob.

Moisi, D. (1995) L'Amérique dans les relations franco-allemandes, in H. Stark (ed.) *Agir pour l'Europe*, Paris: Masson, pp. 26–33.

Moravcsik, A. (1991) Negotiating the Single European Act: national interests and conventional statecraft in the European Community, *International Organization*, **45**, 19–56.

Moravcsik, A. (1993) Preferences and Power in the European Community: A Liberal Intergovernmentalist Approach, *Journal of Common Market Studies*, **31**, 473–524.

Moravcsik, A. (1998) *The Choice for Europe. Social Purpose and State Power from Messina to Maastricht*, Ithaca and London: Cornell University Press.

Moreau-Defarges, P. (1992) L'Allemagne change-t-elle? *Défense nationale*, **48**, 69–76.

Moreau-Defarges, P. (1994) *La France dans le Monde au XXè Siècle*, Paris: Hachette.

Morgan, R. (1991) French perspectives on the new Germany, *Government and Opposition*, **26**, 108–14.

Morgan, R. (1993) France and Germany as partners in the European Community, in P. McCarthy (ed.) *France–Germany 1983–93. The Struggle to Cooperate*, Basingstoke: Macmillan. pp. 93–112.

Morizet, J. (1990a) Coopération franco-allemande et intégration européenne, in R. Picht and W. Wessels (eds) *Motor für Europa. Deutsch–französischer Bilateralismus und europäische Integration*, Bonn: Institut fur Europäische Politik, pp. 251–69.

Morizet, J. (1990b) Le problème allemand vu de France, *Défense Nationale*, **46**, 11–23.

Moscovici, P. (1998) On ne peut pas imposer une version française de l'Europe, *L'Humanité*, 8 December.

Nicoll, A. (1999) Blair calls on Europe to boost military role, *Financial Times*, 3 March.

Noël, G. (1995) *France, Allemagne et 'Europe Verte'*, Bern: Peter Lang.

Northcutt, W. (1986) The domestic origins of Mitterrand's foreign policy, 1981–1985, *Contemporary French Civilisation*, **10**, 233–67.

O'Neill, M. (1996) *The Politics of European Integration. A Reader*, London: Routledge.

Padgett, S. (1994) (ed.) *Adenauer to Kohl*, London: Hurst.

Paolini, M. (1998) Les agriculteurs pourraient patir de l'austerité budgetaire européenne, *La Tribune*, 24 November.

Papcke, S. (1996) Une allemagne européenne ou une Europe allemande? *Allemagne Aujourd'hui*, **135**, 3–20.

Papcke, S. (1997) Quel rôle international pour l'Allemagne? Ni loup, ni agneau, *Allemagne Aujourd'Hui*, **139**, 21–33.

Parkes, S. (1997) *Understanding Germany*, London: Routledge.

Patat, J.-P. (1994) L'Allemagne et la France sur le chemin de l'UEM, *Bulletin de la Banque de France*, **4**, 27–31.

Paterson, W. (1994) The Chancellor and foreign policy, in S. Padgett (ed.) *Adenauer to Kohl*, London: Hurst, pp. 127–56.

Paterson, W. (1998) Helmut Kohl, 'The Vision Thing' and Escaping the Semi-Sovereignty Trap? in C. Clemens and W. Paterson (eds) *The Kohl Chancellorship*, London: Frank Cass, pp. 17–36.

Paxton, R. (1972) *Vichy France. Old Guard and New Order*, New York: Columbia University Press.

Péan, P. (1994) *Une jeunesse française*, Paris: Fayard.

Pedersen, T. (1998) *Germany, France and the Integration of Europe: a Realist Interpretation*, London: Pinter.

Percheron, A. (1991) Les Français et l'Europe, acquiesement de façade ou adhésion véritable, *Revue française de Science Politique*, **41**, 382–405.

Peters, B. G. (1994) Agenda-setting in the European Community, *Journal of European Public Policy*, **1**, 9–26.

Petersen, J. (1995) Decision-making in the European Union: towards a framework for analysis, *Journal of European Public Policy*, **2**, 69–93.

Petersen, J. and Bomberg, E. (1999) *Decision-Making in the European Union*, Basingstoke: Macmillan.

Picht, R., Uterwedde, H. and Wessels, W. (1990) (eds) *Motor für Europa. Deutsch–französischer Bilateralismus und europäische Integration*, Bonn: Institut fur Europäische Politik.

Pierson, P. (1996) The Path to European Integration: A Historical Institutionalist Analysis, *Comparative Political Studies*, **29**, 123–63.

Pruys, K.-H. (1996) *Kohl: Genius of the Present*, Illinois: Edition Q.

Puchala, D. J. (1999) Institutionalism, Intergovernmentalism and European Integration: A Review Article, *Journal of Common Market Studies*, **37**, 317–31.

Pulzer, P. (1995) *German Politics, 1945–1995*, Oxford: OUP.

Putnam, R. (1988) Diplomacy and two-level games, *International Organization*, **42**, 427–60.

Quatremar, J. (1995) Le soutien appuyé de Kohl à Chirac, *Libération*, 9 December.

Quatremar, J. (1999a) Avec Schroder, quelle tête aura l'Europe? *Libération*, 2–3 January.

Quatremar, J. (1999b) Sur la voie d'une Europe Économique, *Libération*, 19 April.

Quilès, P. (1996) Défense européenne et OTAN: la dérive, *Le Monde*, 11 June.

Radaelli, C. (1997) *The Politics of Corporate Taxation. Knowledge and International Policy Agendas*, London: Routledge.

Radaelli, C. (1999) *The Public Policy of the European Union: whither politics of expertise?* Paper presented to the European Community Studies Association conference, Pittsburgh, USA, June 32 pp.

Reeh, K. (1994) France et Allemagne: des démocraties incompatibles? *Le Banquet*, **5**, 237–61.

Reeh, K. (1995) Critique des propositions CDU/CSU, *L'Année Européenne*, 177–83.

Reland, J. (1998) France, in J. Forder and A. Menon (eds) *The European Union and National Macroeconomic Policy*, London: Routledge, pp. 81–104.

Reuillon, M. (1999a) A propos du pacte pour l'emploi, *Documents. Revue des Questions Allemandes*, **54**, 61–3.

Reuillon, M. (1999b) D'une présidence à l'autre: petite chronique d'une gestion européenne, *Documents. Revue des Questions Allemandes*, **54**, 50–2.

Reuters (1998) Text of French–British European Defence statement, Saint-Malo, France, 4 December.

Rhodes, C. and Mazey, S. (1995) Introduction: Integration in Theoretical Perspective, in C. Rhodes and S. Mazey (eds) *The State of the Union, Volume 3*, Harlow: Longman, pp. 1–26.

Rhodes, M. (1999) An Awkward Alliance. France, Germany and Social Policy, in D. Webber (ed.) *The Franco-German Relationship in the European Union*, London: Routledge, pp. 131–48.

Rideau, J. (1975) *La France et Les Communautés Européennes*, Paris: LGDJ.

Rosenzweig, L. (1997) Les responsables de l'OTAN ne croient plus dans un retour prochain de la France, *Le Monde*, 7 June.

Rosselin, J. (1993) L'Allemagne et la France doivent réinventer l'Europe, *Belles Feuilles*, 3, 5–13.

Ruehl, L. (1992) La construction de l'Europe federaliste vue d'Allemagne, *CADMOS*, 58–59, 17–30.

Sabatier, P. (1998) The advocacy coalition framework: revisions and relevance for Europe, *Journal of European Public Policy*, 5, 98–130.

Sabatier, P. and Jenkins-Smith, H. (1993) (eds) *Policy Change and Learning. An Advocacy Coalition Approach*, Boulder, CO: Westview.

Saint-Etienne, C. (1995) L'Union monétaire franco-allemande, in H. Stark (ed.) *Agir pour l'Europe*, Paris: Masson, pp. 106–16.

Sandholtz, W. (1993) Monetary Bargains: the Treaty on EMU, in A. Cafruny and G. Rosenthal (eds) *The State of the European Community. Volume 2*, Harlow: Longman, pp. 125–42.

Sandholtz, W. and Zysman, J. (1989) 1992: Recasting the European Bargain, *World Politics*, 42, 95–128.

Sauron, J.-L. and Asseraf, G. (1999) Le Conseil européen de Cologne des 3 et 4 juin 1999, *Revue du Marché Commun*, 430, 441–7.

Schild, J. (1994) La France, l'Allemagne et l'élargissement aux pays de l'AELE, *Relations Internationales et Strategiques*, 15, 44–62.

Schmidt, S. K. (1999) Mastering differences. The Franco-German alliance and the liberalisation of European electricity markets, in D. Webber (ed.) *The Franco-German Relationship in the European Union*, London: Routledge, pp. 58–74.

Schmidt, V. (1996) *From State to Market? The Transformation of French Business and Government*, Cambridge: Cambridge University Press.

Schmidt, V. (1997) Running on empty; the end of dirigisme in French economic leadership, *Modern and Contemporary France*, 5, 229–42.

Schneider, V. and Vedel, T. (1999) From high to low politics in Franco-German relations. The case of telecommunications, in D. Webber (ed.) *The Franco-German Relationship in the European Union*, London: Routledge, pp. 75–92.

Schosser, F. (1999) Nouvelles technologies et prestations de services. Des perspectives pour la coopération des entreprises françaises et allemandes, *Documents. Revue des Questions Allemandes*, 54, 59–65.

Schröder, G. (1999) L'Allemagne, l'Europe et la défense, *Documents. Revue des Questions Allemandes*, 54, 15–20.

Servent, P. (1995) La défense européenne: quelle ambition et combien de divisions? *L'Annee Européenne*, 64–7.

Simonian, H. (1985) *The Privileged Partnership: Franco-German Relations in the European Community, 1969–1984*, Oxford: OUP.

Smith, G. (1994) The Changing Parameters of the German Chancellorship, in S. Padgett (ed.) *Adenauer to Kohl*, London: Hurst, pp. 187–96.

Smith, M. and Sandholtz, W. (1995) Institutions and Leadership: Germany, Maastricht and the ERM crisis, in C. Rhodes and S. Mazey (eds) *The State of the European Union Vol. 3: Building a European Polity?* Boulder, CO: Lynne Reiner, pp. 245–65.

Sontheimer, K. and Kolboom, I. (1993) L'Allemagne et la France s'interrogent sur leur rôle futur, *Documents. Revue des Questions Allemandes*, 48, 22–37.

Soutou, G.-H. (1991) Le Général de Gaulle, le plan Fouchet et l'Europe, *Commentaire*, 13, 757–66.

Soutou, G.-H. (1996) *L'Alliance Incertain*, Paris: Fayard.

Soutou, G.-H. (1997) Pourquoi la France se rapproche de l'Otan, *Nouvel Observateur*, 6–12 February.

Soutou, G.-H. (1999) La France et l'Allemagne vont-elles continuer à être le moteur de l'intégration européenne? *Géopolitique*, 65, 40–9.

Spencer, T. (1997) *The new Treaty provisions on Common Foreign and Security Policy (CFSP) after the European Council meeting of Amsterdam.* Working Document PE 223.297. Committee on Foreign Affairs, Security and Defence Policy, European Parliament, 21 July, 7 pp.

Stark, H. (1992) Dissonances franco-allemandes sur fond de guerre serbo-croate, *Politique Etrangère*, 57, 329–47.

Stark, H. (1995a) La France et L'Allemagne face à l'Est: le cas Yougoslave, in H. Stark (ed.) *Agir pour l'Europe. Les Relations Franco-allemandes dans l'après-guerre froide*, Paris: Masson, pp. 92–104.

Stark, H. (1995b) *Agir pour l'Europe. Les Relations Franco-allemandes dans l'après-guerre froide*, Paris: Masson.

Stein, G. (1993) The Euro-Corps and Future European Security Architecture, *European Security*, 2, 200–26.

Stephens, P. (1997) The Ragbag Treaty, *Financial Times*, 20 June.

Stone Sweet, A. and Sandholtz, W. (1997) European integration and supranational governance, *Journal of European Public Policy*, 4, 297–317.

Story, J. (1999) Monetary Union. Economic competition and political negotiation, in D. Webber (ed.) *The Franco-German Relationship in the European Union*, London: Routledge, pp. 20–40.

Sur, E. (1993) Maastricht, la France et l'Allemagne, *Hérodote*, 68, 125–37.

Szabo, S. (1990) *The Changing Politics of German Security*, London: Pinter.

Taylor, P. (1983) *The Limits of European Integration*, London: Croom Helm.

Teltschik, H. (1990) Rien sans la France, *Cosmopolitiques*, 16, 67–78.

Thatcher, M. (1997) L'Impact de la Communauté européenne sur la règlementation nationale: les services publiques en France et en Grande-Bretagne, *Politiques et Management Public*, 15, 141–68.

The Economist (1994) Froideur, Angst, or all in the mind? 26 March.

The Economist (1998) A Future without Kohl, 20 June.

Tindemans, L. (1997) *Report on the Gradual Establishment of a common defence policy for the European Union*. European Parliament Committee on Foreign Affairs, Security and Defence Policy. December 10. PE 224.862/B. 11 pp.

Tranholm-Mikkelsen, J. (1991) Neo-functionalism: Obstinate or Obsolete? A Reappraisal in the Light of the New Dynamism in the EC, *Millennium: Journal of International Studies*, 20, 1–22.

Treacher, A. (1996) *France and military intervention in the 1990s*. Paper presented to the Political Studies Association conference, University of Glasgow, April. 13 pp.

Tréan, C. (1991) La France et le Nouvel Ordre Européen, *Politique Etrangère*, 91, 81–90.

Trichet, J.-C. (1997) Entretien avec Jean-Claude Trichet, *Politique Internationale*, 75, 225–36.

Trouille, J.-M. (1994) The Franco-German axis since unification. Paper presented to the Association for the Study of Modern and Contemporary France annual conference, University of Portsmouth, 12 pp.

Trouille, J.-M. (1999) La coopération industrielle Franco-Allemande face à la mondialisation, *Documents. Revue des Questions Allemandes*, 54, 51–60.

Truscott, P. (1997) *Russia First: Breaking with the West*, London: I. B. Tauris.

Truscott, P. (1999) *European Defence Co-operation in the 21st Century*, European Parliamentary Labour Party Discussion Paper, 4 March. 11 pp.

Tsebelis, G. (1990) *Nested Games: Rational Choice in Comparative Politics*, Berkeley: University of California Press.

University of Aix-en-Provence (1998) *La Coopération franco-allemande en Europe à l'aube du XXIe siècle. Colloque du quarantième anniversaire du jumelage Aix-Tübingen*, Aix-en-Provence: Presses Universitaires d'Aix-en-Provence.

Vaillant, J. (1998) Les Relations Franco-Allemandes à l'épreuve: le traité de l'Elysée a 35 ans, *Allemagne Aujourd'hui*, 143, 3–5.

Valence, G. (1990) *Le Retour de Bismarck*, Paris: Flammarion.

Védrine, H. (1996) *Les Mondes de François Mitterrand. A l'Elysée, 1981–1995*, Paris: Fayard.

Vernet, D. (1991) L'Allemagne unie et le couple franco-allemand, *Défense nationale*, 47, 99–114.

Vernet, D. (1995a) La France et l'Allemagne, *Politique Etrangère*, 60, 879–90.

Vernet, D. (1995b) Yougoslavie: Le test raté de la securité européenne, *L'Année Europeénne*, pp. 52–5.

Vernet, D. (1996a) Accord sur la réforme de l'OTAN, *Le Monde*, 12–13 May.

Vernet, D. (1996b) La Révolution stratégique chiraquienne, *Le Monde*, 8 June.

Vernet, D. (1996c) Couacs franco-allemands sur la défense, *Le Monde*, 12 July.

Vernet, D. (1997) L'Europe dans l'engrenage de la monnaie unique, *Le Monde*, 19–20 January.

Wall, I. (1991) Charles de Gaulle, les Etats-Unis et la communauté européenne de défense, 1950–1954, *Espoir*, 76, 73–85.

Wallace, H. (1990) Institutionalized Bilateralism and Multilateral Relations: Axis, Motor or Detonator, in R. Picht, H. Uterwedde and W. Wessels (eds) *Motor für Europa. Deutsch–französischer Bilateralismus und europäische Integration*, Bonn: Institut fur Europäische Politik, pp. 145–57.

Wallace, H. and Wallace, W. (1996) (eds) *Policy-Making in the European Union*, Oxford: Oxford University Press.

Wallace, W. (1990) (ed.) *The Dynamics of European Integration*, London: Pinter.

Wallach, H. and Francisco, R. (1993) *United Germany. The Past, Politics, Prospects*, London: Praeger.

Webb, C. (1983) Theoretical perspectives and problems, in H. Wallace, W. Wallace and C. Webb (eds) *Policy-Making in the European Community*, London: Croom Helm, pp. 1–39.

Webber, D. (1998) High Midnight in Brussels: an analysis of the September 1993 Council meeting on the GATT Uruguay round, *Journal of European Public Policy*, 5, 578–94.

Webber, D. (1999a) (ed.) *The Franco-German Relationship in the European Union*, London: Routledge.

Webber, D. (1999b) Franco-German Bilateralism and Agricultural Politics in the European Union: The Neglected Level, *West European Politics*, 22, 45–67.

Welfens, P. (1993) The New Germany in the EC, in A. Cafruny and G. Rosenthal (eds) *The State of the European Community. Volume 2*, Harlow: Longman, pp. 159–76.

Wiersma, J.-M. (1999) *The Common Foreign and Security Policy: the Way Forward.* Recommendations to the Parliamentary Group of the Party of European Socialists. February. 4 pp.

Williams, P. M. W. (1964) *Crisis and Compromise. Politics in the Fourth Republic*, London: Longman.

Willis, R. (1978) Origins and Evolution of the European Communities, *Annals AAPSS*, 440, 1–12.

Wood, P.-C. (1995) The Franco-German Relationship in the Post-Maastricht Era, in C. Rhodes and S. Mazey (eds) *The State of the European Union Vol. 3: Building a European Polity?* Boulder, CO: Lynne Reiner, pp. 221–43.

Wright, V. (1996) The national co-ordination of European policy-making: negotiating the quagmire, in J. Richardson (ed.) *European Union: Power and Policy-Making*, London, Routledge, pp. 148–69.

Yost, D.-S. (1991) France in the New Europe, *Foreign Affairs*, 69, 107–28.

Young, O. (1991) Political leadership and regime formation: on the development of institutions in international society, *International Organization*, 45, 281–308.

Ziebura, G. (1996) Between appearance and reality. Franco-German relations and the crisis of European Union, *Debatte*, 2, 10–21.

Index